Communication Instruction in the Generation Z Classroom

Communication Instruction in the Generation Z Classroom

Educational Explorations

Edited by
Renee Robinson

LEXINGTON BOOKS
Lanham • Boulder • New York • London

Published by Lexington Books
An imprint of The Rowman & Littlefield Publishing Group, Inc.
4501 Forbes Boulevard, Suite 200, Lanham, Maryland 20706
www.rowman.com

86-90 Paul Street, London EC2A 4NE

Copyright © 2021 by The Rowman & Littlefield Publishing Group, Inc.

All rights reserved. No part of this book may be reproduced in any form or by any electronic or mechanical means, including information storage and retrieval systems, without written permission from the publisher, except by a reviewer who may quote passages in a review.

British Library Cataloguing in Publication Information Available

Library of Congress Cataloging-in-Publication Data Available

ISBN 978-1-7936-2622-6 (cloth : alk. paper)
ISBN 978-1-7936-2624-0 (pbk. : alk. paper)
ISBN 978-1-7936-2623-3 (electronic)

To the dedicated communication faculty, instructors, teachers, and researchers committed to the students of today, shaping the generations of tomorrow, ultimately leading to societal change and a better world

Contents

List of Figures and Tables ix

1 Introduction 1
  Renee Robinson

2 Motivation and Learning: Need-Supportive Teaching Style to Engage Gen Z 9
  Sadia E. Cheema and Jie Zhang

3 Acknowledging the Needs of Gen Z: Opening Spaces for Connection and Care 25
  Kristen T. Christman and Jessica D. McCall

4 A Bridge for Communication: Negotiating Intergenerational Listening Expectations in Face-to-Face Interactions and Digital Platforms 45
  Emeline Ojeda-Hecht and Elizabeth S. Parks

5 Listening Research Shows How Gen Z and Faculty Can Co-Create Engaging Learning Environments 59
  Pamela Sherstad

6 Teaching Digital Natives Where They Live: Generation Z and Online Learning 71
  Troy Cooper and T. Kody Frey

7 The Applied Case Study as a Pedagogical Tool for Educating Today's Generation Z Student Population 85
  Corey Jay Liberman

8	When Learning Is Play: Using Video Games to Educate Gen Z in the Classroom *Gwendelyn S. Nisbett, Newly Paul, and Juli James*	103
9	Getting Outside of the Norm: Adopting Outdoor Adventure Education Pedagogy to Engage Generation Z *R. Tyler Spradley*	115
10	Engaging Generation Z with Communication's Civic Commitments *Spoma Jovanovic, Cristiane S. Damasceno, and Roy Schwartzman*	129

Bibliography	149
Index	173
About the Authors	181

List of Figures and Tables

FIGURES

Figure 2.1	Need-Supportive Instructional Strategies to Engage Generation Z	12
Figure 4.1	Post-Gen Z Focus Group Discourse	52
Figure 4.2	Gen Z Focus Group Discourse	52
Figure 5.1	Listening Tips from Generation Z Students	66
Figure 8.1	Simple Game Design Model	107
Figure 8.2	Core Mechanic Design Model	108
Figure 8.3	Hoaxes and Havoc by Playable Media	110

TABLES

Table 2.1	Instructional Design Strategies and Approaches to Engage Gen Z in Learning	18
Table 4.1	Demographic Traits Perceived to Influence Listening Behaviors	51
Table 9.1	Debriefing Questions to Enhance Soft Skills	123

Chapter 1

Introduction

Renee Robinson

Communication instructors have always been interested in the dynamics and innerworkings of the classroom as it relates to course content and the teaching-learning process. This interest is fueled by the inherent nature of the field. Communication, as a discipline, is broad and consists of, but not limited to, various subareas such as computer-mediated or digital communication, group/team communication, health communication, intercultural communication, interpersonal communication, mass communication, organizational communication, political communication, and speech communication, to name a few. Within each of the subareas, different contexts exist that involve communication dynamics related to the characteristics of each individual involved in the interaction, the roles the individuals play in the communication exchange, and the goals or outcomes of those interactions that were influenced by communication dynamics involving personality traits, verbal, and nonverbal messages. As a result, communication instructors have studied their instructional spaces from a variety of perspectives that involve messages, course content, and/or communication processes and behaviors that occur in an instructional space and that can influence the effectiveness of that space. The disciplinary breadth and diversity of the field has contributed to two general frameworks that define and guide how a teacher might investigate an instructional space: communication education and instructional communication.

While these two areas are related in that they both involve the topic of communication, they are distinctly different. According to McCroskey and McCroskey (2016), communication education "centers on the study of teaching the disciplines of speech and/or communication" (34). However, instructional communication "centers on the role of communication processes in teaching and training contexts in K–12, college, and other organizational environments" (33). While communication education and instructional communication are different, they each have classroom applications and relevancy. Consequently, communication instructors may contemplate or investigate their classrooms from a communication curriculum or pedagogical perspective or a communication process-relationship-effects/outcome perspective. However, communication education is discipline specific and linked to how an instructor might teach communication content while instructional communication applies to any classroom or training space across disciplines and organizational contexts and how communication behaviors and processes impact those spaces. Therefore, it is not confined to educational institutions or the teaching of communication specifically.

Examples of communication education topics published in journals such as Communication Education illustrate studies in instructional preparedness and remote learning (Westwick and Morreale 2021), instructional flexibility during a global pandemic (Tatum and Frey 2021), organizational communication and the basic course (Pace and Ross 1983) and have focused on internships in the discipline (Downs et al. 1976), among many other areas of communication teaching emphasis. Over the decades, communication instructors and scholars have frequently asked research questions about instructional spaces and pursued studies related to communication curriculum and pedagogical ideas, interests, or noted problems of the time.

When considering areas explored by communication instructors and scholars in instructional communication, teacher nonverbal immediacy, use of instructor humor, teacher misbehavior, and instructor communication behaviors as they influence student affective and cognitive learning or motivation to learn are common topics of study. A comprehensive reference for the history and origins of instructional communication and the topics, approaches, and methods affiliated with this aspect of communication studies is the Handbook of Instructional Communication: Rhetorical and Relational Perspectives (Mottet et al. 2016). An understanding of the differences and similarities concerning communication education and instructional education is helpful in comprehending the content and purpose of this book.

TEXT CONCEPTUALIZATION

In keeping with the questions that communication instructors and scholars pose of the discipline, I began contemplating the instructional state of the field from a communication education perspective and an instructional communication perspective. However, my thoughts were further honed during my first semester (2019) as department chair of a large unit comprised of eight undergraduate and two graduate programs offering approximately

200 sections of various courses primarily focused on some aspect of communication (e.g.,digital/interpersonal/organizational/rhetorical communication, journalism, mass/media studies and production, public relations, visual and performing arts) each semester. Additional factors heightening my interest involved diversity in delivery systems (face-to-face, online, and hybrid) and the myriad of communication processes presented. The department, program, college and broader university meetings, I attended or facilitated, focused on the classroom, instruction, and student demographics regarding challenges and opportunities as they intersected with course and programmatic assessment, delivery systems, faculty development, student engagement, and the organizational implications of each topic being discussed by campus faculty and administrator colleagues. These campus conversations reflected national and regional conversations at the discipline's conferences and conventions. They were also topics explored in publications such as The *New York Times, US News and World Report*, and *Wall Street Journal*.

In my own classroom, I began observing differences in students, at both the undergraduate and graduate levels, concerning student communication behaviors and practices, demographics, learning and messaging preferences, and other needs as they impacted my own communication behaviors and pedagogical responses. As a result, research questions concerning generational characteristics intersecting with access to education, communication curriculum, delivery systems, student engagement strategies, technology tools, and instructor-student communication behaviors and practices emerged. Given my role as department chair, I was wondering about how these topics would impact the institution of higher education, instructional spaces, students, and the broader world. These observations led to the exploration of generational literature as it relates to our newest cohort of students in the classroom and those soon to enter the workplace, Generation Z, and how these learners differed from Millennial students.

Generation Z: An Overview

As noted by Seemiller et al. (2021) "studies on Generation Z college students and learning are sparse" (1). Consequently, two key sources were consulted when learning more about Generation Z: Seemiller and Grace's (2016) *Generation Z Goes to College* and the research conducted by the Pew Research Center (2019). Pew generates a host of research focused on US populations, technology use, and related variables. What follows is a brief summary of cohort characteristics and considerations when thinking about Generation Z in US classrooms, future workplaces, and/or broader societies.

Populations and people can be studied from a variety of perspectives. However, the Pew Research Center notes that, generational cohorts give researchers a tool to analyze changes in views over time. They can provide a way to understand how different formative experiences (such as world events and technological, economic and social shifts) interact with the life-cycle and aging process to shape people's views of the world (2019).

Pew has conducted generational research on Baby Boomers (1946–1964), Generation X (1965–1980), and Millennials (1981–1996). Until recently, the focus has been on Millennials and the implications for educational, social, and political environments. Millennials, who are now approaching 40, have a population size of approximately 72 million. They are the largest US generation to date and like other generations, were significantly influenced by some key life experiences: the terrorist attacks (9/11), US warfare, an economic recession, and substantial technology advancement and use (Pew Research Center). This generation has also been referred to as the Me Generation or Generation Y (Seemiller and Grace 2016). Because this generation was the first to be born at the onset of a new century, the term Millennial is most often used when referencing individuals born at or around that time. However, in 2018, the Pew Research Center established a timeline to demarcate a new generational cohort, Generation Z.

When examining the literature on Generation Z, early research referred to them as Homelanders (Howe and Strauss 2014, as cited in *Psychology Today*), Net Generation or iGeneration (Seemiller and Grace 2016), and Post-Millennials (Pew Research Center 2019). The most commonly used term is Gen Z. This book utilizes the term Generation or Gen Z when discussing our newest generation and applies the Pew Research Center's definition of Generation Z as individuals born between 1997 and 2012.

Seemiller and Grace's (2016) text, Generation Z Goes to College, is also a valuable source of information when thinking about the variables that shaped this population and the attitudes, beliefs, and values present. Their work provides a detailed analysis of Generation Z drawing upon various studies and research focused on this population. Seemiller and Grace (2016), coupled with the Pew Research Center (2019) present compelling data that can help instructors better understand their instructional environments when considering the various student identifiers that emerge based on attitudes, beliefs, and values as they intersect with biological, cultural, political, psychological, social, and technological structures and systems. These points of intersection have shaped Generation Z in interesting ways.

For the purposes of this text, a summary of some Pew Research Center (2019) findings relating to Gen Z is included in this introduction as it is especially important to current learning environments. Additional details about Generation Z are also presented in each chapter as they relate to the topic of exploration. As a primer to thinking about Generation Z, demographically speaking, Gen Z consists of approximately 67 million people between the ages of 9 and 24 currently.

This generation is more ethnically and racially diverse than any other generation (for instance, 1 in 4 are Hispanic, 14% Black, 6% Asian, 5% other race or 2 or more races, Pew Research 2019). Familywise, Gen Z is also more likely to have a two parent, married home (66%) with at least one parent possessing a bachelor's degree or higher. When it comes to mental health, Gen Z is more likely than other generation to report mental health as fair or poor (Buthane 2019). Politically speaking, they prefer governments to solve problems as opposed to businesses or people. In Gen Z social connections and networks, they are more likely to know someone who prefers gender-neutral pronouns (35%). Regarding technology, it is the first generation born in a fully digital age. Consequently, they have no recollection of a pre-cable/streaming device world which may be why they generally believe that internet access is a human right.

A potential advantage of Gen Z's constant access to and use of technology involves their increased awareness of cultures, others, and regions. However, they have also been negatively impacted by their constant mediated communication, digital device use, and screen time, which appears to have affected their in-person communication skills, nondigital life experiences, and physical health due to inactivity. A lack of experience coupled with mental health concerns and needs for soft skill development demands special attention to communication in learning spaces. However, Seemiller and Grace's (2016) research also describes Gen Z as open-minded and thoughtful, loyal and responsible, compassionate and determined.

Procedures

The findings of Pew (2019) and Seemiller and Grace (2016) present interesting communication questions, opportunities, and challenges for the study of communication education and instructional communication. This body of research combined with my communication administrator and instructor experiences and observations, informed the following preliminary research question, *what are college/university instructors doing, researching or thinking about in relation to the communication discipline, communication education, and instructional communication as it intersects with Generation Z*. This seemed to be an important question to pose given research or lack thereof on Generation Z in learning spaces (Seemiller et al. 2021).

To probe this preliminary research question, I posted a call for chapter proposals related to Generation Z and the college classroom on the National Communication Association CommNotes site in spring 2020 (pre-pandemic).

The call resulted in this text which contains original research on teacher-student communication processes and behaviors, communication frameworks for thinking about course delivery, and communication education topics that reflect the diverse thinking of US faculty in relation to their classrooms and Generation Z and how instructors are working to express student care and invoke engagement practices leading to effective teaching and learning reliant upon communication processes and practices in instructional spaces.

These topics reflect the work associated with communication education and instructional communication and are for colleagues who currently instruct, or plan to instruct, in communication classrooms or learning spaces in educational institutions or outside the academy to which communication impacts learning outcomes and organizational goals of a younger generation of citizens, students, and future professionals. The topic probes the communication processes required to connect and understand Gen Z as well as activities that advance their learning, develop their skills, and enhance their personal growth.

It is important to note that at the onset of this book's formation, we entered a global pandemic with COVID-19 (March 2020). This worldwide threat significantly impacted countries, people's daily lives at the most basic level, economic systems, health organizations, and travel to name a few. Higher education was not immune to the pandemic or the institutional and structural disruptions it caused. Educational systems were forced to go remote, rely on digital devices, applications, and tools to facilitate instructional and operational practices while striving to educate and support students. Faculty, staff, and school/college/university life as people knew it no longer existed. To complicate matters, a few weeks later, the US experienced significant social unrest and challenges to organizational, political, and societal structures concerning the treatment of people and how institutional and political organizations govern or protect their citizens and constituencies regardless of color, ethnicity, or race.

While this book set out to understand how instructors were communicating with, engaging, instructing, and researching Generation Z in learning spaces in normal times, it didn't initially account for the implications of a pandemic or US unrest concerning race and fair treatment. However, it was a natural progression that this project would begin to raise questions about how the pandemic and the practices of social structures as they intersect with class, privilege, race, and sex would impact Generation Z further as well as communication instruction. As a result, this book presents communication education and instructional communication original research and classroom-tested practices currently at work in the Gen Z college classroom.

It is my hope that the beginning work of this text is carried forward by other researchers interested in how to effectively instruct and collaborate with Generation Z to improve our overall world through the differences each of our generations can potentially make and to explore the communication competencies needed by instructors and students alike.

REFERENCES

Bethune, Sophie. "Gen Z More Likely to Report Mental Health Concerns." Last Updated January 2019. https://www.apa.org/monitor/2019/01/gen-z.

Downs, Cal W., Paul Harper, and Gary Hunt. 1976. "Internships in Speech Communication." *Communication Education* 25 (4): 276–282. DOI: 10.1080/03634527609384641.

Elmore, Tim. 2014. "Homelanders: The Next Generation." Last Updated February 27, 2014. https://www.psychologytoday.com/us/blog/artificial-maturity/201402/homelanders-the-next-generation.

McCroskey, James C., and Linda L. McCroskey. 2016. "Instructional Communication: The Historical Perspective." In *Handbook of Instructional Communication: Rhetorical and Relational Perspectives*, edited by Timothy P. Mottet, Virginia P. Richmond, and James C. McCroskey, 33–47. London: Routledge, Taylor and Francis Group.

Mottet, Timothy P., Virginia P. Richmond, and James C. McCroskey. 2016. *Handbook of Instructional Communication: Rhetorical and Relational Perspectives*. London: Routledge, Taylor and Francis Group. http://search.ebscohost.com/login.aspx?direct=true&AuthType=sso&db=cat00991a&AN=sth.ocn925332681&site=eds-live.

Pace, Wayne R., and Robert F. Ross. 1983. "The Basic Course in Organizational Communication." *Communication Education* 32 (4): 402–412. DOI: 10.1080/03634528309378561.

Pew Research Center. 2019a. "Defining Generations: Where Millennials end and Generation Z Begins." https://www.pewresearch.org/fact-tank/2019/01/17/where-millennials-end-and-generation-z-begins/.

Pew Research Center. 2019b. "Generations and Age." https://www.pewresearch.org/topics/generations-and-age/.

Seemiller, Corey, and Meghan Grace. 2016. *Generation Z Goes to College*. Hoboken, NJ: John Wiley & Sons.

Seemiller, Corey, Meghan Grace, Paula Dal Bo Campagnolo, Isa Mara Da Rosa Alves, and Gustavo Severo De Borba. 2021. "What Makes Learning Enjoyable? Perspectives of Today's College Students in the U.S. and Brazil." *Journal of Pedagogical Research* 5 (1): 1–17.

Tatum, Nicholas T., and T. Kody Frey. 2021. "(In)flexibility During Uncertainty? Conceptualizing Instructor Strictness During a Global Pandemic." *Communication Education* 70 (2): 214–216. DOI: 10.1080/03634523.2020.1857419.

Westwick, Joshua N., and Sherwyn P. Morreale. 2021. "Advancing an Agenda for Instructional Preparedness: Lessons Learned from the Transition to Remote Learning." *Communication Education* 70 (2): 217–222. DOI: 10.1080/03634523.2020.1857416.

Chapter 2

Motivation and Learning

Need-Supportive Teaching Style to Engage Gen Z

Sadia E. Cheema and Jie Zhang

INTRODUCTION

Engagement is vital in academic learning (Turner et al. 1998) as it expresses the behavioral intensity of students' active involvement in learning. It is through engagement that students' motivational processes contribute to their learning and development (Connell and Wellborn 1990), including their skill development and their overall performance in the course (Finn and Rock 1997). In contrast, disengaged students are passive, give up easily when faced with difficulty, express frustration, display negative emotions, struggle with concentration and generally withdraw from the class (Skinner and Belmont 1993). When students are actively engaged in the classroom, there is always something to be said about a teacher's behavior in the classroom. To better understand this, researchers have investigated socio-contextual factors (Skinner et al. 2008), such as the teacher's instructional style, interpersonal communication and classroom management, and their subsequent impact on students' academic engagement and motivation. Several motivational theories, such as the Self-determination theory (SDT) (Ryan and Deci 2002), provide insight on how teacher's instructional styles affect students' engagement and motivation (Ames and Archer 1988). This chapter will specifically address two such engagement-promoting features of teachers' instructional styles: autonomy supportive (versus controlling) and structure (versus chaos). According to SDT, autonomy supportive teachers facilitate students' personal autonomy by integrating their needs, interests, and goals to guide learning and activity which ultimately enhances their engagement level in the classroom. Such teachers are able to provide optimal challenges to students, use interesting and enriching learning activities, and highlight meaningful learning goals to the students (Assor et al. 2002; Reeve and Jang 2006). Furthermore, teachers who provide structure, that is, clarity on performance expectations, are also able to successfully engage students in the classroom.

However, it is important to consider how teachers' instructional styles interact with a new generation of students, Generation Z, born between the mid-1990s and 2012 (Twenge 2017). This new generation of learners includes a unique set of attributes, beliefs, social norms, and experiences that profoundly shape their worldview, and also impact educational approaches used to motivate and engage them in classrooms. Hence, previous pedagogical strategies to engage these learners are likely doomed if the characteristics of this generation of learners is not matched with teaching styles and instructional approaches that can successfully motivate and engage them in classrooms. The purpose of this chapter is to discuss the teacher's instructional styles most critical to engage Generation Z students, and identify their implication on their motivation, and engagement. Additionally, recommendations on instructional strategies aligning with autonomy supportive teaching style best suited for engaging Generation Z students will be discussed.

MOTIVATION AND EDUCATION: A SELF-DETERMINATION THEORY PERSPECTIVE

For students, interactions with their teachers are central to learning. These student teacher interactions also intersect with students' motivation and engagement in classrooms. One theoretical framework that connects this student-teacher interaction and provides insight on how teacher's motivating styles affect students' engagement (Ames and Archer 1988) is self-determination theory (SDT) (Deci and Ryan 2000). The basic premise of the theory is that social contexts of interactions can either be supportive or thwart students' motivation and engagement. In this context, need support becomes a crucial concept. Within SDT, the satisfaction of three psychological needs: *autonomy, competence, and relatedness*, positively affect motivation and engagement (Ryan and Deci 2000). In the context of education, *autonomy* involves students' being given more choice with regards to using instructional materials for assignments. *Competence* refers to recognizing students' need to understand their coursework. Lastly, *Relatedness* refers to recognizing students' need for personal support and need for belonging in their school relationships. Classroom environments and teaching styles can either facilitate or thwart these needs (Deci and Ryan 1985). Accordingly, the theory postulates that students' engagement in activities in the classroom is dependent on the satisfaction of these psychological needs (Stefanou et al. 2004). Consequently, it becomes critical for teachers to formulate pedagogical approaches that satisfy these needs in a classroom, that is, need supportive teaching. Within SDT, three dimensions of need supportive teaching are discussed: *autonomy support, structure, and involvement*. These dimensions of need support originate from the three psychological needs of autonomy, competence and relatedness, and complement each other in terms of their effect on students' experiences of satisfaction of such needs (Connell and Wellborn 1990).

The first dimension is autonomy support, that is, an inherent desire for students to experience learning as a self-chosen act reflective of their values and needs. According to SDT, teachers' motivating styles range from controlling to autonomy supportive (Deci et al. 1981). Specifically, in controlling style, teachers define how students should think, feel, and work on tasks which ultimately interferes with students' inner motivations to actively engage in classroom activities. In contrast, autonomy-supportive teachers create classroom opportunities to facilitate the needs, interests, and preferences of students that guide their learning and engagement in activities (Reeve et al. 2004). Additionally, this teaching style encourages teachers to show respect (Belmont et al. 1992), allow criticism (Assor and Kaplan 2001), and use informational language to pressurize students to accomplish tasks. Particularly in academic settings, researchers have found that students of autonomy-supportive teachers compared to controlling teachers exhibit greater conceptual understanding (Grolnick and Ryan 1987), and higher academic performance (Boggiano et al. 1993). In other words, autonomy-supportive teachers can facilitate positive educational outcomes and are better at engaging students and enhancing their intrinsic motivation during classroom instruction (Hardre and Reeve 2003).

The second dimension is structure which is associated with the satisfaction of need for competency. This dimension argues that students' level of competency is enhanced if they feel they have more control over their educational outcomes. Previous researchers have theorized this dimension into four components (Jang et al. 2010). First, teachers can provide structure by focusing on clarity that is, giving clear and detailed instructions. Second, teachers can provide guidance by offering help or support on on-going activities. Third, teachers can offer support and encouragement by communicating positive expectations from coursework (Belmont et al. 1992). Fourth, they can offer informational feedback to students that ultimately lets them experience control over their valued educational outcomes.

The third dimension of involvement is associated with need for relatedness which is an inherent desire of students to develop and maintain strong interpersonal relationships (Baumeister and Leary 1995). Within the context of education, teacher-student relationships do not satisfy the students' needs for interpersonal relatedness which have a strong correlation with students' emotions, motivational beliefs and achievement (Ahmed et al. 2010). In other words, students feel respected and cared for when teachers express involvement in their lives. Teachers can express involvement by showing affection, attunement, dedicating resources (e.g., time), and supportive behaviors.

This chapter focuses on the engagement-promoting aspect of teaching style, that is, autonomy supportive (vs. being controlling), and structure that make important contributions to support students' classroom engagement. Previous literature has found the relationship between autonomy-supportive and structure as antagonistic (Daniels and Bizar 1998), curvilinear (deCharms 1984), independent (Skinner and Belmont 1993), and complementary (Jang et al. 2010). The relationship is antagonistic when the provision of one interferes with the provision of another, for example, structure (i.e., rules and detailed guidelines) will diminish teachers' autonomy-supportive (i.e., provision of choice) behavior to guide learning. On similar lines, it is curvilinear

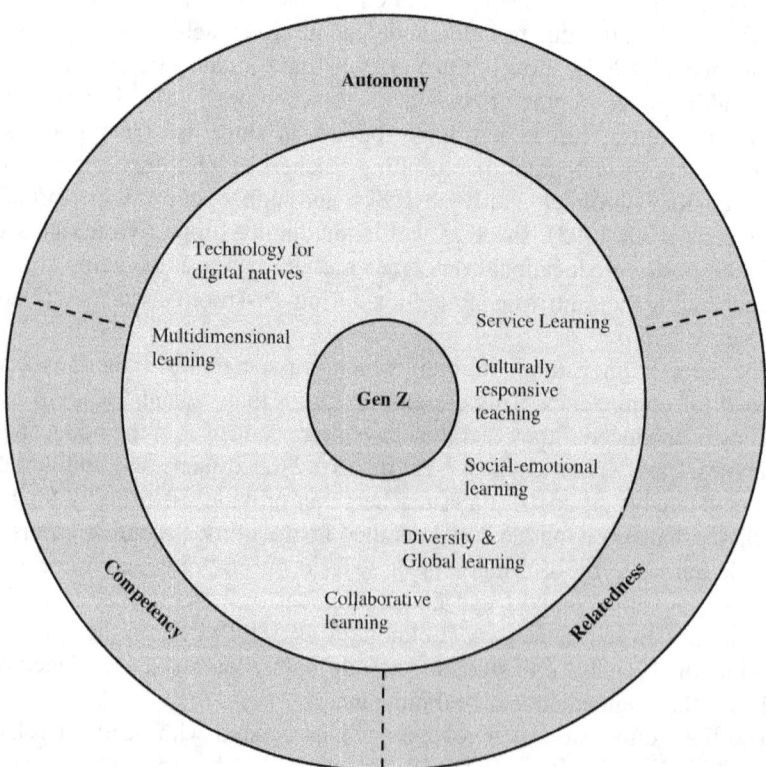

Figure 2.1 Need-Supportive Instructional Strategies to Engage Generation Z. *Source:* Cheema and Zhang 2021.

when teachers with moderate levels of structure have a high level of autonomy support that yields optimal classroom engagement (deCharms 1984). When this relationship is independent, the assumption is that structure and autonomy- support uniquely contribute to students' motivation and engagement. However, it can become complementary when structure is provided in an autonomy supportive way (Jang et al. 2010).

In this chapter, a complementary relationship between autonomy-support and structure is suggested to yield an optimal level of student classroom engagement for Generation Zers who are heavily influenced by technology and social media, have a low attention span, are constantly multitasking, struggle with under-developed interpersonal skills, have increased risk of mental health issues, and desire convenience and immediacy in learning (See fig. 2.1).

In the following section, various autonomy-supportive and structural teaching-learning design strategies are discussed to optimally motivate and engage Generation Zers in the classrooms.

INSTRUCTIONAL DESIGN STRATEGIES TO SUPPORT GENERATION Z

Generation Z, born between 1997 and 2012 (Livingston and Barroso 2019), are identified as digital natives as they grew up with the rapid development of the World Wide Web, smartphones (Parker and Igielnik 2020), internet, and social media (technology, Generation Z use t Dimock 2019). As such, they desire learning that is technologically advanced. Additionally, compared to other generational cohorts before them (e.g., Millennials, Generation X), Generation Z students are more racially, ethically, and culturally diverse student population (Chicca and Shellenbarger 2018) who desire learning approaches that correlate with their social, political, and economical experiences. As this generation infiltrates colleges, they bring these unique characteristics, interests, preferences to learning environments as well, making it challenging for teachers to keep them engaged in classrooms. Hence, it is urgent for faculty to consider Gen Z's learning styles and communication preferences when selecting the instructional strategies to optimally motivate and engage them.

Technology for Digital Natives

Growing up with technology, Generation Z use technological tools frequently and are accustomed to the digital world (Chicca and Shellenbarger 2018). Anderson and Jiang (2018) reports that 95% of American teens have access to smartphones while Shatto and Erwin (2016) report that on average, Generation

Z spend nine hours on cell phones every day. Eighty-nine percent of American teens reported being online "almost constantly" or at least "several times a day," and their most favorite online platforms are YouTube, Instagram, and Snapchat (Anderson and Jiang 2018). Emotional attachment to the internet and electronic devices is also reported. The Generation Z teenagers between 13 and 17 years of age reported that they would get more upset when being taken away access to the internet or connections with friends through cell phone or texting than prevention from allowance money or new video games (Palley 2012). To Gen Zers, internet and technology have become an essential part of their life and digital intelligence has emerged into Gardner's multiple intelligences theoretical framework (Adams 2004).

Accordingly, teachers need to consider ways to harness technology to supplement educational activities. This generation has been exposed to electronic books, video lessons, digital media, and visual teaching materials through their K–12 educational experience. Hence, relying on text-based materials and traditional lecture-based classrooms will be unappealing, and reduce their motivation and engagement in learning activities. Other, more technologically advanced learning tools, such as e-learning instructional materials, software, internet-guided learning, digital storytelling, social media, educational badges (Abramovich et al. 2013), and infographic syllabus can be used as multi-dimensional instructional approaches to ensure an optimal learning environment for this generation (Mocek 2017).

In particular, Gen Zers are reported as frequent users of social media, so instructors could incorporate such platforms in teaching to encourage peer interactions, promote self-reflection, support long-term retention of content, and contribute to deeper learning (Samuels-Peretza et al. 2017). Studies report the effectiveness of using social media, including blogs (Yang and Chang 2012), wikis, Facebook (Hemmi et al. 2009), twitter (Junco 2013), Google docs (George et al. 2013), and many more. Technology platforms, such as Skype, Facetime, Google Hangout, WhatsApp, Facebook Messenger, and Zoom, allow instructors and students to meet virtually online, share resources, exchange ideas, collaborate on joint projects, and keep connected anytime and anywhere (Zhang and Pearlman 2018), especially in a COVID-19 world when remote teaching and social distancing become the new normal. Such approaches will also make the learning environment autonomy-supportive, providing an optimal level of structure in the classroom to enhance the motivation and engagement of Generation Zers.

Multidimensional Learning

Constantly surrounded by various technological tools and ways to access information, Generation Z tend to engage in multitasking and pay continuous partial attention rather than being fully engaged in and focusing on one task (Firat 2013). They are reported to have a shorter attention span of eight seconds, compared to the Millennials' twelve seconds (Shatto and Erwin 2016). Internet and powerful web search engines allow Gen Z to find answers or get connected quickly, resulting in their inclination toward convenience and immediacy, or instant gratification (Chicca and Shellenbarger 2018). Instead of checking the accuracy and reliability of the information, they show a tendency to believe and use the first source they found. They may get easily frustrated when immediate answers are not available. These characteristics lead to a less efficient and higher stressful working process, impatience, and expectations of prompt feedback (Firat 2013). As such, virtual connectivity will probably be the best solution to immerse these multitaskers into a learning activity. This can be achieved by envisioning ways to incorporate the use of technology in- and outside- of the classroom. For example, holding virtual office hours can be substituted for face-to-face meetings, and using social media for course announcements and reminders instead of solely relying on emails. Use of such familiar and preferred technologies will motivate students and keep them engaged.

Additionally, transitioning between learning modalities, such as lecture, discussion, audio-visual content, demonstrations, and peer learning low stakes activities will provide short bursts of teaching and support this generation to stay attentive. This strategy can also be supplemented with finding course materials that seem relevant to this generation and integrating them into the curriculum. For example, issues pertaining to activism, and equal rights are of special interest to generation Z as they are more racially and ethnically diverse than previous generations (Pew Research Center 2020). Additionally, the use of active-learning techniques, such as concept mapping, flipped classroom, case studies, low stakes assignments with short-term learning objectives, problem-based learning, and gamification tools such as Jeopardy, Kahoot, and Quizizz will reduce their constant desire for immediacy and convenience by giving them response and feedback in real time. This can help students to find answers using multiple learning techniques that also help them meaningfully engage with the material presented. By creating the above-mentioned opportunities, teachers are being autonomy-supportive, providing a moderate level of structure to enhance the inner motivations of students so they are optimally engaged in the classroom.

Service Learning, Collaborative Learning, and Diversity and Global Learning

The National Association of Colleges and Employers (NACE) Center for Career Development and Talent Acquisition (2018) identifies eight career readiness competencies, including professionalism and work ethic, oral and written communication, teamwork and collaboration, critical thinking and problem solving, global and intercultural fluency, leadership, digital technology, and career management. Furthermore, the NACE Center (2018) reports lower proficiency rates from the employers in all eight areas than the students' self-ratings, and universities need to do more to better prepare their students for careers. Comparably, the Association of American Colleges and Universities (AAC&U) recognizes ten high-impact practices (HIPs) being effective in improving student retention, learning, engagement, and career preparation in a new global century (Kuh 2008). Among those ten HIPs, service learning, collaborative learning, and diversity and global learning are three practices that specifically support Gen Zers' learning needs and career readiness.

Compared to the previous generations, Generation Z learn more efficiently through observation and practice (Shatto and Erwin 2016) and prefer hands-on activities in which they can apply knowledge and skills to real life immediately (Donaghy 2014). To meet Gen Zers' pragmatic nature, teachers need to incorporate hands-on activities, experiential learning, and service learning opportunities for students to connect college curriculum with real life practice and to make learning more authentic and meaningful. Such activities will help students demonstrate their understanding of the content knowledge and apply their learned knowledge and skills beyond college classrooms to the community, analyze and connect different ideas, evaluate to make decisions, and create new ideas, following the revised Bloom's Taxonomy (Anderson and Krathwohl 2001).

Due to an increasing amount of time spent in a virtual environment versus declined time in the real world, Generation Z experience difficulty interacting face-to-face, which hinders the development of their social skills and relationship (Chicca and Shellenbarger 2018). Collaborative projects using technology is an effective way to counter this problem and build their teamwork and interpersonal skills. Moreover, when working with people from diverse backgrounds, students gain better understanding about themselves and others, and develop intra- and interpersonal skills through collaboration on a joint project toward a common goal. A technology enhanced Collaborative Online International Learning (COIL) course could be a cost-effective solution for universities to integrate experiential learning, collaborative learning, diversity and global learning into one course. The instructors at the international partner universities work together to provide students global learning opportunities with collaboration and diversity competencies (Zhang and Pearlman 2018). Technology enhanced COIL courses enable students to learn course content, build interpersonal competencies, develop interpersonal relationships, and demonstrate their learning and growth through experiential, collaborative, diversity learning in a global context.

To offer any of these service learning, collaborative learning, and diversity and global learning opportunities, the instructors need to carefully design the activities and projects, closely align them with learning objectives, attentively monitor student progress, offer specific and immediate feedback and support, and provide ample opportunities for students to reflect throughout the process. All of these three HIPs provide students opportunities to support autonomy, increase personal and academic competency, develop interpersonal relationships, and get ready for career.

Culturally Responsive Teaching and Social-emotional Learning

Generation Z have been growing up with the impact of the financial hardships and stressors at home. The Great Recession nationally and globally from 2007 to 2009 resulted in a widened income gap, shrinking middle class, and higher unemployment rate (Turner 2015). Now COVID-19 has led to even greater uncertainty socially, politically and economically. Compared to the other generations, a significantly higher percentage, or 50% to be specific, of the oldest Gen Zers with the age range from 18 to 23 reported job loss or pay cut either themselves or someone in the household due to the coronavirus outbreak (Pew Research Center 2020). All these factors lead to concerns with emotional, physical, and financial safety. Because of that, Gen Zers are pragmatic, cautious, and at higher risk for isolation, insecurity, anxiety, and depression (Chicca and Shellenbarger 2018).

Being a content expert is not sufficient for today's university faculty. To meet the changing needs of their student population, faculty need to find ways to convey care to connect with their students and to make learning more relevant and meaningful. Research indicates that faculty caring is one of the four important factors to engage Generation Z students in learning, motivate them to work, and increase the likelihood for them to be successful (Miller and Mills 2019). Thanks to technology, faculty could work on relationship building with their students beyond face-to-face classroom settings through emails and messaging tools within the Learning Management System (LMS) such as Blackboard Announcements. They could initiate interactions with students even before the beginning of the semester, maintain frequent interactions with students, provide additional support to clarify questions and offer guidance in a more timely manner. Open communication is one strategy that faculty could implement to assure students that they are approachable and willing to listen and support, which contributes to a caring and supportive learning environment. Researchers express concerns regarding the amount of additional time and work faculty will spend in communicating and providing guidance to students (Varallo 2008). Conversely, students report positive and

Table 2.1 Instructional Design Strategies and Approaches to Engage Gen Z in Learning

Gen Z Characteristics	Instructional Design Strategies to Engage Gen Z
Digital natives relying on technology	*Strategy:* Technology for digital natives *Learning outcome:* To encourage peer interactions, promote self-reflection, support long-term retention of content, and contribute to deeper learning by including: • e-learning instructional materials such as, softwares, internet-guided learning, digital storytelling, social media, educational badges, and infographic syllabus. • using social media platforms, such as Skype, Facetime, Google Hangout, WhatsApp, Facebook Messenger, and Zoom, allow instructors and students to meet virtually online, share resources, exchange ideas, collaborate on joint projects.
Multitaskers who desire convenience & immediacy	*Strategy:* Multidimensional learning *Learning outcome:* To demonstrate information literacy concepts, and learn ethical principles related to confidentiality and social media use by including: • multidimensional learning modalities such as lecture, discussion, audio-visual content, demonstrations, peer learning, and active-learning techniques in the classroom to provide timely response and feedback in real-time.
Pragmatic	*Strategy:* Service Learning, Collaborative Learning, and Diversity and Global Learning *Learning outcome:* To develop career readiness competencies of professionalism and work ethic, oral and written communication, teamwork and collaboration, critical thinking and problem solving, and global and intercultural fluency by including: • experiential learning, collaborative learning, diversity and global learning, and service learning opportunities.
Heterogenous & multicultural group who are at higher risk of developing mental health issues	*Strategy:* Culturally responsive teaching and Social emotional learning *Learning outcome:* To identify and manage emotions, develop self-awareness and responsible decision making, build empathy and respect toward others, establish and maintain relationships. This can be achieved by: • frequent use of Learning Management Systems (LMS). • student-centered teaching repertoires.

Source: Cheema and Zhang (2021).

professional faculty-student interactions help them feel welcome, ease anxiety, and engage in learning, which lead to increased retention and improved learning outcomes (Miller and Mills 2019).

Instructors could provide student-centered teaching through culturally responsive teaching, in which they start with knowing self, the students and the context, and tailor the instructional materials and assessments to the students' backgrounds (Ladson-Billings 1994; Gay 2000). A teacher may conduct an icebreaker at the beginning of the semester, in person or online, to learn about each individual student's background and interests. During the semester, the teacher could offer options for students to propose topics of research projects or jigsaw mini-lessons based on their interests and strengths. Thus, the teacher encourages students to be actively engaged in learning and develop competencies through autonomy support.

In social-emotional learning (SEL), Collaboration for Academic, Social, and Emotional Learning (CASEL) reports that students identify and manage their own emotions, develop self-awareness and responsible decision-making, build empathy and respect toward others, establish and maintain relationship (2000). Research shows the effectiveness of implementing SEL in reducing stress and anxiety while improving students' attitudinal, behavioral and educational performance (Durlak et al. 2011; Stocker and Gallagher 2019). When students get anxious and stressful because of family, work, well-being, financial situations on top of the academic demands, it would be helpful if the instructor is willing to work with the students to find possible solutions with caring and understanding. University faculty could create a positive environment through open communication, clear guidance and expectations, culturally responsive teaching and social emotional learning to support autonomy, increase personal and academic competency, develop interpersonal relationships, and facilitate students' growth. table 2.1 summarizes some instructional design strategies to get Gen Z engaged in learning.

CONCLUSION

While examining the literature, numerous Generation Z characteristics were identified, including: a) digital natives relying on technology; b) multitaskers who desire convenience and immediacy in learning environments; c) pragmatic; d) largely heterogeneous, multicultural group who are at higher risk of developing mental health issues. These generational characteristics immensely impact their inner motivations and learning aptitudes, thus requiring a shift in the role of teachers in educational environments. To help this generation meaningfully engage in classrooms, teachers need to focus on two instructional style dimensions: a) being autonomy supportive and b) provide a moderate level of structure in curriculum. The incorporation of these dimensions will make the educational environments enriching and relevant for this generation which leads to a higher level of engagement in the classroom.

To keep Generation Z engaged:

1) Harness technology to supplement education activities such as e-learning instructional materials, software, internet-guided learning, digital storytelling, social media, educational badges, and infographic syllabus.

2) Rely on multidimensional learning modalities such as lecture, discussion, audio-visual content, demonstrations, peer learning, and active-learning techniques that will reduce their constant desire for immediacy and convenience by giving them timely response and feedback in real-time.
3) Inclusion of experiential learning, collaborative learning, diversity and global learning, and service-learning opportunities for students to connect college curriculum with real life practice and to make learning more authentic and meaningful.
4) Culturally responsive teaching and social-emotional learning that addresses Gen Z's emotional, physical, and financial safety.

REFERENCES

Abramovich, Samuel, Christian Schunn, and Ross Mitsuo Higashi. 2013. "Are Badges Useful in Education?: It Depends Upon the Type of Badge and Expertise of Learner." *Educational Technology Research and Development* 61 (2): 217–232. DOI: 10.1007/s11423-013-9289-2.

Adams, Nan B. 2004. "Digital Intelligence Fostered by Technology." *Journal of Technology Studies* 30 (2): 93–97. DOI: 10.21061/jots.v30i2.a.5.

Ahmed, Wondimu, Alexander Minnaert, Greetje van der Werf, and Hans Kuyper. 2010. "Perceived Social Support and Early Adolescents' Achievement: The Mediational Roles of Motivational Beliefs and Emotions." *Journal of Youth and Adolescence* 39 (1): 36–46. DOI: 10.1007/s10964-008-9367-7.

Ames, Carole, and Jenner J. Archer. 1988. "Achievement Goals in the Classroom: Students' Learning Strategies and Motivational Processes." *Journal of Educational Psychology* 80 (3): 260–267. DOI: 10.1037/0022-0663.80.3.260.

Anderson, Lorin W., and David R. Krathwohl (Eds). 2001. *A Taxonomy for Learning, Teaching, and Assessing: A Revision of Bloom's Taxonomy of Educational Objectives*. New York: Longman.

Anderson, Monica, and Jingjing Jiang. 2018. "Teens, Social Media & Technology 2018." *Pew Research Center*. Last Modified May 31, 2018. https://www.pewresearch.org/internet/2018/05/31/teens-social-media-technology-2018/.

Assor, Avi, and Haya Kaplan. 2001. "Mapping the Domain of Autonomy Support: Five Important Ways to Enhance or Undermine Students' Experience of Autonomy in Learning." In *Trends and Prospects in Motivation Research*, edited by Anastasia Efklides, Richard Sorrentino, and Julius Kuhl, 99–118. Dordrecht, The Netherlands: Kluwer.

Assor, Avi, Haya Kaplan, and Guy Roth. 2002. "Choice is Good, But Relevance is Excellent: Autonomy-Enhancing and Suppressing Teacher Behaviours Predicting Students' Engagement in Schoolwork." *British Journal of Educational Psychology* 72 (2): 261–278. DOI: 10.1348/000709902158883.

Baumeister, Roy F., and Mark R. Leary. 1995. "The Need to Belong: Desire for Interpersonal Attachments as a Fundamental Human Motivation." *Psychological Bulletin* 117 (3): 497–529. DOI: 10.1037/0033-2909.117.3.497.

Belmont, Michael J., Ellen A. Skinner, James G. Wellborn, and James P. Connell. 1992. *Two Measures of Teacher Provision of Involvement, Structure, and Autonomy Support (Technical Report)*. Rochester, NY: University of Rochester.

Boggiano, Ann K., Cheryl Flink, Ann Shields, Aubyn Seelbach, and Marty Barrett. 1993. "Use of Techniques Promoting Students' Self-Determination: Effects on Students' Analytic Problem-Solving Skills." *Motivation and Emotion* 17: 319–336. DOI: 10.1007/bf00992323.

Chicca, Jennifer, and Teresa Shellenbarger. 2018. "Connecting with Generation Z: Approaches in Nursing Education." *Teaching and Learning in Nursing* 13 (3): 180–184. DOI: 10.1016/j.teln.2018.03.008.

Collaboration for Academic, Social, and Emotional Learning (CASEL). "CASEL's Widely Used Framework Identifies Five Core Competencies." Accessed June 25, 2020. https://casel.org/what-is-sel/.

Connell, James P., and James G. Wellborn. 1990. "Competence, Autonomy and Relatedness: A Motivational Analysis of Self-System Processes." In *Minnesota Symposium on Child Psychology* 23, edited by Megan R. Gunnar and L. Alan Sroufe, 43–77. Hillsdale, NJ: Lawrence Erlbaum Associates, Inc.

Daniels, Harvey, and Marilyn Bizar. 1998. *Methods That Matter: Six Structures for Best Practice Classrooms*. Portland, ME: Stenhouse.

deCharms, R. Christopher. 1984. "Motivation Enhancement in Educational Settings." In *Research on Motivation in Education: Student Motivation* 1, edited by Russell Ames and Carole Ames, 275–310. Orlando, FL: Academic Press.

Deci, Edward L., Allan J. Schwartz, Louise Sheinman, and Richard M. Ryan. 1981. "An Instrument to Assess Adult's Orientations Toward Control Versus Autonomy in Children: Reflections on Intrinsic Motivation and Perceived Competence." *Journal of Educational Psychology* 73 (5): 642–650. DOI: 10.1037/0022-0663.73.5.642.

Deci, Edward L., and Richard M. Ryan. 1985. *Intrinsic Motivation and Self-Determination in Human Behavior*. New York: Plenum.

Deci, Edward L., and Richard M. Ryan. 2000. "The 'What' and 'Why' of Goal Pursuits: Human Needs and the Self-Determination of Behavior." *Psychological Inquiry* 11 (4): 227–268. DOI: 10.1207/S15327965PLI1104_01.

Dimock, Michael. 2019. "Defining Generations: Where Millennials End and Generation Z Begins." *Pew Research Center*. Last Modified January 17, 2019. http://www.pewresearch.org/fact-tank/2019/01/17/where-millennials-end-and-generation-z-begins/.

Donaghy, Roger. 2014. "Innovation Imperative: Meet Generation Z." Last Modified November 18, 2014. https://news.northeastern.edu/2014/11/18/innovation-imperative-meet-generation-z/.

Durlak, Joseph, Roger P. Weissberg, Allison Dymnicki, Rebecca Taylor, and Kriston K. Schellinger. 2011. "The Impact of Enhancing Students' Social and Emotional Learning: A Meta-Analysis of School-Based Universal Interventions." *Child Development* 82 (1): 405–432. DOI: 10.1111/cdev.2011.82.issue-1.

Finn, Jeremy D., and Donald A. Rock. 1997. "Academic Success Among Students at Risk for School Failure." *Journal of Applied Psychology* 82 (2): 221–234. DOI: 10.1037/0021-9010.82.2.221.

Firat, Mehmet. 2013. "Multitasking or Continuous Partial Attention: A Critical Bottleneck for Digital Natives." *Turkish Online Journal of Distance Education* 14 (1): Article 23. DOI: 10.17718/tojde.52102.

Gay, Geneva. 2000. *Culturally Responsive Teaching*. New York: Teachers College Press.

George, Daniel R., Tomi D. Dreibelbis, and Betsy Aumiller. 2013. "How We Used Two Social Media Tools to Enhance Aspects of Active Learning during Lectures." *Medical Teacher* 35 (12): 985–988. DOI: 10.3109/0142159X.2013.818631.

Grolnick, Wendy S., and Richard M. Ryan. 1987. "Autonomy in Children's Learning: An Experimental and Individual Difference Investigation." *Journal of Personality and Social Psychology* 52 (5): 890–898. DOI: 10.1037/0022-3514.52.5.890.

Hardre, Patricia L., and Johnmarshall Reeve. 2003. "A Motivational Model of Rural Students' Intentions to Persist in, Versus Drop out of, High School." *Journal of Educational Psychology* 95 (2): 347–356. DOI: 10.1037/0022-0663.95.2.347.

Hemmi, A., S. Bayne, and R. Land. 2009. "The Appropriation and Repurposing of Social Technologies in Higher Education." *Journal of Computer Assisted Learning* 25 (1): 19–30. DOI: 10.1111/j.1365-2729.2008.00306.x.

Jang, Hyungshim, Johnmarshall Reeve, and Edward L. Deci. 2010. "Engaging Students in Learning Activities: It is Not Autonomy Support or Structure but Autonomy Support and Structure." *Journal of Educational Psychology* 102 (3): 588–600. DOI: 10.1037/a0019682.

Junco, Reynol. 2013. "Comparing Actual and Self-Reported Measures of Facebook Use." *Computers in Human Behavior* 29 (3): 626–631. DOI: 10.1016/j.chb.2012.11.007.

Kuh, George D. 2008. *High-Impact Educational Practices: What They Are, Who Has Access to Them, and Why They Matter*. Washington, D.C.: American Association of Colleges and Universities.

Ladson-Billings, Gloria. 1994. *The Dreamkeepers: Successful Teachers of African American Children* (1st Ed.). San Francisco: Jossey-Bass Publishing Company.

Livingston, Gretchen, and Amanda Barroso. 2019. "For U.S. Teens Today, Summer Means More Schooling and Less Leisure Time Than in the Past." *Pew Research Center*. Last Modified August 13, 2019. https://www.pewresearch.org/fact-tank/2019/08/13/for-u-s-teens-today-summer-means-more-schooling-and-less-leisure-time-than-in-the-past/.

Miller, Amy, and Brooklyn B. Mills. 2019. "'If They Don't Care, I Don't Care': Millennial and Generation Z Students and the Impact of Faculty Caring." *The Journal of the Scholarship of Teaching and Learning* 19 (4): 78–89. https://files.eric.ed.gov/fulltext/EJ1234123.pdf.

Mocek, Evelyn Anne. 2017. "The Effects of Syllabus Design on Information Retention by At-risk First Semester Students." *Syllabus* 6 (2). Accessed June 25, 2020. http://www.syllabusjournal.org/syllabus/article/view/222/Mocek.

National Association of Colleges and Employers (NACE) Center for Career Development and Talent Acquisition. 2018. "Are College Graduates 'Career Ready'?" Last Modified February 19, 2018. https://www.naceweb.org/career-readiness/competencies/are-college-graduates-career-ready/.

Palley, Will. 2012. "Gen Z: Digital in Their DNA." Last Modified April 23, 2012. http://www.jwtintelligence.com/wpcontent/uploads/2012/04/F_INTERNAL_Gen_Z_0418122.pdf.

Parker, Kim, and Ruth Igielnik. 2020. "On the Cusp of Adulthood and Facing an Uncertain Future: What We Know About Gen Z So Far." *Pew Research Center.* Last Modified May 14, 2020. https://www.pewsocialtrends.org/essay/on-the-cusp-of-adulthood-and-facing-an-uncertain-future-what-we-know-about-gen-z-so-far/.

Pew Research Center. 2020. "Worries About Coronavirus Surge, as Most Americans Expect a Recession – or Worse." Last Modified March 26, 2020. https://www.people-press.org/2020/03/26/worries-about-coronavirus-surge-as-most-americans-expect-a-recession-or-worse/.

Reeve, Johnmarshall, and Hyungshim Jang. 2006. "What Teachers Say and Do to Support Students' Autonomy During a Learning Activity." *Journal of Educational Psychology* 98 (1): 209–218. DOI: 10.1037/0022-0663.98.1.209.

Reeve, Johnmarshall, Hyungshim Jang, Dan Carrell, Soohyun Jeon, and Jon Barch. 2004. "Enhancing Students' Engagement by Increasing Teachers' Autonomy Support." *Motivation and Emotion* 28 (2): 147–169. DOI: 10.1023/B:MOEM.0000032312.95499.6f.

Ryan, Richard M., and Edward L. Deci. 2000. "Self-Determination Theory and the Facilitation of Intrinsic Motivation, Social Development, and Well-Being." *American Psychologist* 55 (1): 68–78. DOI: 10.7717/peerj-cs.230/fig-3.

Ryan, Richard M., and Edward L. Deci. 2002. "Overview of Self-Determination Theory: An Organismic Dialectical Perspective." In *Handbook of Self-determination Research*, edited by Edward L. Deci and Richard M. Ryan, 3–33. Rochester, NY: University of Rochester.

Samuels-Peretza, Debbie, Lana Dvorkin Camielb, Karen Teeleyc, and Gouri Banerjeed. 2017. "Digitally Inspired Thinking: Can Social Media Lead to Deep Learning in Higher Education?" *College Teaching* 65 (1): 32–39. DOI: 10.1080/87567555.2016.1225663.

Shatto, Bobbi, and Kelly Erwin. 2016. "Moving on From Millennials: Preparing for Generation Z." *The Journal of Continuing Education in Nursing* 47 (6): 253–254. DOI: 10.3928/00220124-20160518-05.

Skinner, Ellen, Carrie Furrer, Gwen Marchand, and Thomas Kindermann. 2008. "Engagement and Disaffection in the Classroom: Part of a Larger Motivational Dynamic?" *Journal of Educational Psychology* 100 (4): 765–781. DOI: 10.1037/a0012840.

Skinner, Ellen A., and Michael J. Belmont. 1993. "Motivation in the Classroom: Reciprocal Effects of Teacher Behavior and Student Engagement Across the School Year." *Journal of Educational Psychology* 85 (4): 571–581. DOI: 10.1037/0022-0663.85.4.571.

Stefanou, Candice R., Kathleen C. Perencevich, Matthew DiCintio, and Julianne C. Turner. 2004. "Supporting Autonomy in the Classroom: Ways Teachers Encourage Student Decision Making and Ownership." *Educational Psychologist* 39 (2): 97–110. DOI: 10.1207/s15326985ep3902_2.

Stocker, Shevaun L., and Kristel M. Gallagher. 2019. "Alleviating Anxiety and Altering Appraisals: Social-Emotional Learning in the College Classroom." *College Teaching* 67 (1): 23–35. DOI: 10.1080/87567555.2018.1515722.

Turner, Anthony. 2015. "Generation Z: Technology and Social Interest." *The Journal of Individual Psychology* 71 (2): 103–113. Accessed May 25, 2020. DOI: 10.1353/jip.2015.0021.

Turner, Julianne C., Debra K. Meyer, Kathleen E. Cox, Candice Logan, Matthew DiCintio, and Cynthia T. Thomas. 1998. "Involvement in Mathematics: Teachers' Strategies and Students' Perceptions." *Journal of Educational Psychology* 90 (4): 730–745. DOI: 10.1037/0022-0663.90.4.730.

Twenge, Jean M. 2017. *iGen: Why Today's Super-Connected Kids are Growing Up Less Rebellious, More Tolerant, Less Happy-and Completely Unprepared for Adulthood*. New York, NY: Atria.

Varallo, Sharon M. 2008. "Motherwork in Academe: Intensive Caring for the Millennial Student." *Women's Studies in Communication* 31 (2): 151–157. DOI: 10.1080/07491409.2008.10162527.

Yang, C., and Y. S. Chang. 2012. "Assessing the Effects of Interactive Blogging on Student Attitudes Towards Peer Interaction, Learning Motivation, and Academic Achievements." *Journal of Computer Assisted Learning* 28 (2): 126–135. DOI: 10.1111/j.1365-2729.2011.00423.x.

Zhang, Jie, and Ann Giralico Pearlman. 2018. "Expanding Access to International Education Through Technology Enhanced Collaborative Online International Learning (COIL) Courses." *The International Journal of Technology in Teaching and Learning* 14 (1): 1–11. https://sicet.org/main/wp-content/uploads/2019/03/1_Zhang_Jie.pdf.

Chapter 3

Acknowledging the Needs of Gen Z
Opening Spaces for Connection and Care
Kristen T. Christman and Jessica D. McCall

RECOGNIZING THE SPACE

Early March 2020

I was listening to student speeches in my CST 105 course and something started to happen. We were about the third person in and one of my students leaned over to me and said, "I didn't expect this," and I just smiled. She was referring to the openness and vulnerability of my students when sharing deep and even dark stories and connections to their lives in front of virtually "strangers" in their very first speech only weeks into the semester. No one in the class knew each other, so why would they share things about themselves that otherwise they normally keep hidden Family violence, abuse, coming out, drugs and low self-esteem etc., were all revealed in 3 speeches; 22 more to come.

This moment was powerful. I was thrilled to have students open up, to share, and to be brave. I felt for a minute that maybe, just maybe, I had helped to create an environment where they feel comfortable sharing these delicate subjects. I hope for this moment in all of my classes where everyone feels "ok" being themselves and knowing that this is a place where they will be welcomed and supported and acknowledged.

We all have a need and a desire to be connected, to have a purpose, and to be
 acknowledged. Without acknowledgment, there is "the possibility of being isolated, marginalized, ignored, and forgotten by others" (Hyde 2006, 1). While college students are often connected with and finding purpose through their digital devices, they are conversely disconnected from the classroom

community and intentional relational development. Many instructors have seen an increase in stress, depression, and anxiety (Twenge 2017, 93). These circumstances may suggest the necessity of supportive and intentional acknowledgment in educational spaces. As instructors, we believe it is necessary to bridge the space between ritualistic recognition and acknowledgment, but research has not thoroughly explored what our students think about this. Do they care about acknowledgment? Does it matter? What does acknowledgment look like to them?

THE CRISIS SPACE

As we set out to consider the importance of acknowledgment within the traditional face-to-face classroom, mid-March 2020 brought COVID-19, and forced higher education to entirely online platforms. This pandemic changed teaching and learning for the foreseeable future and our study of acknowledgment.

Mid-March 2020

I remember being in class one day and telling my students that the very next week there would be no class and for the rest of the semester, we would be all online. I wouldn't see them again, maybe ever.

On the same day, at the end of one of my courses, after sharing this information and assuring them we would figure this out together and they would be "OK," a few students came up to thank me and even to give me a hug and say they were going to miss being in class. It was such a nice moment, until one of my students got very emotional and apologetically explained her emotion sharing with us that her mother was in China and she wasn't sure when she would see her again. It was at that moment that whatever I thought COVID-19 was, became all the more real and the connections we have to one another became all the more important for me to maintain online.

Instead of considering the importance of acknowledgment in a face-to-face context, we were now dealt with the complexity of also looking at acknowledgment in online environments. We know that previous research has focused on the importance of teacher-student interaction in developing and maintaining student engagement in online learning spaces (i.e., Morreale, Thorpe, and Westwick 2020; Martin and Bolliger 2018; King 2014; Dixson 2010; Gayton and McEwen 2007). As noted by Martin and Bolliger (2018), "Online learners want instructors who support, listen to, and communicate with them" (218). What we didn't know is how a worldwide pandemic would alter student expectations and needs. We found ourselves in the trenches of what Morreale et al. (2020) recognize as "crisis pedagogy" (117). We believe acknowledgment is always of critical importance in this relationship, especially when courses have moved from face-to-face delivery to entirely online in the matter of a week (or even less). In addition to courses changing to platforms that students "did not sign up for," students were instructed to leave their dorms and move home, all while continuing their coursework online. To say this was a stressful time is an understatement. One student shares his concerns in an email:

> *I am currently struggling to understand how to navigate to the lectures, the assignments, and find out how to do them through canvas. I need a video conference of what to do and how to do it. There is no tutorial on how to find assignments on canvas so can you help me figure this thing out before I fail the semester and the school bars me from returning? I really do need help because I am not used to online education and I can only learn via face to face. I have considered dropping out one too many times I can't use canvas right now except on my phone because I can't get XXX to come fix the internet in my housing assignment, so right now I have no internet.*

Pfefferbaum and North (2020) remind us that "mass home-confinement directives (including stay-at-home orders, quarantine, and isolation) are new to Americans and raise concern about how people will react individually and collectively" (para.5). While many students were likely fearful of the potential illness during the pandemic there were many other stress inducing factors (e.g., lack of school structure, stress of dorm evacuation, increased working hours, job loss, caring for sick relatives). Mangiapane and Viscuso (2020) share that "the state of Pandemic, therefore, has activated in the majority of the populations a survival modality with primordial defense mechanisms such as attack or flight, coming from the activation of the sympathetic nervous system" (981). One could consider the impact of the pandemic to be a traumatic event for many of these students. Life as they knew it changed entirely.

THE NATURAL-FORCED SPACE

Late March 2020

> *I was constantly analyzing and processing what and how I could help my students. I knew realistically that there was little I could say or do to help ease the anxiety, or the overwhelming sense of chaos; the comfort and security that I normally create in my physical classroom had vanished. In its place was an*

> *online platform that students seemed to check sporadically. As an educator with close to two decades of experience and a human with 4 decades of life experience, my own motivation and sense of direction was fleeting.*
>
> *But these students are digital natives; they should be fine, right? They were born for this! Perhaps it was just the Late Gen X/Early Millennial in me that was panicking.*
>
> *I was worried about creating a space for students to engage and learn. I was worried about guiding students with authenticity; I needed to inspire them to focus on both health and academics. But what if I couldn't give them the gift of time and devotion needed as they navigated this time of chaos and social change (Hyde 2006, 165). This wasn't just online learning with Gen Z, this was about my insecurities and inability to connect with my students during a time of complete uncertainty.*

As twenty-first century educators, we believe students benefit from the acknowledgment we provide; however, it would be remiss of us to assume students recognize the acknowledgment we intend to send. Coming from generations prior to the current Generation Z students, we certainly find ourselves bringing our own framework and narratives to the teacher-student relationship. In the spirit of constructive and other oriented communication (Hyde 2006; Freire 1970, 1998; hooks 1994; Levinas 1972) we developed an initial study to explore student perceptions of acknowledgment in student-teacher relationships.

Early April 2020

> *COVID-19 threw us all for a loop, to say the least. When I sat down, at home, at the beginning of every week to post a weekly update/check-in with each of my classes, I debated many times how much I should share about my life during COVID-19. My life was, as I would put it, a hot mess. With 4 kids 10 and under at home and my courses carrying on online, it was quite a juggling act. I felt like sharing a funny video of my kids running half naked through the kitchen or dancing to Taylor Swift would lighten the mood, but I worried about what was appropriate to share. I often wondered if the students truly missed the in-class interactions as much as I did. Did they care that I was reaching out to remind them of course updates, but also make sure they were doing okay amidst moving off campus, losing their jobs, and caring for sick family members?*

Historically, traditional teaching pedagogies view the teacher as the sender and student as the receiver, but more constructivist pedagogies and scholarship suggest creating learning environments where all can connect, engage, inspire and transform. Hyde (2006) calls us all to be devoted to the use of competent acknowledgment in the classroom (5;187). Other scholars (i.e., Freire 1970, 1998; hooks 1994; Levinas 1972) would support the call to build supportive and meaningful classroom relationships. Hyde (2006) defines acknowledgment as "a communicative behavior that grants attention to others and thereby makes room for them in our lives" (1). Hyde states, "Teaching requires a commitment to being-for others . . . engaging others in an activity believed to be life-giving. The teacher is someone who must enter the scene bearing gifts" (164). While experience tells us that students do appreciate these invitations to engage and move beyond customary norms of polite interaction, little research has wrestled with the college student's perception of acknowledgment. Mills and Miller (2019) share that, "Despite the growing scholarship on both generational differences and the centrality of teacher caring to student success, little research has connected these two areas" (1).

LISTENING SPACE

Even though many scholars endeavor to incorporate the constructivist practices mentioned above, the academy does not always prioritize innovative or relational teaching (McMurtrie 2019). Limited funding, limited time, and the expectation that a college education is a product to be purchased leaves little room for life-giving pedagogy and relationships. Our current collegiate rituals to develop authentic connections and create "dwelling spaces" in which acknowledgment may thrive, may only be serving as a facade and may not be appreciated at all. We could argue that our current Generation Z students may be immune to recognition- even the historic practices of phatic communication have been automatized and the rituals of recognition abound (i.e., automated email responses, trophies for participation, interactive digital systems). Students live in a society where recognition is often seen as all that is necessary and perhaps even where recognition is not expected at all. Inspired by the work of Michael Hyde (2005, 2006), we set out to uncover how Gen Z students experience acknowledgment and listen to their voices to determine how this acknowledgment may benefit them. We needed to know what students wanted and if they even felt acknowledged at all. A phenomenological approach encouraged us to ask these questions (Creswell and Poth 2016, 78): 1) If acknowledgment is only defined by the receiver, what do students recognize as acknowledgment?; 2) Do current Generation Z students believe acknowledgment from instructors is important?; 3) and How do Gen Z students benefit from acknowledgment?

In order to understand Generation Z expectations during spring 2020 and prior, we used a single- phase mixed methods approach in which we included both quantitative and qualitative questions in one survey instrument (Creswell and Plano Clark 2006, 58) (see appendix 3.1). We hoped to understand what percentage of students did experience acknowledgment from instructors and complement this with specific examples to further understand student reality. Additionally, with the spring 2020 Pandemic affecting all educational spaces, we sought to discover how acknowledgment may differ during crisis/challenging times.

As we began crafting our study—originally designed to be distributed in various classes at a single university—the 2020 COVID-19 pandemic began to dominate the lives and minds of students across the United States; the world of education quickly became an entirely virtual endeavor. Knowing that students across the United States were experiencing a similar transition to online crisis-education, we decided to widely distribute the survey to any undergraduate student currently taking (or recently having finished) classes online during spring 2020. While we assumed students would be overwhelmed with change and fear, we also assumed that they may be in need of more acknowledgment during this time. We sought to complete a phenomenological study that captures student beliefs about and experiences with acknowledgment. As noted by Creswell and Poth (2016), this approach allows us to focus on the students' reality as it is understood by and within them (78). To protect the students, instructors, and universities, we decided to keep the survey as anonymous as possible and collect very little identifiable information. Following distribution of the survey via email and social media, 68 students agreed to complete the survey. We believe the mental state of students and instructors likely impacted participation. All data was analyzed through a thematic content analysis utilizing emergent coding (Creswell and Poth 2016, 181). After careful consideration of the quantitative and qualitative results, the study does provide some insight into the needs of students. Self-reported data suggests a fairly diverse sample that roughly reflects the overall college student population (see Appendices 2 and 3). The sample does include more perspectives from Freshmen and Sophomores than from Juniors and Seniors/Recent Grads. Close to twice as many participants identified as female than male. Finally, approximately half of the students identified as minority (Black & African American, Asian, Hispanic, and MENA) and half identified as White.

When asked if students received acknowledgment from at least one instructor during spring 2020, 94.12% of the sample replied affirmatively. This can be compared to the 88.24% that replied affirmatively to the question asking if students received acknowledgment from at least one instructor prior to spring 2020 (likely traditional university setting classes) (see appendix 3.4). This suggests that most students do believe they are receiving acknowledgment from university instructors regularly. The slightly higher response rate referencing the time during spring 2020 is important to note as it may suggest that either instructors were more inclined to give acknowledgment or students were more open to receiving and/or seeking acknowledgment.

In describing the types of acknowledgment received, student responses were categorized into themes (see appendices 5 and 6). There are several important results in the data that we hope to highlight. The data showcased both the channel/delivery system through which acknowledgment was received as well as the factors creating acknowledgment. First, students recognized that email and learning management systems were critical in students receiving acknowledgment both before and during the spring 2020 Pandemic. While almost twice as many students referenced these emails/announcements as important during the Pandemic than prior to (21 references versus 11 references), this seemed to be an important means of delivery in both situations. Not surprisingly, interactions in and out of class were referenced fairly frequently as a means prior to the Pandemic, but not referenced at all during the Pandemic. A few students did mention the importance of Google meet/Zoom interactions during the Pandemic which may be considered a substitute for typical in-class interaction.

When asked about the means of acknowledgment prior to spring 2020, students referenced examples of *care and concern* (25.8%); *appreciation and praise* (13.7%); *availability and connection* (12.1%); and *conversations* (12.1%). When thinking about the spring 2020 semester, students still referenced general statements of *care and concern* (27.6%) and *availability and connection* (10.3%); however, the other themes were not present. Instead, spring 2020 responses presented themes around recognition of *difficulty and stress* (20.7%). Additionally, data suggested that acknowledgment in the form of course requirement updates and *leniency with assignm*ents (17.2%) was particularly important during spring 2020. Neither the *recognition of difficulty and stress* nor the *course requirement updates and leniency* were common themes in the responses concerning time prior to the Pandemic.

When comparing the frequency of themes, it is important to recognize that far more students recognized the course updates, leniency with assignments, and recognition of the difficulty of the experience and overall stress during the spring 2020 Pandemic. Conversely, far more students recognized appreciation and praise, conversations with instructors, and attention to timeliness with assignments/feedback as forms of acknowledgment before the spring 2020 Pandemic. Finally, it is important to recognize that the frequency counts of responses mentioning general check-ins and/or care and concern, and the counts of students referencing connection and availability, were almost identical in both questions. This suggests that it is important for instructors to show care and concern and showcase their availability and willingness to connect regardless of the circumstances. This may make students feel more acknowledged.

While all of this data is quite interesting to consider, we also discovered a few general ideas concerning overall student perceptions regarding importance of and satisfaction with acknowledgment. All students (100%) believed acknowledgment was *either moderately* to *very important* during spring 2020-during the Pandemic (see appendix 3.7). Specifically, almost 90% of students found acknowledgment to be *very important* during this time. When considering the time prior to spring 2020, less than 2% of students reported that acknowledgment from instructors was not important. Statements made to support this may include: "I don't care for or against acknowledgment unless it can benefit me in my future career" and "It is not really expected . . . college professors are just to present the material and do not care about the students."

Finally, students were asked to consider their level of satisfaction with the acknowledgment they have received from instructors prior to and during spring 2020. The responses suggested that most students are *moderately* to *highly satisfied* with acknowledgment they have received. The percentage of students reporting *high satisfaction* during a typical semester was slightly higher than those reporting *high satisfaction* during spring 2020 (see appendix 3.8).

To gather a better understanding of how acknowledgment benefits students, we strategically chose to ask this question directly. The responses were divided into two categories: 1) personal/relational & holistic benefits (e.g., motivation, confidence, being understood/heard, support and not being alone) and 2) instrumental and course related benefits (e.g., better organization, more learning, future references, clarity of information/class standing) (see appendix 3.8). A frequency count showed that students care about both of these categories as 71.4% of respondents recognized "personal/relational & holistic benefits" and 67.9% referenced "instrumental and course related benefits." Approximately 37.5% recognized the connection between these two benefits with statements such as, "It encourages me to work harder in class because I know they actually care" and acknowledgment is "valuable in building a professional contact with an adult who a student can use for future references for a job or any other life opportunity." Students also recognized the lack of acknowledgment with statements like, "It's important to be acknowledged so the instructors and students can build a relationship. I believe that some of my classes would have ended differently if more professors acknowledged me."

Finally, common themes emerging from student beliefs about the benefits of acknowledgment include: being motivated and encouraged by instructors, knowing that instructors care and have a student's best interest and/or success in mind, gaining confidence and belief in success, enhancing learning and/or the environment, and enabling students to work harder, improve and/or push through. As stated by one student, "It lets me know that I have support and that we aren't alone. The person who is taking the time to educate me, actually cares and is passionate about what they are doing. It truly makes a difference because college can be hard enough as it is especially being so young and trying to understand the world around us."

With this study, we sought to explore how students see acknowledgment and the overarching value they seem to place on this pedagogy/approach. To say that we have gained insight into this phenomenon would be a drastic understatement. In many ways, the confirmation of the need for acknowledgment has been "life giving" during a very challenging time. To answer the original questions we presented, we can confidently say that Gen Z students recognize and appreciate some form of acknowledgment in the "classroom." Students typically understand the importance of acknowledgment and recognize the role it can play in both instrumental and relational ways. While some student responses suggested the level of "sustained openness" expressed by Hyde (2006, 4), many statements seemed to reflect what Hyde (2006) might consider "recognition"(3) as their comments did not always suggest the intensity and depth that would allow the interaction to be "life-giving" or "life-draining" (2). This challenges us to reconsider our understanding of how acknowledgment is received. The study presented a variety of themes suggesting how students receive acknowledgment and how this benefits them. While there are certainly some broad categories that were mentioned by the majority of students, there were few specific examples of teacher actions/behaviors that were commonly recognized by participants and none that were recognized by a "majority."

UNCOMFORTABLE SPACE

The limitations to our study push us to continue working. We hope to gather more participants to enhance validity and increase generalizability. While this survey was open to any university student, we suspect that most data was obtained from a few class clusters. Furthermore, we would like to understand how acknowledgment is perceived differently by individual demographics and cohorts. While this study does explore student perceptions during an unprecedented time, we believe it provides a snapshot of what students may find to be meaningful during traditional semesters as well. While Hyde (2006) does morally call instructors to "create openings where people can dwell, deliberate, and know together what is right, good, just and truthful," very few students overtly recognized the obligation as a moral or ethical responsibility (7). This does not negate the importance of acknowledgment but suggests that students have not thought about this from an ethical or moral perspective. Several of the student responses did suggest that instructors were able to "grant[s] people hope, the opportunity for a new beginning, a second chance, whereby they might improve their lot in life" (Hyde 2006, 7) through pedagogical practices. As noted by one student,

> I have been too scared [to] apply for scholarships before. I have had the grades, I was always doing extracurricular activities outside academics, but it wasn't until my professor encouraged me that I felt I could do it. It's like I didn't feel strong enough. . . . The confidence to reach out to more professors came from the one professor that became interested in my education.

Many students recognize the time that instructors dedicated to them, the extra effort and intentionality behind the check ins, and how much the support and motivation helped. Future research may enable us to focus more specifically on the ethical and moral instructor obligations and the specific ways in which the acknowledgment provided a new beginning. Expanding our study should allow us to gather more examples and ways to begin differentiating positive acknowledgment from negative and absent states (Hyde 2006, 2). We neglected to focus specifically on the challenges and difficulties of sitting within positive acknowledgment, and the pain and isolation students may feel without it.

In future research, one area we hope to pursue is the role of acknowledgment in facilitating resiliency and consequently retention. When a student calls you a decade after they graduate to tell you they are engaged, you know you have been critical in supporting the student's long-term success. When you receive texts and emails saying, "thank you for believing in me" we suspect that resiliency has been impacted positively. We all face adversities at varying degrees, but the ways in which we respond and "bounce back" from these experiences can be tremendous learning experiences. According to the American Psychological Association, 2012 "Becoming more resilient not only helps you get through difficult circumstances, it also empowers you to grow and even improve your life along the way" (APA 2012, para. 5). From our own experience and narratives of others, we know many Gen Z students are sincerely appreciative of the life-giving acknowledgment they receive. Now we must continue the commitment required to both give and receive the gift (164).

EXTRAORDINARY AND EXTRAORDINARY SPACE

As our study closed, the COVID-19 pandemic continued to have a global impact. Stay-at-home orders and restrictive measures were in place to attempt to slow the infection rate. In addition to the pandemic, nationwide uprisings began in response to racial injustice and police brutality against black people. In referencing the trauma and fear that was also prevalent twenty-years prior during 9/11, Poulos wrote "At least by our old definitions we live in *extra*-ordinary times. In these days of hatred and retaliation, of vitriol and violence, as daily life overflows with the rhetoric of war, the call to dialogic civility, the need for honoring all humans, has never been more urgent" (2004, 538). The call is even louder and more necessary today. We live in a world riddled with anxiety and hatred and a lack of compassion for *the Other* (Levinas 1972). Whether we are facilitating an "extra-ordinary" time or a traditional semester, acknowledgment becomes an extraordinary means of survival and ultimately creates a place where students can thrive. Tompkins (2015) shares that acknowledgment is closely "entwined" in communication and ethics and further states, "The *ethos* of acknowledgment establishes an environment wherein people can take the time to "know together (con-scientia)" some topic of interest and, in the process, perhaps gain a more authentic understanding of those who are willing to contribute to the development of this environment" (242). It is within this idea of authenticity that spaces can be co-created to support the wholeness of everyone involved and a breeding ground for authentic acknowledgment is created.

June 2020

I know I need to say something. I haven't even tried to craft an email yet. The collection of stories I am hearing on the news of racial injustice, horrific murders, triumphant marches, conspiracy theories, COVID-19 deaths, and unemployment rates is suffocating my abilities to open up- my ability to give life. I am broken and working overtime to uphold the facade that the material I am "teaching" to my students is of priority right now.

I am an educated and privileged white female with twice the number of years of experience of my students- I will never truly understand the brokenness that many of my students are experiencing. I fear my words do not even recognize my students, let alone acknowledge them. I have built in assignments for students to talk about how much they appreciate each other- hopefully this will help. All I can really manage to say is, "I am here, and I will listen."

A day or two later, I received this email from one of the student class groups:

"Our group enjoyed the team appreciation activity you suggested for the weekly Zoom meetings and we decided to put our own spin on things. We created a google doc so that we are able to revisit all the wonderful things our group members have to say about one another. We also thought it was important to include things we appreciate about our professor who makes all these awesome learning opportunities possible. . . . We wanted you to know that XXXXX and all of XXXXX appreciates you!"

While societal circumstances will change, educators can always seek ways to acknowledge and build relationships with students. As Roll (2020) shares, "the relationships between students and staff affects everything from student satisfaction to their capacity to take risks and excel, to a sense of personal efficacy and sustained curiosity" (para. 4). Modeling acknowledgment for our students also encourages them to acknowledge others, thus enhancing reciprocity within relationships. When educators seek to acknowledge their students, they speak to this relational desire that so many of our students seek and need. Students appreciate the relationships built with instructors for both instrumental and more holistic reasons. They do not want to be "alone or forgotten." In creating a classroom that embodies acknowledgment, we are creating a space where connection is key and students aren't alone or forgotten, but instead are part of the fabric of the community you have created. When you know a little bit more about a student you can ask how their family is doing, how work is, or other questions that connect to who they really are. They will share what they want, but they will appreciate you asking about more than just academic matters. One study participant shared, "One of my professors always checked in on me after I once told him I had trouble sleeping due to anxiety." Another student stated, "This professor facilitates our talks by asking if I am doing okay and making sure I am mentally in a good head space . . . sometimes I am not always okay."

As shown in this final Google Hangout example, students seem to embrace the instructor acknowledgment and appreciate the more personal connection.

Student: Thanks for introducing Rizzo (the family dog) by the way! Tell him he's doing a great job for me.
Me: Yah! Thanks for waiting. I have a new one to upload.
Student: Can't wait to see it! I never expected to get an inside look at all of my professor's lives, but then again I never thought any of you would see us sitting in our living rooms either!
Me: Honestly, I've been thinking a lot about this. I like having some anonymity so this has me wondering what it will feel like to be in classes in the fall with students who know me well. LOL.
Student: Personally, I like having things on a more personal level, I have met two children, a dog, and a cat so far and I'm loving it! As for fall, it will definitely take some adjustment for everyone, but then again so has the past two weeks.
Me: Absolutely agree.

Arnett (2008) emphasizes, acknowledgment is a life-giving gift. Furthermore, Hyde (2006) pulls in the works of Levinas (xiii) and Kenneth Burke (5) and sees the importance of attending to others and being open to their interests. Acknowledgment is feeling a part of something, having a sense of place (Hyde 2006, 10). In this sense, we can create courses that are spaces where students can feel a part of something and be acknowledged as a critical piece of the whole; we need to be open to connection and care and listen to one another (Lipari 2004, 122). Our experiences and pilot data suggest that Gen Z students desire connection, encouragement, and acknowledgment of their being. As instructors, we are called to create physical and digital spaces for connection and care. We invite you to consider your own relational dynamics with students. As Dannels (2015) reminds us, student-teacher relationships are both exciting and potentially challenging (138). While many of us are familiar with strategies of affinity seeking, immediacy, and self-disclosure, we must also consider acknowledgment as a core element of our relationships with students. By continuously seeking an understanding of how acknowledgment is being perceived and received, we are better equipped to organically and intentionally acknowledge our Gen Z students and create an extraordinary space to give life.

APPENDICES

Appendix 3.1 Survey Questions

Q1.	Consent (yes/no)
Q2.	Choose one or more races that you consider yourself to be (multiple choice)
Q3.	What is your sex? (multiple choice)
Q4.	What is your Academic Classification (multiple choice)
Q5.	For the purposes of this survey, we are defining Acknowledgment as "an act that provides ongoing attention, time, and openness for the development of a caring and supportive relationship." We consider acknowledgment to be an action that goes beyond recognition. We are defining recognition as "a preliminary step." Ex: Recognition is when someone says "hi, how are you?" and you reply with "good, how are you?" Acknowledgment offers more time and genuine appreciation for others. This definition is inspired by Michael Hyde's work (Hyde 2006). During the spring 2020 Semester and the COVID-19 Pandemic (after universities moved classes online), did you receive acknowledgment from at least one of your instructors?
Q6.	If yes, in what ways did you feel acknowledged by any of your college instructors?
Q7.	Now consider the time you spent with instructors PRIOR to the COVID-19 Pandemic (face-to-face during any semester). During the typical college semester, did you receive acknowledgment from at least one of your instructors?
Q8.	If yes, in what ways did you feel acknowledged both in and out of the college classroom?
Q9.	How important is acknowledgment from college instructors? (likert scale)
Q10.	How satisfied are you with the level of acknowledgment from college instructors? (likert scale)
Q.11	How does acknowledgment from college instructors support/benefit you as a student?
Q.12	Please provide any additional thoughts on acknowledgment from college instructors.

Source: Christman and McCall (2021).

Appendix 3.2 Survey Responses to Academic Classification Question

Self-reported Classification	N	% of Sample
Freshman	26	38.24%
Sophomore	19	27.94%
Junior	13	19.12%
Senior	10	14.71%

Source: Christman and McCall (2021).

Appendix 3.3 Survey Responses to Race/Ethnicity Classification Question

Self-reported Classification	N	% of Sample
White	37	50.00%
Black or African American	23	31.08%
Asian	6	8.11%
Hispanic	4	5.41%
MENA	1	1.35%

Source: Christman and McCall (2021).

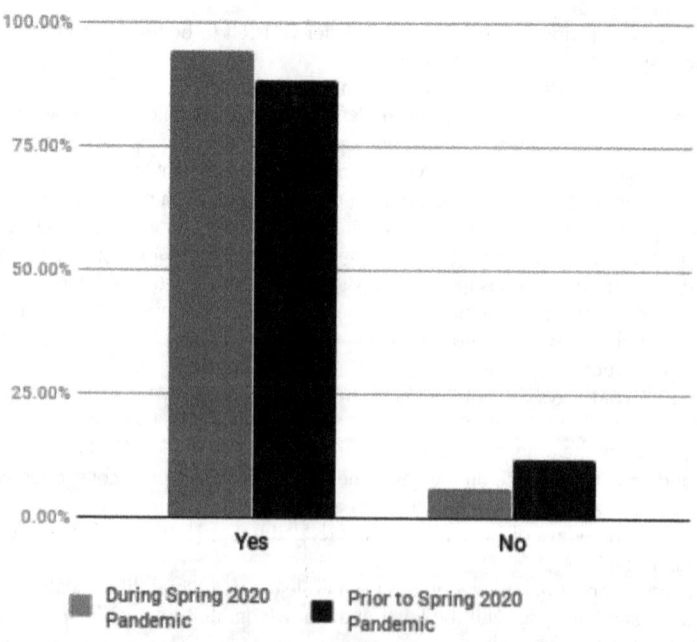

Appendix 3.1 Acknowledgment Prior to and during Spring 2020. During the Spring 2020 Semester and the COVID-19 Pandemic (after universities moved classes online), did you receive acknowledgment from at least one of your instructors? Source: Christman and McCall (2021).

Appendix 3.4 Ways Acknowledgment Was Received during Spring 2020

Theme Identified	Codes Developed and Supporting Data

Channel/ Delivery for Acknowledgment	• Email/Canvas
	  ○ "Kept me updated with emails"
	  ○ "All of my professors reached out to my class via email and canvas to express appreciation for our hard work"
	• Google Meet/Zoom/Chats
	  ○ "I had many zoom class where the professors would check on how we were doing"
	  ○ "Multiple of my professors held online chats"

Means of Acknowledgment	• Course Requirement Considerations
	  ○ Course Updates/Assignment Reminders
	    ○ "regular email updates; updates on grades"
	    ○ "the instructor was very helpful in teaching how [the course] works"
	  ○ Extensions and Leniency
	    ○ "The professor for my online class acknowledged the extra stress we may be feeling and cut back on the workload of the course"
	    ○ "More time was allotted to finish assignments/tests toward the end of the class"
	• Recognition of Difficulty and Stress
	  ○ "They understood it was a hard time for students, and have sympathy"
	  ○ "Most of my college instructors would send weekly emails acknowledging my stressors during the pandemic. They expressed concern for my well-being and offered resources that were available to me if needed."
	• Expressing Care and Concern
	  ○ "Checking in on me from the start of the shutdown . . . until now. I am grateful for them for reaching out since I have not felt my best in weeks."
	  ○ "I had a forum where we put how we were doing and the professor responded to each one of us engaged in what we had to say"
	• Availability and Connection
	  ○ "She has offered a wide chunk of her time for her students to talk and try to come up with positive solutions to get things done"
	  ○ "If I need the instructor for anything, I will text her or invite her on Zoom, or Google Meet"

Source: Christman and McCall (2021).

Appendix 3.5 Ways Acknowledgment Was Received Prior to Spring 2020

Theme Identified	Codes Developed and Supporting Data

Channel/Delivery	• Email/Canvas
	  ○ "my instructors responded to emails within 1 day"
	  ○ "by getting emails every day, updates . . . very easy to get a response in a timely manner"
	• Interactions—During Class & Outside of Class
	  ○ "before the pandemic hit . . . I used to meet with her during her office hours"
	  ○ "my voice was heard during class discussions"

Means of Acknowledgment	• Expressing Care and Concerns
	  ○ "they cared about me as a person and asked how I was doing"
	  ○ "my professors showed genuine concern for the things we had going on outside of the their classroom and always told us that they were happy to be teaching out class"
	• Availability and Connection
	  ○ "availability and mutual respect"
	  ○ "he took his time to talk to everyone and was available outside of class"
	• Appreciation and Praise
	  ○ "my XX teacher said I always had something intelligent to say in class. My XX teacher said she loved the way my mind worked and how organized my work is"
	  ○ "congratulating me on grades/scores as well as starfish kudos"
	• Conversations
	  ○ "they just talked to us"
	  ○ "in class, some instructors encouraged conversations on how we were doing and coping with classes"

Source: Christman and McCall (2021).

Appendix 3.6 How Important Is Acknowledgment from College Instructors?

	Very important	Moderately Important	Not Important
During a Typical Semester	58.82%	39.71%	1.47%
During the Spring 2020 COVID-19 Pandemic	89.55%	10.45%	0%

Source: Christman and McCall (2021).

Appendix 3.7 How Satisfied Are You with the Level of Acknowledgment from College Instructors?

	Very Satisfied	Moderately Satisfied	Not Satisfied
During a Typical semester	57.35%	38.24%	4.41%
During the COVID-19 Pandemic	50.00%	46.97%	3.03%

Source: Christman and McCall (2021).

Appendix 3.8 How Does Acknowledgment from College Instructors Support/Benefit You as a Student?

Broad Categories	Themes Discovered and Supporting Data

Instrumental & Course Related	• Better organization/More focused
	  ○ "I know how to keep organized"
	  ○ "keep us in line with assignments and updates"
	• Enhanced Learning/Environment
	  ○ "creates a supportive and caring classroom environment that fosters learning"
	  ○ "helps me as a student to learn what I am not doing the best and to correct that with direct help and comments"
	• Work harder/Do better/Push through
	  ○ "could help motivate students and make them feel like they can put forth their best work"
	  ○ "I'm going to make it through the next semester"

Personal/ Relational and/or Holistic	• Motivation/Encouragement
	  ○ If a student is having a rough time, they can think back to the acknowledgment and remember the positive feeling it gave them with hopes further instructors will do the same"
	  ○ "it helps them to want to learn more not just sit there because they have to"
	• Confidence/ Feeling Successful/Pride
	  ○ "gives me more confidence in my work"
	  ○ "I feel a sense of pride. I feel as though I am important and this benefits me as a student because it drives encouragement and self-esteem"
	• Being Supported/Not alone/Connected
	  ○ "being not only seen and heard, but also understood is very valuable for morale and reaffirmed my ability to push through"
	  ○ "it makes you feel like you are not so alone and that the people at the university want you to succeed"
	• Knowing instructors care/Instructors have best interest in mind
	  ○ "makes me feel like my instructor cares about me as an individual and in my overall development, not just in their class"
	  ○ "it shows that they care about our well being first and foremove above academics'

Source: Christman and McCall (2021).

REFERENCES

American Psychological Association. 2020. "Building Your Resilience." Accessed July 21, 2020. http://www.apa.org/topics/resilience.

Arnett, Ronald. 2008. "Pointing the Way to Communication Ethics Theory: The Life-Giving Gift of Acknowledgment." *Review of Communication* 8 (1): 21–28.

Buhs, Eric S. 2005. "Peer Rejection, Negative Peer Treatment, and School Adjustment: Self-Concept and Classroom Engagement as Mediating Processes. *Journal of School Psychology* 43 (5): 407–424. DOI: 10.1016/j.jsp.2005.09.001.

Buskirk-Cohen, Allison, and Aria Plants. 2019. "Caring About Success: Students' Perceptions of Professors' Caring Matters More Than Grit." *International Journal of Teaching and Learning in Higher Education* 31 (1): 108–114. https://files.eric.ed.gov/fulltext/EJ1206948.pdf.

Creswell, John W., and Cheryl N. Poth. 2016. *Qualitative Inquiry and Research Design: Choosing Among Five Approaches*. California: Sage Publications.

Creswell, John W., and Vicki Plano-Clark. 2006. *Designing and Conducting Mixed Methods Research*. California: Sage Publications. https://www.sagepub.com/sites/default/files/upm-binaries/10982_Chapter_4.pdf.

Dannels, Deanna P. 2015. *8 Essential Questions Teachers Ask: A Guidebook for Communicating with Students*. New York: Oxford.

Dixson, Marcia D. 2010. "Creating Effective Student Engagement in Online Classes: What Do Students Find Engaging?" *Journal of Scholarship of Teaching and Learning* 10 (1): 1–13.

Freire, Paulo. 1997. *Pedagogy of the Oppressed*. New York: Continuum. (Originally published 1970).

Gayton, Jorge, and Beryl C. McEwen. 2007. "Effective Online Instructional and Assessment Strategies." *American Journal of Distance Education* 21 (3): 117–132. DOI: 10.1080/08923640701341653.

"Generation Z Goes to College: How They Compare to Previous Generations." 2018. *Lendkey*. Accessed July 20, 2020. https://www.lendkey.com/blog/paying-for-school/generation-z-goes-to-college-how-they-compare-to-previous-generations/.

hooks, bell. 1994. *Teaching to Transgress: Education as the Practice of Freedom*. New York: Routledge-Falmer.

Hyde, Michael J. 2005. "Acknowledgment, Conscience, Rhetoric, and Teaching: The Case of Tuesdays with Morrie." *Rhetoric Society Quarterly* 35 (2): 23–46. https://www.jstor.org/stable/40232462.

Hyde, Michael J. 2006. *The Life-Giving Gift of Acknowledgment: A Philosophical and Rhetorical Inquiry*. West Lafayette, IN: Purdue University Press.

King, Stephanie B. 2014. "Graduate Student Perceptions of the Use of Online Course Tools to Support Engagement." *International Journal for the Scholarship of Teaching and Learning* 8 (1). DOI: 10.20429/ijsotl.2014.080105.

Kozinsky, Sieva. 2017. "How Generation Z Is Shaping the Change in Education." *Forbes*. Accessed July 20, 2020. https://www.forbes.com/sites/sievakozinsky/2017/07/24/how-generation-z-is-shaping-the-change-in-education/#ffdb15d65208.

Lee, Joyce. 2020. "Mental Health Effects of School Closures During Covid-19." *The Lancet Child and Adolescent Health* 4. Accessed July 20, 2020. https://www.thelancet.com/action/showPdf?pii=S2352-4642%2820%2930109-7.

Levinas, Emmanuel. 1972. *Humanism of the Other*. Translated by Nidra Poller. Chicago: University of Illinois Press.

Lipari, Lisbeth. 2004. "Listening for the Other: Ethical Implications of the Buber-Levinas Encounter." *Communication Theory* 14 (2): 122–141. DOI: 10.1111/j.1468-2885.2004.tb00308.

Mangiapane, Ernesto, and Gabrielle Ilse Viscuso. 2020. "Pandemic Covid-19: Psychodynamic Analysis of a Global Trauma: Clinical Considerations Pre/Post Lock Down." *Journal of Medical Research and Health Sciences* 3 (6): 976–990. DOI: 10.15520/jmrhs.v3i6.194.

Marron, Maria. B. 2015. "New Generations Require Changes Beyond the Digital." *Journalism & Mass Communication Educator* 70 (2): 123–124. DOI: 10.1177/1077695815588912.

Martin, Florence, and Doris U. Bolliger. 2018. "Engagement Matters: Student Perceptions on the Importance of Engagement Strategies in the Online Learning Environment." *Online Learning* 22 (1): 205–222. DOI: 10.24059/olj.v22i1.1092.

McMurtrie, Beth. 2019. "Many Professors Want to Change Their Teaching But Don't. One University Found Out Why." *The Chronicle of Higher Education*. Last Modified March 21, 2019. https://www.chronicle.com/article/Many-Professors-Want-to-Change/245945?cid=at&utm_source=at&utm_medium=en&cid=at.

Miller, Amy, and Brooklyn B. Mills. 2019. "If They Don't Care, I Don't Care': Millennial and Generation Z Students and the Impact of Faculty Caring." *The Journal of the Scholarship of Teaching and Learning* 19 (4): 78–89. https://files.eric.ed.gov/fulltext/EJ1234123.pdf.

Mirivel, Julien C. 2014. *The Art of Positive Communication: Theory and Practice*. New York: Peter Lang.

Morreale, Sherwyn, Janice Thorpe, and Joshua N. Westwick. 2021. "Online Teaching: Challenge or Opportunity for Communication Education Scholars?" *Communication Education* 70 (1): 117–119. DOI: 10.1080/03634523.2020.1811360.

Pfefferbaum, Betty, and Carol S. North. 2020. "Mental Health and the Covid-19 Pandemic." *The New England Journal of Medicine*. DOI: 10.1056/NEJMp2008017. https://www.nejm.org/doi/full/10.1056/NEJMp2008017#article_introduction.

Poulos, Chris. 2004. "Disruption, Silence, and Creation: The Search for Dialogic Civility in the Age of Anxiety." *Qualitative Inquiry* 10 (4): 534–547.

Roll, Kate. 2020. "Lecturer and Student Relationships Matter Even More Online Than on Campus." *The Guardian*. Last Modified June 8, 2020. https://www.theguardian.com/education/2020/jun/08/lecturer-and-student-relationships-matter-even-more-online-than-on-campus?fbclid=IwAR3UEXOlJd1aJ6JwUTM2L95DaSF1BtZsfMY5tjDbtQWbJCtk57jigKVwwGo.

Seemiller, Corey, and Meghan Grace. 2016. *Generation Z Goes to College*. Hoboken, NJ: John Wiley & Sons.

Tinto, Vladimir. 1987. "The Principles of Effective Retention." Paper Presented at Fall Conference of the Maryland College Personnel Association (LARGO, MD, November 20, 1987): 1–15. https://eric.ed.gov/?id=ED301267.

Twenge, Jean M. 2017. *iGen: Why Today's Super-Connected Kids are Growing Up Less Rebellious, More Tolerant, Less Happy-and Completely Unprepared for Adulthood.* New York, NY: Atria.

Zumbrunn, Sharon, Courtney McKim, Eric Buhs, and Leslie R. Hawley. 2014. "Support, Belonging, Motivation, and Engagement in the College Classroom: A Mixed Method Study." *Instructional Science* 42 (5): 661–684.

Chapter 4

A Bridge for Communication

Negotiating Intergenerational Listening Expectations in Face-to-Face Interactions and Digital Platforms

Emeline Ojeda-Hecht and Elizabeth S. Parks

Digital technologies, specifically email, have become so commonly used between students and instructors that many faculty already believed that email had replaced most face-to-face meetings with students early in this millennium (Duran et al. 2005). In 2020, this became undeniable as the onset of coronavirus disease and ensuing physical distancing to slow the spread of the disease caused colleges and universities around the world to shift face-to-face engagement exclusively to digital spaces. The new realities of social distancing forced instructors and students to quickly learn how to teach and learn through technology, even for those who preferred face-to-face engagement. Rather than dropping into an instructor's office hours in a building, video conferencing, email exchanges, and online educational platforms became their main communication tools. With this pervasive technological shift, digital channels of connection are likely to remain common pedagogical practice.

As the world considers how this health crisis impacts globalization on a holistic level (Altman 2020), educational institutions wrestle with discrimination and exclusion in individual and systemic forms. A "shadow pandemic" that perpetuates exclusion of others based on their nondominant identities undeniably co-exists with coronavirus. People are no less diverse in online spaces; rather, communication through and about diverse identities may be expressed and received differently in online and offline worlds (Mani 2020). Far from disappearing with online education, injustice is just as (if not more) present in digital spaces as compared to face-to-face ones and it is imperative that we better learn how to inclusively communicate in all instructional contexts. *Listening*, as one type of communication, influences educational success. Instructors utilize relational behaviors in their teaching practices to build relationships with their students; diverse practices are valued by different students in different ways and ultimately contributes to student learning motivation (Frymier and Houser 2000). Similarly, research has shown that student's affective learning, communication satisfaction, and classroom participation is impacted by listening practices (Goodboy and Bolkan 2009).

In this chapter, we expand communication scholarship by exploring how generational differences might inflect and inform the ways that we listen better together in both online and offline instructional spaces. Grounded in online surveys and generation-based face-to-face focus group dialogues, we explore the following research question (RQ): *How does Generation Z and older generations' values about listening compare, especially in the context of instructional interactions, online and offline communication, and negotiation of diverse identities?* In the sections that follow, we first offer a brief theoretical framing for this study, then outline our IRB approved two-stage research process conducted at a large public research university in Fall 2019, briefly discuss of the results and implications of our findings for intergenerational listening with Generation Z in online and offline instructional spaces, and conclude with tips for how better to listen with generational difference in mind.

INTERGENERATIONAL LISTENING AND TECHNOLOGY

Generation is one type of identity categorization that is often overlooked in research about diversity, difference, and communication across cultures. Yet, diverse generations have their own shared system of norms and values for the ways they communicate and interact within the world, thus creating unique cultural systems (Cennamo and Gardner 2008). Recent research has shown that there are significant differences between the ways that Generation Z conceptualizes good listening and the ways that older generations conceive what "listening" means and how it should be enacted. For example, Generation Z is more likely to conceptualize listening as *evaluative*—involving communicative activities such as being critical, arguing, conceding, and answering—as compared to older generations and Generation Z and Generation X appear to have the most saliently (and statistically) different conceptualizations of what good listening entails (Parks 2020). In other words, how a particular generational cohort expects to listen relationally may differ from another generation's values. This can have real-world implications for instructional spaces when assumptions about whether and how a person is listening is made from specific individual standpoints, social positions, and power structures.

Listening may happen in a variety of spaces, including face-to-face contexts (e.g., classroom settings) and digital platforms (e.g., email communication), with each inflecting communication practices as its distinct medium (Seemiller and Grace 2016). Despite increased digital platform use in education, students and teachers are often unaware that listening with and through technology is an active process to which they must attend just as closely as spoken words and messages (Bond 2012). Indeed, listening is pervasively underestimated and under taught, but remains an essential skill for relational well-being. The ways that we expect to listen to each other can minimize or perpetuate interpersonal understanding and conflict between students and instructors in both face-to-face and digital instructional spaces. Thus, diverse generations must navigate individual and group expectations, as well as the need to accommodate across their cohort's cultures.

Expectancy Violation Theory (EVT), as developed by Judee K. Burgoon (1993; Burgoon and Jones 1976), asserts that individuals hold expectations for how they and others "should" interact in a given situation, and when those expectations are violated (a behavior that deviates from the expectations), it typically results in a chain of psychological reactions by the one interpreting the perceived violation to explain the violation's occurrence. These expectations can be assigned to both face-to-face interactions, as well as digital communication interactions, such as email (Ramirez and Wang 2008). Technological innovations continuously shape how individuals interact in our workplaces, with families, and even within our education systems (Berry 2016; Hassini 2006). Furthermore, the use of technology in communication interactions may be perceived differently based on one's own cultural and social identities (Palfrey and Gasser 2016). For example, values that determine professionalism, which communication platforms are preferred, and what makes one feel listened to can also differ among the generational cohorts. Thus, educational institutional members find themselves navigating new ground when using digital technologies to connect inside and outside of their workplaces.

Across generations, students and instructors are making conscious and unintentional choices about how to negotiate their own and other's expectations and how best to accommodate each other to create positive communication climates. They may choose to hold a member of a different generational cohort to their own generation's values or do the work of accommodating diverse listening expectations. As Howard Giles (1973; Gallois et al. 2005) explains in his articulation of Communication Accommodation Theory (CAT), people may choose whether or not to adapt to stated and implicit expectations based on desires to align their identity with another person or group or the wish to signal that they are different—and this is no less true among diverse generational cohorts. Individuals from different generational cultures may, in other words, choose to listen with similar affective and behavioral norms (accommodate) or listen in ways that they signal their differing generational position (divergence). This study works to explore these intergenerational expectations and accommodations in the instructional context.

STUDY PROCEDURE

Our research goal was to learn how to better listen across difference in both online and offline instructional contexts, with specific focus on listening expectations between Generation Z and older generations. To achieve this, we conducted a two-part study including an online survey and generation-based focus group dialogues. For both parts, we used the Pew Research Center's generational definitions to distinguish between two generational categories—Generation Z (those born after 1996, and hereafter Gen Z) and generations older than Generation Z (those born through 1996, and hereafter Post-Gen Z) (Pew Research Center 2019). In this section, we describe the research process for both the online survey and focus group discourse.

Part 1: Online Survey

Online survey participants were recruited through flyers posted in the local university and surrounding community, word-of-mouth, and snowball sampling. Participant involvement was incentivized with a randomized $20 gift-card drawing, and consent was required to participate. The survey included basic social demographic (e.g., race, ethnicity, and gender identities) and close-ended measures designed to probe distinct listening perceptions. Survey participants ($N = 133$) ranged from 18 to 72 years of age ($M = 26.53$, $SD = 11.09$). 74.1% of participants identified with she/her pronouns, 25.2% with he/him pronouns, and 0.7% with they/their pronouns (0.07%). 30.8% of participants identified as a member of the LGBTQA+ community. Reflective of the demographics of the surrounding regional area, the majority of the participants identified as white/Caucasian (76.3%); other racial and/or ethnic identities included Hispanic or Latinx (10.1%), Black or African American (5.0%), Asian Pacific Islander, Native Hawaiian or Polynesian (3.6%), Mixed Race (1.4%), Native American (0.7%), and Other/None (2.9%). 11.9% of participants indicated multiple racial identities.

The 10–15 minute online survey was conducted through Qualtrics and included items from the revised Listening Concepts Inventory (LCI-R) (G. Bodie 2011), the revised Listening Styles Profile (LSP-R) (G. D. Bodie et al. 2013), and several new questions designed to measure perceptions of listening within the instructor/student, online and offline, and diverse identity affinity. Some of these questions were framed in ways reflecting the following theme: "How do you think your racial and/or ethnic identity impacts how you listen to professors/students of color (or how they listen to you) in face-to-face/email contexts?" Following this series of questions, participants ranked specific demographic factors in order of perceived impact on listening behaviors toward others in instructional settings. For our chapter's purposes, we only relate findings from this third set of education-related survey questions.

Survey data was exported and organized in Microsoft Excel for simple statistical analysis. We utilized a two-sample t-test assuming unequal variances and compared responses from participants who identified as ages that we categorized as Gen Z and Post-Gen Z cohorts to explore statistically significant differences in generational listening perceptions related to student/instructor communication in face-to-face and online contexts. We also performed a relative ranking analysis of the questions measuring demographic factors that are perceived to affect listening behaviors in instructional settings by calculating the total sums of participants' categorical demographic relative ranking and comparing these total sums with the totals of the other identity categories. We then compared the relative ranking of Gen Z and Post-Gen Z to compare generational listening expectations with each other.

Part 2: Focus Groups

The second stage of our research process moved from quantitative online survey responses to a mixed quantitative (corpus linguistics) and qualitative (thematic analysis) approach to focus group discourse. Survey participants who indicated wanting to join conversations about listening were invited to focus group dialogues, one consisting of people who identified as Gen Z and one of older generations (Post-Gen Z). After the date and location and core group of participants was set, the original list of participants in each generational cohort were notified of the location, time, and place in case they were able/wanted to attend. Participants were thanked with a $25 gift card for their involvement in the focus group dialogue. The generational focus groups included seven total participants. The Gen Z focus group included three participants, one self-identified as she/her, Asian (aged 19), and two as he/him and white/Caucasian (both aged 21). The Post-Gen Z focus group included four participants, two self-identified as he/him and white/Caucasian (aged 63 and 49), one as she/her and Native American and white/Caucasian (aged 54), and one as she/her and Mixed Race, Asian, and white/Caucasian (aged 38).

Each focus group conversation lasted 45-55 minutes. Participants consented, and then trained facilitators followed an interview protocol which led participants through a conversation that included introductions and four sets of questions designed to prompt conversation about listening. Question Set 1 included prompts such as "When you think of a good/bad listener, what traits do they have?" and "How do people listen differently with technology?" Question Set 2 included prompts such as "Think of a person or group you feel it is hard/easy to listen to. What makes it this way?" and "Is there ever a time when you should/choose not to listen to someone? If so, when?" Question Set 3 included prompts related to listening and difference, all framed around the question "How do you think a person's gender (or race, ethnicity, socio-economic status, disability, etc.) impacts their listening and the ways others listen to them?" Question Set 4 included prompts such as "How does it feel to you to listen to people with different perspectives and backgrounds than your own in <this town>? When is it easy? When is it hard?" and "If you had 30 seconds to give advice to someone about how to listen to you well, what would you say?" Participants were encouraged to discuss any questions that they find most interesting and did not need to answer them all. Focus group dialogues were video recorded and then transcribed with the ELAN annotation tool, resulting in two transcripts.

Transcripts were analyzed using thematic analysis and basic corpus linguistics. Thematic analysis was used to identify similarities, trends, and differences among the two generational cohort focus groups regarding listening, connection, difference, and technology in the data as related to the research question. To perform our thematic analysis, we followed Terry, et al.'s six-step analytic process (Terry et al. 2017). We transcribed the dialogues, listened to them multiple times, summarized the content, generated codes from the notes, and built meaning from the coded discourse. Based on our focus on listening, generation, and technology, we also used the freeware corpus analysis software AntConc to perform a basic lexical analysis using both interview transcripts as a small corpus (18,453 word tokens representing 1,684 word types).

RESULTS

Online survey results show both overlapping and divergent perspectives between Gen Z and Post-Gen Z perspectives on listening behaviors. Based on perceived impact of a variety of identity categories, participants of both generational cohorts indicated that the most salient identity traits impacting listening in the classroom are people's personality traits and personal values, whereas dis/ability, socio-economic status, and sexuality were ranked as least salient. See table 4.1 below for complete rankings.

In contrast to these survey results which suggest that both generational cohorts consider socio-economic status and dis/ability to minimally impact

Table 4.1 Demographic Traits Perceived to Influence Listening Behaviors

Ranking	Gen Z	Post-Gen Z
1	Personality Traits	Personal Values
2	Personal Values	Age
3	Education Level	Political Affiliation
4	Age	Gender
5	Political Affiliation	Occupation
6	Occupation	Ethnicity
7	Gender	Race
8	Race	Education Level
9	Native Language(s)	Native Language(s)
10	Ethnicity	Religious Affiliation
11	Religious Affiliation	Personality Traits
12	Sexuality	Sexuality
13	Socio-economic Status	Socio-economic Status
14	Dis/ability	Dis/ability

Source: Ojeda-Hecht and Parks (2021).

listening, focus group dialogues consider both (and other) demographic categories as significantly impacting listening. Consider, for example, the Post-Gen Z and Gen Z focus group dialogues related below (pseudonyms used) in figure 4.1.

As can be seen above, three Post-Gen Z participants consider race and ethnicity to impact listening, but also that socio-economic status and/or disability can also impact listening expectations and behaviors. The Gen Z focus group dialogue also expresses this belief, as seen in Case 2 figure 4.2 below:

As Mia stated (and was affirmed by the other Gen Z focus group members), communicating between differing socio-economic classes can make it hard to listen to others, while having a shared identity with another person (such as a student) creates "a bridge for communication."

However, generations were not similar on all listening perceptions. When considering listening in face-to-face offline contexts and emailing in online ones, survey results suggest that Gen Z and Post-Gen Z cohorts may hold distinct beliefs about the ways that their racial and/or ethnic identities impact how they *listen to others*. Based on responses to contextual and identity based questions "How do you think your racial and/or ethnic identity impacts how you listen to other people in <X> situation?" with professors or students, face-to-face or email exchanges, and whether or not the person avowed or ascribed a person of color identity. Statistically significant differences appear between Gen Z and Post-Gen Z. The data showed that Gen Z is less likely to perceive their racial and/or ethnic identities to impact their listening to others in the following contexts: 1) emailing with professors of color, 2) face-to-face with students of color, 3) face-to-face with white/Caucasian students, and 4) emailing with white/Caucasian students.

John   Yeah and I think these different kind of you know, in the groups or kind of thing, I think also have uh an boldness to call other people out with say let's say race or ethnicity. If you know maybe not doing a job of- of listening or being heard or you know socioeconomic status you know with the people that are on the upper-end of the economy scale obviously not you know giving a voice to people who that are poor and whatnot. Or you know disability or similar kind of things, um.

Lucy   Mmhmm. Or just not having a sense of their experience so you know when they're communicating even you think you're listen- listening but just not having that perspective or being aware that there is another perspective, you know.

John   Mmhmm. Yeah.

David Well I'm gonna go back to where I was before. Kind of hung up on the listening thing versus race or ethnicity impacts listening. I think there- unless there's something I can't think of anything on race that would impact listening ethnicity I guess that would be more cultural, you know. Whether you're talking to somebody you know from New York whether as opposed to someone from L.A. okay maybe- I guess you get a cultural difference there when they want different things or they might expect different things so they're trying to listen in different ways.

John   Mmhmm.

Lucy   Yeah, but you don't think that people of different races when they're interacting like you Know… let's say I was a black woman. I can't speak for that cause I'm not. But you know that would add a layer of how you and I would communicate. Cause I have two intersectional minorities, you know, and what I might say or how I might listen or respond to you is reflective of your still traditional as a wh- as a white male in society.

David How you communicate I think that was the key in your discussion here but how do you listen? yeah, I don't know you know your- your all your experiences everything that you grew up with kind of impacts how you listen. If you were rich if you were poor, you know if you're from the south. Kay that might impact how you listen a little bit. I think it- especially if like you're from the northeast you know and you wanna- let's go let's go or like you're talking to someone from Alabama and you're going oh my god spit it out, you know.

Figure 4.1 Post-Gen Z Focus Group Discourse. *Source:* Hecht and Parks (2021).

Mia   But to like actually answer the question, umm I don't. I think its easier to listen to a different perspective and background when like its almost relatable and it feels personal. Like if its like someone who is now fifty-seven and is a billionaire and is trying to talk to me about like how they got there, I'm like what the fuck d- like how is that applicable to me at all? Like when a professor is like "when I was your age," I'm like dude, I don't know when that was. I have no idea when that was. And like but when there is something like connecting you guys, like being a student, and like going through the motions and stuff its like. It kind of creates like a bridge for communication to actually happen. Cause we're all completely different. There's no way for all of us to have lived the exact same life you know.

Figure 4.2 Gen Z Focus Group Discourse. *Source:* Ojeda-Hecht and Parks (2021).

Additionally, Gen Z and Post-Gen Z cohorts also differ in how they perceive their racial and/or ethnic identities impacting how *other people listen to them*. Based on the survey question "How do you think your racial and/or ethnic identity impacts how other people listen to you in <X> situation?" with professors or students, face-to-face or email exchanges, and whether or not the person avowed or ascribed a person of color identity, significant differences were found between generations, with Gen Z as less likely to perceive their racial and/or ethnic identities to impact how other people listen to them in the following contexts: 1) emailing with professors of color, and 2) emailing with white/Caucasian professors, 3) emailing with students of color, and 4) face-to-face with students of color. Notably, no statistically significant differences appeared between generations for questions related to face-to-face conversations with either white/Caucasian students or professors of color, pointing to the need for additional research about listening through digital communication mediums in instructional contexts.

To further explore this role of technology in instructional contexts, we pursued thematic analysis of an overarching *Listening and Technology* theme. Participants referenced four important "subthemes," including 1) quantity and quality of understanding, 2) generational differences in use and perception, 3) listening limitations through technology, and 4) listening strengths through technology. These subthemes were articulated by participant expressions of technology inhibiting understanding by simply getting in the way (e.g. having headphones in and not being able to hear someone), or technology facilitating understanding (e.g. when one person shares internet references with a person of the same generation). Post-Gen Z participants expressed that their preferences for how to use technology is perceived differently by people of younger generations. Participants also expressed that listening through technology has both strengths (e.g., being able to connect with people from a distance) and limitations (e.g., misunderstanding somehow based on how they used technology different from one might prefer). These subthemes inform us of the balance when communicating through technology with others that Post-Gen Z and Gen Z members negotiate.

Results from our corpus linguistic analysis also suggest that each generational cohort may each conceptualize and discuss technology in different ways. Terms such as "technology" and "phone" were mentioned by both generational cohorts, with "technology" mentioned twice as many times in the Post-Gen Z group as the Gen Z group (9/5, respectively) and "phone" mentioned twice as many times by the Gen Z as the Post-Gen Z group (4/2, respectively). Of special note, however, is that the word "email" or "emailing" was referenced 7 different times in the transcripts, but only by the Post-Gen Z group; it was not referenced at all by the Gen Z group. This suggests that generations may not only diverge in how they conceptualize listening itself, but the digital mediums that they consider important for the listening and communication process may differ as well.

In summary, online survey and focus group discourse results together help us better understand intergenerational listening expectations and possible needs for accommodation. Results show that both generations perceive their racial and/or ethnic identities to impact how *they listen to others* and how *others listen to them* when emailing and in face-to-face conversations within the instructor-student relationship. Both generational cohorts perceive that listening (whether in-person or online) across racial and/or ethnic identity differences can be difficult, despite initial online survey results where participants initially indicated that these (and some other) identities may not be the most important factors impacting interpersonal listening.

DISCUSSION

Gen Z, making up a large part of today's college student body, and older generations, making up a large part of instructors, consistently express that listening across difference can be difficult for them. As students and instructors communicate through digital technologies, they are negotiating multiple, personal, and potentially differing, expectancies. Burgoon's Expectancy Violation Theory involves communication expectancies derived from communicator characteristics (demographics, physical appearance, personality), relationship factors (familiarity, liking, similarity), and context characteristics (privacy, formality, task orientation) (Burgoon 1993). These communicator characteristics and factors can each prescribe certain interaction behaviors and dictate the expectancies in a given encounter. Given that these communicator characteristics are conceptualized by both generational cohorts as factors of listening across difference (including race and ethnicity/physical appearance, socio-economic status/demographics) and listening across technology (including formality, privacy, formality) the implications that expectancies have on the instructor-student relationship are substantial. Our study shows that Gen Z and Post-Gen Z cohorts differ in their perception of the ways of the ways that their racial and/or ethnic identities impact how *other people listen to them*, making it increasingly important for instructors and students alike to be aware of the expectations they are bringing to online and face-to-face interactions and to which they hold others accountable.

Both generations also expressed that listening across technology will never be the same (or as good) as listening in person, because of its lack of immediacy and the crucial face-to-face layers of nonverbal cues, like eye contact, vocal tone, and body language. Significantly, both generations indicated that generational differences also occur in technology use and ways of listening through technology. Giles' Communication Accommodation Theory (CAT) explores the act of accommodation as a process in which interactants adjust their communication to either diminish or enhance social and communicative differences (Giles 1973). The process of accommodation can be enacted through a variety of communicative modes, be it face-to-face or mediated communication (as via telephone, email, or texting). Communicators can engage in either accommodative or nonaccommodative moves among a multitude of communicative modes, such as nonverbal posture or tone, topics to pursue, or even choice of listening medium (Gallois et al. 2005). Both focus groups expressed that nonverbal cues are an integral part of listening that is often missed when using digital technologies yet nonverbal cues are integral to being a good listener. The lack of familiar nonverbal cues may make it harder for communication accommodation to take place but could also generatively result in both students and instructors attempting to find new ways to accommodate one another's choice of and communication through diverse digital technologies.

As the world continues to adapt to the use of technology and works to become increasingly inclusive of all identities, Generation Z and older generations find themselves exploring the digital world to connect with others. Students and instructors, typically coming from two different generational cohorts—each with their own cohort's cultural expectations—are using digital tools to connect now more than ever. It is clear that shared and contrasting concerns exist between generational cohorts in the instructional context about listening in online and offline communication and negotiation of a multiplicity of diverse identities.

15 INTERGENERATIONAL LISTENING TIPS

It is on this final note about diversity that we conclude. Our study consistently showed that people of all generations often find it difficult to discuss diversity and difference, regardless of whether the communication medium is face-to-face or digital. We thus offer readers a final set of themes from our analysis in order to provide meaningful steps forward for intergenerational listening between Generation Z and older generations in any instructional space.

1. Listen to understand.
2. Be slow to argue.
3. Develop appropriate empathy.
4. Resist fear and fixing.
5. Choose to be an engaged listener in both individual and group settings.
6. Intentionally listen to people who you do not agree with or understand.
7. Expand your horizons and develop shared context with more diverse others.
8. Learn how to listen differently to people from different backgrounds than you.

9. Build resilience for holding others' stories of marginalization and oppression.
10. Pursue shared and reciprocal listening and speaking in your conversations.
11. Determine relational listening expectations.
12. Attend to nonverbal cues.
13. Find ways to know when you are being listened to, even when it does not feel like it.
14. Develop strategies for listening to extreme emotions, beliefs, and ideas.
15. Attend to your own communication resources so that you can listen well when needed.

REFERENCES

Altman, Steven A. 2020. "Will Covid-19 Have a Lasting Impact on Globalization?" *Harvard Business Review*, May 20, 2020. https://hbr.org/2020/05/will-covid-19-have-a-lasting-impact-on-globalization.

Berry, Gregory R. 2016. "Can Computer-Mediated Asynchronous Communication Improve Team Processes and Decision Making? Learning from the Management Literature." *The Journal of Business Communication (1973)*, September. DOI: 10.1177/0021943606292352.

Bodie, G. D., D. L. Worthington, and C. C. Gearhart. 2013. "The Listening Styles Profile-Revised (LSP-R): A Scale Revision and Evidence for Validity." *Communication Quarterly* 61 (1): 72–90. DOI: 10.1080/01463373.2012.720343.

Bodie, Graham. 2011. "The Revised Listening Concepts Inventory (LCI-R): Assessing Individual and Situational Differences in the Conceptualization of Listening." *Imagination, Cognition and Personality* 30 (3): 301–339.

Bond, Christopher D. 2012. "An Overview of Best Practices to Teach Listening Skills." *International Journal of Listening* 26 (2): 61–63. DOI: 10.1080/10904018.2012.677660.

Burgoon, Judee K. 1993. "Interpersonal Expectations, Expectancy Violations, and Emotional Communication." *Journal of Language and Social Psychology* 12 (1–2): 30–48. DOI: 10.1177/0261927X93121003.

Burgoon, Judee K., and Stephen B. Jones. 1976. "Toward a Theory of Personal Space Expectations and Their Violations." *Human Communication Research* 2 (2): 131–146. DOI: 10.1111/j.1468-2958.1976.tb00706.x.

Cennamo, Lucy, and Dianne Gardner. 2008. "Generational Differences in Work Values, Outcomes and Person-Organisation Values Fit." Edited by Keith Macky, Dianne Gardner, and Stewart Forsyth. *Journal of Managerial Psychology* 23 (8): 891–906. DOI: 10.1108/02683940810904385.

Duran, Robert L., Lynne Kelly, and James A. Keaten. 2005. "College Faculty Use and Perceptions of Electronic Mail to Communicate with Students." *Communication Quarterly* 53 (2): 159–176. DOI: 10.1080/01463370500090118.

Frymier, Ann Bainbridge, and Marian L. Houser. 2000. "The Teacher-Student Relationship as an Interpersonal Relationship." *Communication Education* 49 (3): 207. DOI: 10.1080/03634520009379209.

Gallois, Cindy, Tania Ogay, and Howard Giles. 2005. "Theorizing About Intercultural Communication." In *Theorizing About Intercultural Communication*, edited by W. B. Gudykunst, 121–148. Thousand Oaks: Sage.

Giles, Howard. 1973. "Accent Mobility: A Model and Some Data." *Anthropological Linguistics* 15: 87–105.

Goodboy, Alan K., and San Bolkan. 2009. "College Teacher Misbehaviors: Direct and Indirect Effects on Student Communication Behavior and Traditional Learning Outcomes." *Western Journal of Communication* 73 (2): 204–219. DOI: 10.1080/10570310902856089.

Hassini, Elkafi. 2006. "Student–Instructor Communication: The Role of Email." *Computers & Education* 47 (1): 29–40. DOI: 10.1016/j.compedu.2004.08.014.

Mani, B. Venkat. 2020. "Inclusive Teaching Is Needed to Help Combat the Xenophobia, Racism and Discrimination Brought on by COVID-19." *Inside Higher Ed*. Last Modified May 14, 2020. https://www.insidehighered.com/views/2020/05/14/inclusive-teaching-needed-help-combat-xenophobia-racism-and-discrimination-brought.

Palfrey, John, and Urs Gasser. 2016. *Born Digital: How Children Grow Up in a Digital Age* (Revised, Expanded Ed.). New York: Basic Books.

Parks, Elizabeth S. 2020. "Listening Through the Ages: Measuring Generational Listening Differences with the LCI-R." *International Journal of Listening* 34 (3). DOI: 10.1080/10904018.2020.1748503.

Pew Research Center. 2019. "Generations and Age." https://www.pewresearch.org/topics/generations-and-age/.

Ramirez, Artemio, and Zuoming Wang. 2008. "When Online Meets Offline: An Expectancy Violations Theory Perspective on Modality Switching." *Journal of Communication* 58 (1): 20–39. DOI: 10.1111/j.1460-2466.2007.00372.x.

Seemiller, Corey, and Meghan Grace. 2016. *Generation Z Goes to College* (1st Ed.). San Francisco, CA: Jossey Bass.

Terry, Gareth, Nikki Hayfield, Victoria Clarke, and Virginia Braun. 2017. "Thematic Analysis." In *The SAGE Handbook of Qualitative Research in Psychology*, edited by Carla Willig and Wendy Stainton Rogers, 17–36. London: SAGE Publications Ltd. DOI: 10.4135/9781526405555.n2.

Chapter 5

Listening Research Shows How Gen Z and Faculty Can Co-Create Engaging Learning Environments

Pamela Sherstad

Recognizing the attention struggles of students in higher education classrooms piqued an interest in listening and communication scholarship. Gaining the listening attention of college students is not a new challenge. Through the decades, communication scholars have signaled, or shouted, a need for more education and research focused on listening (Beall et al. 2008; Wolvin 2012). However, the mix of a digital age, COVID-19 pandemic, racial tensions, political chaos, etc. demonstrates the need may be even more acute for Generation Z. The findings from a recent case study indicate Generation Z students are aware that their listening processes are hindered because of their digital bond to the Internet and the handheld devices used to access it (Sherstad 2019). Take a moment and think back to when you were a student. What classes did you most look forward to, and why? And, which professors did you connect with and why? Keep those answers tucked in your mind as you continue reading. We will circle back to your memories in the conclusion. First, however, the question of how professors can embrace the higher education challenge of listening, which has been exasperated during the COVID-19 pandemic, will be addressed.

An assumption, because you are reading this book, is that you genuinely care about the educational growth of students and recognize differences between Gen Z and other generations. Another reality is how behavioral changes during the COVID-19 pandemic has elevated adverse mental health conditions of young adults (Centers for Disease Control and Prevention 2020). While this chapter ends with a bullet list of suggestions to increase effective listening specifically for face-to-face classrooms, it is essential to understand that the co-creation of an effective educational community is a team effort that involves professors and students. The emphasis is on face-to-face educational environments, but the principles are adaptable to online environments.

Information on what makes today's college students different than previous generations will set the foundation followed by technology's influence on listening in higher education. The conclusion emphasizes pedagogy to co-create engaging and effective learning environments. Be encouraged that recent research shows that Generation Z students want to learn from their professors. To begin, let us explore more in-depth about what can be learned about Gen Z.

TODAY'S COLLEGE STUDENT: GENERATION Z

It has been pointed out that Generation Z is a generation which differs significantly from generations of the past. The use of technology is one of the defining characteristics of Gen Z, in addition, the world-wide COVID-19 pandemic has effected young adults. In an August 2020 report, the Centers for Disease Control and Prevention stated because of COVID-19, "Mental health conditions are disproportionately affecting specific populations, especially young adults…" (par. 8). Higher education with COVID-19 has forced changes for the safety of stakeholders. These changed have relied heavily on technology. Virtual class meetings, learning management systems, and text messages replaced face-to-face classes, physical handouts, and office hours. Higher education with COVID-19 has also changed the way Gen Z listens.

Growing up in a highly digitalized media environment has influenced not only Gen Z's views of education but also their views on social issues and life in general. Elmore (2017) explains seven major shifts for Generation Z: 1) confidence shifted to caution, 2) idealism shifted to pragmatism, 3) attacking an education shifted to hacking one, 4) spending money shifted to saving money, 5) consuming media shifted to creating media, 6) viral messages on social media shifted to vanishing messages, and, 7) text messaging shifted to iconic messaging (47–49). These changes point to a different mindset and directly or indirectly influence higher educational environments. Growing up as "digital natives" (Rickes 2016, 21) provides unique challenges to Gen Z in higher education environments specifically for listening. Now put in the mix the stresses of living during a time of COVID-19.

Shatto and Erwin (2016) note, "This reliance on mobile technology affects not only how this generation learns, it also drastically affects how instructors should be delivering instructional material" (253). According to Seemiller and Grace (2017), "The individual nature of technology has helped Generation Z become comfortable and accustomed to learning independently. Whether reading an article or an eBook, completing an online module, or watching an instructional video, students can typically engage in many educational practices in an individual setting" (23). Nemko (2015) notes, "Z'ers having grown up with a smartphone has led them to expect information and entertainment on-demand, instantly, and in phone-sized bites" (par. 2). It seems relatively clear that Generation Z's learning experiences have been different than those of other generations. It is their pervasive access to digital communication technologies that have been an essential reason for this.

More so than any other generation, Generation Z is "even more technologically advanced and equipped usually with more than one device at the same time" (Jaleniauskienė and Jucevičienė 2015, 41). With an average of nine hours a day using cell phones and other media consumption, students graze content, bypassing the details, focusing on headlines and pictures. Jaleniauskienė and Jucevičienė state, "This generation will be engaged and at the same time bored with technology, therefore, educators should think of new ways to employ technology" (50). Elmore (2017) asserts Generation Z has an attention span of six to eight seconds. An inability to focus for an extended period may seem contrary to some educational environments; however, this shifting attention could "aid in the ability to sort information quickly assisting in processing" (Cameron and Pagnattaro 2017, 318).

Generation Z can sense immediate satisfaction from social networks; these students can also feel bullied or rejected instantly (Turner 2015). According to Clarkson (2018), Generation Z is the first generation to live their lives online; this reality may include feelings of being watched and judged always. Studies show that experience linked to the Internet has made Generation Z anxious and uneasy (Stillman 2016), affecting listening. Gamble and Gamble (2013) describe mindful listening as being fully present, focused, and attentive. Generation Z's use of smartphones, laptops, or other devices to communicate online reportedly negatively affects their ability to talk face-to-face (Turkle 2013), which has implications in the higher education classroom. Being fully present for learning appears to take a backseat to the prominence of social connections. Hope (2016) explains social links are critically important to this generation. The frequently used acronym FOMO, fear of missing out, is an example. If Generation Z cannot be physically present with their friends and family's activities, their online engagement helps them feel virtually present. Identifying students physically present, but mentally checked-out of the class discussion can become like a game for instructors which leads to "randomly" directing questions to those who appear less than fully engaged.

Generation Z students have grown up in an environment with more communication technology and information than any previous generation

(Dimock 2019); this engagement with technology has implications for higher education environments. "The image of the multitasking teenager is rapidly becoming ingrained in the public consciousness, as parents and other adults simultaneously marvel at and worry about young people juggling two, three, or four different media activities concurrently" (Kaiser Family Foundation 2010, 33). Earlier generations have described technology as a handy tool for communicating or working; Generation Z describes communication technology as an essential part of life comparable to air and water (Elmore 2017). Next, we will look specifically at technology's influence on listening in higher education environments.

TECHNOLOGY'S INFLUENCE ON LISTENING IN HIGHER EDUCATION

Because listening plays a critical role in learning (Tindall and Nisbet 2008) and effective listening leads to academic success (Beall et al. 2008), student engagement in higher education needs to be addressed. Trenholm (2018) observes that "listening is the forgotten part of communication, yet being able to listen well is one of the most essential communication-related skills" (47). Dolby (2012) purports, "'Listening' is at the center of an education: It takes many forms (visual, auditory, sensory), but is the only way to understand another's life and experience" (par. 8). Gen Z students bring their technology to higher education learning environments. As high school students, they may have been required to keep their smartphone, tablet, or laptop in their school locker, but college is different and may provide the freedom to keep their technology nearby or use that technology in the classroom for educational purposes. Recognizing how technology influences effective listening in postsecondary institutions is essential because listening is fundamental to learning. The study of technology in the classroom is not new, and lines in the sand have been drawn.

Wireless Internet falls on the spectrum between being a benefit, by keeping students engaged, to a temptation, by disrupting students from listening in class. Ridberg (2006), a contributor to *The Christian Science Monitor*, interviewed law professors who deemed Internet wired classrooms as too distracting. Others in higher education recognize distracted students is not a novel concern; every generation has struggled with not being mentally present in classrooms. Before the Internet, students read newspapers, passed notes, or mentally checked-out by daydreaming (Ridberg 2006).

Here is one example of how technology can keep a student from being mentally present. During the spring 2019 semester, a student's behavior during a Communication Skills class stood out. With 10 students in the class, discussions typically involved everyone. When it was "Jake's" (not the student's real name) turn to contribute, he mentioned he agreed with another classmate, rehashing what was already said. What Jake missed was the student he agreed with had, only moments before, reversed his position and explained the rationale. Jake was on his computer during a critical few minutes of the class discussion. When it was pointed out what he missed, Jake sheepishly readjusted himself and appeared to be paying closer attention. After class, Jake apologized for not listening; explaining he was responding to an email and that he "normally doesn't do that in class." For a variety of reasons, including similar stories to the one shared, views on technology in the higher education classroom vary. For more than a decade, the debate on whether laptop computers help or hinder in-class learning has conflicting opinions. Some have argued communication technology allows for more instructor-student interactions (Barak et al. 2006), and this additional interaction is said to increase engagement and learning. Fried (2008), however, found in-class laptop use was a distraction. The distraction extended beyond the individual using the laptop to the effect this had on other classmates. "This research raises serious concerns about the use of laptops in the classroom. Students admit to spending considerable time during lectures using their laptops for things other than taking notes. More importantly, the use of laptops was negatively related to several measures of learning. The pattern of the correlations suggests that laptop use interfered with students' abilities to pay attention to and understand the lecture material, which in turn resulted in lower test scores" (Fried 2008, 911).

More recently, Thompson (2017) explored the negative relationship between frequent use of communication technologies and academic performance. Part of the research on student use of communication technology included the in-class use of technology. Thompson stated:

> The negative relationship between communication technology use and concentration found in the study seems intuitively logical, but the data from this study do not provide a way of determining causal relationships. It is possible that frequent use of communication technologies habituates cognitive behaviors inconsistent with concentration, or that people with poor concentration skills gravitate to using communication technologies. (2017, 265)

Returning to how Gamble and Gamble (2013) describe mindful listening with the three characteristics of being fully present, focused, and attentive, can lead educators to co-creating an engaging and effective learning environment for the benefit of all students, an environment that is more conducive to listening.

PEDAGOGY TO CO-CREATE ENGAGING AND EFFECTIVE LEARNING ENVIRONMENTS

Consider that Generation Z students have grown up in a continually changing, highly mediated communication environment that has provided more information than any previous generation (Dimock 2019; Seemiller and Grace 2017). Their connected world has implications for listening and learning in higher education environments. Handheld technology is described by students and faculty as the number one distraction to effective listening for Generation Z in today's higher education classrooms (Sherstad 2019). According to students and faculty, the highest-ranked immunity against distraction is class discussions and in-class activities (Sherstad). These findings imply faculty and students recognize the challenge of effective listening for Generation Z and have identified strategies to co-create engaging and effective learning environments to promote competent listening.

Cultivating a culture of listening for the sake of learning involves students and faculty coming together to take steps on a path of purpose. Students and faculty acknowledge that handheld technology is a distraction that hinders listening in the classroom; putting away personal technology was considered essential to aid classroom listening (Sherstad 2019). This result relates to what Cronon (1998) shared over 20 years ago. In a distracted and overly busy age, an educated person puts in the effort to "follow an argument, track logical reasoning, detect illogic, hear the emotions that lie behind both the logic and the illogic, and ultimately empathize with the person who is feeling those emotions" (Cronon 1998, 76). Based on recent findings, it appears Generation Z students and faculty members recognized this level of engagement is rarely happening because of technology use in the classroom (Sherstad). When students were asked about a tip to help classmates be an effective listener in school, the majority of student responses suggested putting away media devices (Sherstad).

Instructors should be encouraged to hear students' state technology should be tucked away during class. They recognize their in-class online shopping or checking of sports scores is not contributing to their education. This finding is significant coming from a generation who has grown up with and lives life close to their handheld technology. That is excellent news. However, an obvious question follows. If students know how important it is to put handheld technology away while in class, why don't they do it?

Again, scholarship shows Generation Z has relied on communication technology for nearly every aspect of their lives (Elmore 2017; Dimock 2019). One general finding shows being interested in what was being taught in the classroom was a critical factor in aiding effective listening (Sherstad, 2019). However, students said they reach for their media devices while in class (and outside class as well) because they are bored (Sherstad). Lack of interest in the classroom subject matter, together with the proximity of an entertainment device and notification alerts that are visible, audible, and physical (vibration), creates the perfect distraction storm. Let's explore how a professor's communication can positively influence the education environment.

Staton-Spicer and Marty-White (1981) identified a connection between instructor communication concerns and classroom behavior with the educational environment in mind. The instructional communication theory framework provides a lens for guiding pedagogy in higher education classrooms today which include Gen Z and technology. Staton-Spicer and Marty-White reported three communication concerns of educators: self, task, and impact. In Staton-Spicer and Marty-White's research, *self* as a communication concern in the classroom focused on the instructor's credibility and flexibility; *task* as a communication concern was addressed before the start of the semester and involved how to make abstract concepts concrete. Applying what was discovered from a recent study about the higher educational listening experience of Generation Z, Staton-Spicer and Marty-White's communication concern of *impact* was applicable. *Impact* is described as a concern for student understanding. According to Staton-Spicer and Marty-White, "A teacher who expresses the impact concern of student understanding is likely to engage in a variety of behaviors to facilitate such understanding." (365) While Staton-Spicer and Marty-White's findings were published before Internet wired classrooms and students' access to handheld technology, their conclusions have an application to Generation Z's listening in the fact that educational concern and behavior in the classroom have a communication link. To approach teaching from the communication concern of impact, faculty must listen to their students. When students feel listened to, they respond with higher engagement and a sense of involvement, thereby reducing boredom and the pull of handheld technology to entertain (Sherstad 2019).

The question needs to be asked: What communication behaviors can instructors employ to best facilitate Generation Z's effective listening for subject understanding? Staton-Spicer and Marty-White found instructors' concern for students' understanding resulted in behaviors such as facilitating student interaction, eliciting student responses, and using questions to engage thinking. Other findings point to a similar suggestion. Twenge (2009) emphasizes that "students frequently need the purpose and meaning of activities spelled out for them. Previous generations had a sense of duty and would often do what they were told without asking why. Most young people no longer respond to appeals to duty; instead, they want to know exactly why they are doing something and want to feel they are having a personal impact" (404).

As promised, let's return to the questions asked of you at the beginning of this chapter. As a college student, what classes did you most look forward to, and why? And, which professors did you connect with and why? Your responses to those questions can help guide you as you plan to engage today's postsecondary students. Generation Z students listen most effectively during class discussion and in-class activities, two teaching techniques that do not require technology (Sherstad 2019). Using recommendations from Staton-Spicer, Marty-White, and Twenge, instructors can encourage effective listening by crafting meaningful discussions and in-class activities that communicate the relevance of the subject. Be encouraged knowing that recent research shows Generation Z students do want to learn from their professors. In addition, figure 5.1 shows the recommendations from college students on how to be an effective listener in class (Sherstad). By recognizing when students feel listened to, they respond with higher engagement and a sense of involvement, and by sharing the suggestions of Gen Z students about how to be an effective listener in class, a foundation for co-creating an academic community that enhances listening and learning begins.

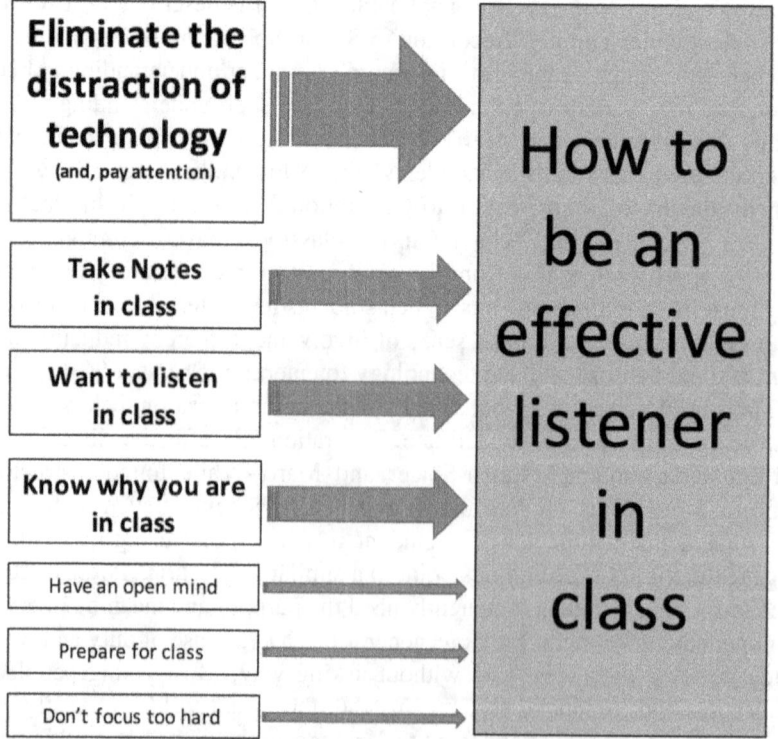

Figure 5.1   **Listening Tips from Generation Z Students.** *Source:* Sherstad 2021.

THE ROLE OF LISTENING IN CO-CREATING AN EFFECTIVE ACADEMIC COMMUNITY

Co-Cocreating an effective academic community with Generation Z that aids successful listening includes steps before, during and after a course. Below are suggestions to begin the thinking process.

BEFORE THE SEMESTER OR TERM BEGINS

1. Ascertain if your institution has a policy regarding student use of handheld technology (phones, tablets, and laptops) in the classroom. Clarify in the course syllabus any additions to the institution policy or your policy regarding student use of handheld technology during class. Be prepared to convince students of the learning benefits of this policy. It is vital to remember instructors are in charge of the classroom environment. If you choose to limit students' access to handheld technology, consider a "technology break" during the class period, allowing students to access their handheld technology for social media, etc. That may help alleviate some of Generation Z's anxiety from being separated from their technology during class.
2. Identify how you will communicate the steps students can take that will help them prepare for your class meetings. For example, will students need paper notebooks and writing utensils, the course textbooks, articles printed in advance, and so on? Information that will help students mentally prepare for being in class aids in effective listening. Plan how you will articulate course requirements clearly.
3. Make plans to help students understand what they are learning in class can be applicable to the present and future. Before the semester beings is the time to develop discussions and activities that will engage the students with the course subject.
4. Learn the names of the students in the class. If possible, introduce yourself and help students know your passion and excitement for teaching them.

DURING CLASS

1. Be welcoming by acknowledging students and addressing students by name.
2. At the beginning of class, explain your handheld technology policy and why you have that policy for their learning benefit.

3. Talk to your class about the suggestions from other college students (figure 5.1) on how to be an effective listener in class. Do your students have other suggestions?
4. If possible, involve every student during every class. Whether that includes discussion questions, small group activities, or impromptu questions that allow students to pull from their experience, help students understand how their presence and participation is valuable for the class as a whole. Students may not be accustomed to this level of participation, but don't give up on intentionally engaging students in the classroom.
5. When students are asking questions during class, allow the students to finish the questions before responding. Show appreciation for the student asking the question; this small act encourages others to ask questions. Approach questions and interactions as teaching opportunities.
6. When possible, consider using teaching techniques that include handheld technology to reach educational objectives. For example, Kahoot or a quick Internet search for subject-related content to jumpstart a discussion can be fun and engaging.

AFTER CLASS

1. When possible, continue course topic conversations after class in the hallway or via email. Share your excitement about the course you are teaching with the students.
2. Acknowledge students outside of class, helping them know you value them as a person, which has potential to increase their listening to you in the classroom.
3. Use technology to engage students in the subject. For example, post interesting videos or content with hashtags that will add to the classes' understanding of the subject and provide starting points for future conversations between you and students, and between students within the class.

REFERENCES

Barak, Miri, Alberta Lipson, and Steven Lerman. 2006. "Wireless Laptops as Means for Promoting Active Learning in Large Lecture Halls." *Journal of Research on Technology in Education* 38 (3): 245–263. DOI: 10.1080/15391523.2006.10782459.

Beall, Melissa, Jennifer Gill-Rosier, Jeanine Tate, and Amy Matten. 2008. "State of the Context: Listening in Education." *International Journal of Listening* 22 (2): 123–132. DOI: 10.1080/10904010802174826.

Cameron, Elizabeth, and Marisa A. Pagnattaro. 2017. "Beyond Millennials: Engaging Generation Z in Business Law Classes." *Journal of Legal Studies Education* 34 (2): 317–324. DOI: 10.1111/jlse.12064.

Centers for Disease Control and Prevention. 2020. "Mental Health, Substance Use, and Suicidal Ideation During the COVID-19 Pandemic – United States, June 24–30, 2020." August 13, 2020. https://www.cdc.gov/mmwr/volumes/69/wr/m m6932a1.htm.

Clarkson, Natalie. 2018. "How is Mental Health Affecting Generation Z's Ability to Achieve?" *Virgin Group*, January 18.

Cronon, William. 1998. "'Only Connect . . .' The Goals of a Liberal Education." *The American Scholar* 67 (4): 73–80.

Dimock, Michael. 2019. "Defining Generations: Where Millennials End and Generation Z Begins." *Pew Research Center*. Last Modified January 17, 2019. http://www.pewresearch.org/fact-tank/2019/01/17/where-millennials-end-and-g eneration-z-begins/.

Dolby, Nadine. 2012. "There's No Learning When Nobody's Listening." *The Chronicle of Higher Education*. http://eres.regent.edu:2048/login?url=https://se arch-proquest-com.ezproxy.regent.edu/docview/1026558027?accountid=13479.

Elmore, Tim. 2017. *Marching Off the Map: Inspire Students to Navigate a Brand New World*. Atlanta: Poet Gardener Publishing.

Fried, Carrie B. 2008. "In-Class Laptop Use and Its Effects on Student Learning." *Computers & Education* 50 (3): 906–914. DOI: 10.1016/j.compedu.2006.09.006.

Gamble, Teri, and Michael Gamble. 2013. *Communication Works* (11th Ed.). New York: McGraw-Hill.

Hope, Joan. 2016. "Get Your Campus Ready for Generation Z." *Student Affairs Today* 19 (7): 1–7. DOI: 10.1002/say.30253.

Jaleniauskienė, Evelina, and Palmira Jucevičienė. 2015. "Reconsidering University Educational Environment for the Learners of Generation Z." *Social Sciences* 88 (2): 38–53. DOI: 10.5755/j01.ss.88.2.12737.

Nemko, Marty. 2015. "Generation Z." *Psychology Today*. Last Modified October 25, 2015. https://www.psychologytoday.com/us/blog/how-do-life/201510/genera tion-z.

Rickes, Persis C. 2016. "Generations in Flux: How Gen Z Will Continue to Transform Higher Education Space." *Planning for Higher Education* 44 (4): 21–45. http://eres .regent.edu:2048/login?url=https://search-proquest-com.ezproxy.regent.edu/doc view/1838982286?accountid=13479.

Ridberg, Maia. 2006. "Professors Want Their Classes 'Unwired'." *The Christian Science Monitor*, May 4, 2006. http://eres.regent.edu:2048/login?url=https://se arch-proquest-com.ezproxy.regent.edu/docview/405555725?accountid=13479.

Rideout, Victoria J., Ulla G. Foehr, and Donald F. 2010. *Generation M2: Media in the Lives of 8–18-Year Olds*. Menlo Park: Kaiser Family Foundation. https://www .kff.org/other/event/generation-m2-media-in-the-lives-of/.

Seemiller, Corey, and Meghan Grace. 2017. "Generation Z: Educating and Engaging the Next Generation of Students." *About Campus: Enriching the Student Learning Experience* 22 (3): 21–26. DOI: 10.1002/abc.21293.

Shatto, Bobbi, and Kelly Erwin. 2016. "Moving on From Millennials: Preparing for Generation Z." *The Journal of Continuing Education in Nursing* 47 (6): 253–254. DOI: 10.3928/00220124-20160518-05.

Sherstad, Pamela S. 2019. "Exploring the Higher Education Listening Experiences of Generation Z." PhD Dissertation, Regent University.

Staton-Spicer, Ann Q., and Cheryl R. Marty-White. 1981. "A Framework for Instructional Communication Theory: The Relationship Between Teacher Communication Concerns and Classroom Behavior." *Communication Education* 30 (4): 354–366.

Stillman, Jessica. 2016. "Gen Z is Anxious, Distrustful, and Often Downright Miserable, New Poll Reveals." Inc., March 23, 2016. https://www.inc.com/jessica-stillman/gen-z-is-anxious-distrustful-and-often-downright-miserable-new-poll-reveals.html.

Thompson, Penny. 2017. "Communication Technology Use and Study Skills." *Active Learning in Higher Education* 18 (3): 257–270. DOI: 10.1177/1469787417715204.

Tindall, Evie, and Deanna Nisbet. 2008. "Listening: A Vital Skill for Learning." *International Journal of Learning* 15 (6): 121–127. DOI: 10.18848/1447-9494/CGP/v15i06/45802.

Trenholm, Sarah. 2018. *Thinking Through Communication: An Introduction to the Study of Human Communication* (8th Ed.). New York: Routledge.

Turkle, Sherry. 2012. "Connected, But Alone?" Filmed February 2012 in Long Beach, California. TED video, 19:32. https://www.ted.com/talks/sherry_turkle_connected_but_alone?language=en.

Turner, Anthony. 2015. "Generation Z: Technology and Social Interest." *The Journal of Individual Psychology* 71 (2): 103–113. Accessed May 25, 2020. DOI: 10.1353/jip.2015.0021.

Twenge, Jean M. 2009. "Generational Changes and Their Impact in the Classroom: Teaching Generation Me." *Medical Education* 43 (5): 398–405.

Wolvin, Andrew D. 2012. "Listening in the General Education Curriculum." *International Journal of Listening* 26 (2): 122–128. DOI: 10.1080/10904018.2012.678201.

Chapter 6

Teaching Digital Natives Where They Live

Generation Z and Online Learning

Troy Cooper and T. Kody Frey

INTRODUCTION

A 2018 Pearson report noted that "GenZ has been so immersed in technology in every aspect of their lives that they no longer see it as a transformative phenomenon, but rather as a normal, integral part of life" (16). Unlike the generation(s) before them, Generation Z (Gen Z) students have grown up in a world in which they have virtually always been connected to digital culture; Gen Z is composed of digital natives. This distinction applies not only to the well-documented use of technology and social media among this generation, but to nearly all aspects of their lives—including education. Indeed, the number of "virtual schools," fully online high schools, is increasing in number rapidly to meet the demands of this generation (Molnar et al. 2019). So, too, have colleges and universities adapted to meet the growing demand for online learning (National Center for Education Statistics 2019). Although this seems a normal evolution, there are many pedagogical considerations that must be addressed to effectively provide instruction for digital natives in the digital format. For example, the same Pearson report (2018) indicated that 55% of Gen Z students say that YouTube has contributed to their education, and 59% cite YouTube as their preferred learning method. This provides a unique opportunity for instructors to reassess the viability of current online course instruction methods and to adapt to account for the learning preferences of Gen Z students.

Therefore, this chapter presents an integrative framework that blends contemporary research on Gen Z characteristics, applications to online learning, and recommendations for future faculty development in order to ensure the preparedness of educators teaching digital natives in digital spaces. We begin by exploring existing trends in online learning in relation to Gen Z students. Presently, little research has empirically examined the preferences and attitudes of Gen Z students toward online pedagogy; however, research has suggested the various methods, systems, and forms of instruction that might appeal to this demographic. Next, we synthesize literature concerning Gen Z learning preferences alongside knowledge of effective online teaching. The vast majority of incoming first-year college students—characterized largely as Gen Z—still come from traditional, face-to-face educational backgrounds. Practitioners must recognize and appreciate that despite growing up with and through technology, many Gen Z students still harbor unique communicative shortcomings that may prevent them from engaging online. Moreover, increasingly ineffective teacher behaviors online could lead to increased student challenge behavior, dissent, or apathy. Finally, we offer recommendations for university administrators concerning faculty development and training. Scholars argue that Gen Z students can quickly become frustrated when their expectations of technology are not met, prompting Shatto and Erwin (2016) to assert that "resources must be devoted to acquiring new technologies as well as faculty development on its use" (254). Universities must be equipped to prepare the professoriate to meet this need. Based on an examination of past research and our own experiences as online instructors, we offer tangible advice for better engaging digital natives in digital platforms.

OVERVIEWING GEN Z LEARNING PREFERENCES

To meet the challenge of teaching digital natives in their own unique spaces, it is important to first review the learning trends and preferences relevant to this group. Across a variety of studies, it appears that three general characteristics describe Gen Z students' attitudes toward their learning: Personalization, Autonomy, and Practicality. In this first section, we expand upon each category and highlight important trends that may impact how learning occurs online for this group of students.

Personalization

Gen Z students prefer learning that is personalized. According to Fry and Parker (2018), Gen Z students are the most racially and ethnically diverse group to enter the college classroom. This implies a multitude of personal, social, and cultural experiences permeating instructional spaces. Moreover, the Gen Z student experience is characterized by busy schedules, growing concerns about mental health, and increased levels of different types of stress (e.g., economic, social), among other things (Mintz 2019). As a result, scholars have called for educators to shift the focus of pedagogy to be less engrossed in instructor dissemination of knowledge and more tailored to students' individualized experiences (Chicca and Sellenberger 2018; Hartman et al. 2018). Said differently, despite the clear importance of instructor message behaviors, the nature of the prototypical Gen Z student suggests that scholars and instructors should begin thinking less about how instructors send messages and more about how students receive them (Pousson and Myers 2018).

This *student-centric* approach implies that instructors put forth time and effort to adjust content to students' needs to create authentic and effective learning environments. Instructors must recognize and understand their students' individual needs in order to personalize their pedagogy. This is not limited strictly to students' content expectations, but includes several factors like the system of pedagogy (i.e., lectures, videos, interaction; Genota 2018), the types of technology used (Chicca and Sellenberger 2018), or even the extent to which their students desire a relationship with them (Asikainen et al. 2018).

For example, perhaps instructors can increase the use of video-based instruction on platforms like YouTube or incorporate a greater variety of communication technologies that are preferred by Gen Z students (Seemiller and Clayton 2019). Further, rather than holding traditional office hours, Gen Z students may benefit from virtual meetings or sharing of class announcements through social media instead of email. The existing research concerning Gen Z student learning preferences ultimately proposes that "faculty may even want to consider offering some customized learning that allows students to select from a menu of possible learning activities, all of which enable achievement of learning outcomes" (Chicca and Sellenberger 2018, 183).

Autonomy

Second, Gen Z students value *autonomy* in their learning. As noted, Gen Z has grown up in the digital world, helping them to become avid and competent users of technology. However, this immersion in the digital world has also resulted in Gen Z students developing an increased comfort working and interacting independently (Chicca and Sellenberger 2018). Seemiller and Grace (2017) argued that Gen Z students prefer intrapersonal experiences where they can reflect on, relate to, or understand content according to their own experiences. In other words, Gen Z students prefer to explore course concepts on their own before applying them in unique, nuanced ways that can make a difference in their own lives. Similar to the argument made regarding personalization, Pousson and Myers (2018) describe the Gen Z mindset as one that perceives instructors as not just agents of knowledge but guides who facilitate and make sense of an abundance of information.

Importantly, this does not mean Gen Z students want to avoid team-based, group, or collaborative learning. Instead, the research found that Gen Z students want to make sense of instructional content on their own before working with others. Seemiller and Clayton (2019) reflected this idea in their synthesis of Gen Z learning preferences. The researchers provide several strategies for modifying content and pedagogy to meet Gen Z students' autonomy learning needs. This includes providing students with opportunities to observe others completing tasks before attempting the experience independently, allowing students to choose topics that are meaningful to them, helping students make connections between course content and their future careers, or giving dedicated time for individual reflection.

The researchers also highlight the importance of scaffolding content so that students can keep track of their individual development. This scaffolding refers to a system of pedagogy designed for students to complete several small assignments as precursors to larger applications of knowledge. After each step in the scaffolding process, students can reflect on content relative to their unique, personal experiences before moving on. This should help students become more confident in their own abilities by thinking critically about where they both succeeded and failed in their pursuits of learning. Summatively, instructors can enhance the learning process for Gen Z students through autonomy-supportive instruction that does not explicitly tell students content but allows them to discover meaning on their own.

Practicality

Gen Z students tend to prefer instruction that is directly applicable to everyday life. Demonstrating the *practicality* of a given lesson or concept is an important consideration for instructors of this generation. Although this is not a new concept, as logically all students wish to see the value of their education, Gen Z is more narrowly focused on the practicality of education. These students seek out skill-focused material. According to Schwieger and Ladwig (2018), "Gen Zers realize the importance of building skills at a young age— 89% of those surveyed indicated that part of their free time activities were devoted to productive and creative endeavors, rather than just 'hanging out'" (47). Many, between the ages of 7 and 17, were already developing productivity skills such as graphic design and app development (Deep Focus 2015). This forward-thinking mentality emerges in many of the surveys of Gen Z.

Not only do Gen Z students expect practicality in the learning process, they see it as an integral part of moving beyond the classroom. Seemiller and Grace (2017) note that Gen Z students "want their educational experience to incorporate practical learning experiences from the beginning" (25) and to carry throughout the college experience. They suggest that college programs provide more internal and external opportunities for students to obtain practical hands-on experience through experiential learning and internships. As Gen Z enters the arena, the expectation is that they will hit the ground running equipped with tangible, useful experience. The expectation is that college will prepare them directly for career success.

Gen Z is also service-oriented. Aside from hands-on learning and practicality, Gen Z students are drawn to experiential and service-learning (see Gardner et al. 2018; Plochocki 2019). Transformative learning is attractive to students of this generation, as is evident from the increasing amount of volunteer and service-learning experience students entering college possess. Given that students are actively seeking out opportunities for meaningful, hands-on learning experiences, it is vital that college faculty and administrators provide opportunities for the incoming generation of students to meaningfully learn.

APPLICATIONS TO EFFECTIVE ONLINE INSTRUCTION

Apart from simply understanding the aforementioned preferences of Gen Z learners, it is also important to reflect on instructional practices and pedagogical strategies that will meet the needs of this generation of students. Because Gen Z students expect technology to be implemented effectively, online instruction that violates expectations can lead to negative experiences or mitigate students' learning experiences. We paint a broader picture of the types of pedagogical adjustments necessary for effective instruction by comparing what scholars argue constitutes effective online instruction (for a review, see Sellnow and Kaufmann 2018) to the expectations of Gen Z learners. Three questions guide this section: (1) How do instructors practice student-centric pedagogy online? (2) How do instructors practice autonomy-supportive instruction online? and (3) How do instructors promote the practicality of concepts online?

Practicing Student-Centric Pedagogy Online

We believe instructors should strive to be student-centric when teaching Gen Z students online. Perhaps this was best articulated by Shearer et al. (2020), who conducted focus groups with both faculty and students in order to identify expectations and needs for online learning in today's landscape: "from a pedagogical perspective, the image the student participants depicted shows that they want a personalized and adaptive learning experience, which is sensitive to learners' needs and preferences" (47). This could include a variety of approaches, including the use of multiple modes of content delivery, increased visibility of learner analytics, shorter content that accommodates a limited attention span, and customizable learning interfaces (e.g., emojis, memes, interactive profiles). From our perspective, relationship-building in online spaces might also appeal to the needs of Gen Z learners. We offer several practical behaviors that will allow instructors to transform their current pedagogy into more student-centric online environments suited to Gen Z students.

Building Immediacy

Instructors can set the groundwork for adaptive pedagogy by thinking critically about communicating *immediacy* in online spaces. O'Sullivan et al. (2004) defined immediacy in online contexts (i.e., mediated immediacy) "as communicative cues in mediated channels that can shape perceptions of psychological closeness between interactants" (471). For example, Dixson et al. (2016) discovered that instructors could boost student engagement online by strategically enhancing the visual aesthetic of the course structure and increasing responsiveness across communicative areas. Specifically, instructors who added color, used figurative language, incorporated fun fonts or emoticons, or contributed more regularly to forms/discussion posts created more engaged communities (Kaufmann et al. 2016). Building immediacy should also create a more collaborative and supportive online climate where students feel comfortable taking personal responsibility over their learning, asking questions, and discussing their intrapersonal reflections (Kaufmann et al. 2018).

Brief Student Assessments

In order to adapt effectively, instructors should consider brief, non-invasive instructional strategies that provide insights into students' classroom expectations. Prior to enrollment in an online course, some scholars have suggested screening that can identify traits (e.g., anxiety or apprehension) that may interfere with the online learning process (Wombacher et al. 2018). One author of this chapter incorporates a similar process by providing students with a series of questions (designed to be completed in less than five minutes) as an accompanying component of the course syllabus (i.e., a syllabus contract). This provides a concrete reference for each individual student that can be used to tailor content, pedagogy, or infrastructure appropriately. As a baseline, perhaps instructors can focus primarily on video-based instruction to appeal to students' general preference for observation (Seemiller and Grace 2017) yet adapt to other methods where deemed appropriate through the brief assessments.

Instructional Flexibility

Instructors can also practice student-centric pedagogy by listening to student feedback and broadening the scope of how students meet course learning outcomes. In an online setting, it may be possible for instructors to adapt office hours based on students' virtual accessibility. This simple adaptation may help Gen Z students navigate busy schedules and increased forms of stress (Mintz 2019). Similarly, instructors may focus on utilizing free, open-access, or familiar technologies that students recognize prior to the course. If Gen Z students are comfortable with a type of technology and can access it effectively, perhaps it would be prudent for students themselves to dictate how that technology is used relative to learning objectives. Moreover, we have had success allowing students to choose topics or activities relative to their own interests, provided those choices will not deter from overall course or assignment outcomes. In one composition assignment, students choose to apply one of three communication theories to an area of interest to them (i.e., uses and gratifications, spiral of silence, or relational dialectics). Students appreciate having the option to choose a theory that resonates with them and apply it to a context in which they have genuine interest, all the while still maintaining a focus on developing writing skills, critical thinking, and understanding applied communication.

Autonomy-Supportive Instruction Online

Along with student-centric learning, we also posit that promoting student autonomy online is important to educating Gen Z. Research on student-regulated learning (SRL) shows that in online classes, higher levels of autonomy are important for student learning, especially as there is less instructor presence in the class (Lehmann et al. 2014). Many online courses are run asynchronously, which necessitates more autonomy and self-motivation from students. In a broad study of MOOCs, Wong et al. (2018) found that prompting, providing feedback, integrating support systems, and encouraging self-monitoring all led to student success. These strategies all point to increased autonomy for the students. In practice, we offer the following as suggestions for promoting student autonomy in online classes.

Discussion Board Priming

One practice that may encourage autonomy in the online classroom is the strategic use of discussion boards. Student-led discussions, perhaps with minimal prompting, can provide a sense of ownership and autonomy. For instance, as the instructor you might assign a broad discussion board topic that allows for a broad diversity of response (e.g., "This week we are discussing pathos.

Describe an instance of pathos that you've noticed in the past two days"). Giving students the opportunity to engage with the course material before the instructor dives in can be a great way to foster agency in learning.

Learning Contracts

Providing students with the authority to engage in the planning and grading process is another way to foster autonomy. Learning contracts come in many different forms and can be applied in a number of contexts. For instance, an instructor can use a learning contract to organize a group project, in which the group must devise a set of rules, deadlines, etc. for the group to follow. On a broader scale, an instructor could choose to design the entire course around a learning contract. For example, an instructor might allow students to weigh assignment grades differently based on their perceived strengths. Allowing students to have a say in the maintenance of the course is a good way to promote investment in the material.

Student Examples and Reviews

Using past examples of student work is a good way to introduce students to the process of a course or assignment. As an instructor, transparency is a good way to get buy-in from students. For example, having students "grade" former students' assignments (with permission, of course), gives students the opportunity to see how the assessment process works. In our experience, student assessments of writing and public speaking are nearly always more critical than the instructor's initial assessment. The conversations that follow such a practice provide students with useful information regarding how they can succeed on an assignment. By giving students a look behind the curtain, they become better prepared to perform.

Modules/Self-Pacing

Depending on the course and material, allowing students to work at their own pace is another great way to promote autonomy. Obviously, some subjects would lend themselves better to this process than others, but a consideration of pacing is absolutely necessary for student success. Does the course work better as a weekly module with all assignments due at the end of the week? Does the material require more frequent check-ins for understanding? How much communication is necessary/expected from students in this particular subject? These are all questions that must be considered when designing a course.

Promoting Practicality and Utility Online

Finally, we believe Gen Z learning experiences online can be enhanced through pedagogy that promotes the practicality and relevance of course concepts. Gen Z students are motivated to make a difference in the lives of others; however, they also value finding connections between the content, their careers, and social good on their own terms (Seemiler and Grace 2019). A variety of strategies, such as e-service (Strait and Sauer 2004; Guthrie and McCracken 2010), flipped classrooms (Strelan et al. 2020), and designated reflection (Chang 2019) may help Gen Z students use their individual passions for community advocacy. We offer several strategies for implementing this idea into online courses for digital natives.

Service-Learning

Engaging Gen Z students through service-learning opportunities is a great way to demonstrate the practicality of course content. In online classes, the coordination of such an effort is more difficult, but it also affords some added benefits to the learning experience. For instance, making volunteer hours a requirement of the course and then tailoring assignments toward the service-learning experience helps to show how content from the course can be applied beyond the classroom. Students can reflect and share on their service-learning experiences through writing, speeches, or multimedia projects in the online forum. Demonstrating the connection between the "outside world" and the classroom drives home the utility of course content.

Flipped Classroom

Flipping the traditional classroom can be another way to demonstrate the utility of course content. Thus, there can be a combination of online and face-to-face instruction. By pre-loading lecture content online via a learning management system, the limited face-to-face time can be better used to apply material to specific situations. For instance, one might post a lecture online at the beginning of the week, and then during the classroom time that week students can discuss concepts and apply them to different situations/scenarios with classmates face-to-face. This allows the instructor to spend more time on practical issues in the classroom while simultaneously giving students a better sense of how the content can be applied.

Reflection

Reflection is an important part of everyday life, but can be very valuable in the classroom setting as well. Giving students the opportunity to reflect on their own work and the work of others provides a method of learning that encourages growth and evolution. The reflection process allows students to see how their work has affected their perceptions of certain concepts and course material. In some cases, reflection that allows students to connect content to real world issues and experiences can be a more valuable tool for Gen Z than online discussions. Instructors might also consider scaffolding assignments or using technological resources to keep students aware of their individual progress. For example, some learning management systems allow students to anonymously compare how well they performed on classroom assignments relative to their classmates. Either way, digital natives in digital spaces may benefit through opportunities to reflect on connections between content and issues they are passionate about, as well as their individual successes or failures as a platform for future development.

RECOMMENDATIONS FOR UNIVERSITY ADMINISTRATION

First, university administrators need to prepare faculty to meet the learning needs of Gen Z. Nearly all college campuses house some sort of center for the enhancement of pedagogy and learning. One of the central ways that administrators can foster success with Gen Z students is through offering workshops for instructors detailing the best practices for teaching Gen Z students. This can be done at the university level with a broad base of information that can be applied to multiple disciplines; it could also be implemented at the unit-level, with a more tailored approach to teaching within a specific discipline. Workshops would also be useful during new faculty orientation sessions, so that new instructors gain a sense of the audience they will be teaching. Potential workshops could include topics such as: Gen Z demographics; Gen Z technology usage; Gen Z mindset; and so on.

Second, university administration can prepare faculty to teach Gen Z online by promoting the accessibility and utility of currently existing university resources. Many instructors may not be aware of all their university has to offer in terms of pedagogical assistance, nor do they know of the subject-matter experts who may be willing to help. Further, some instructors may know about such assistance but choose not to act on it due to perceived inaccessibility or the time required to take part. Institutions can improve the visibility of such resources by connecting individually with programs or departments. Units that specialize in online content creation, video production, or instructional design can help instructors in areas known to affect climate and progression through online courses outside of interpersonal interactions with students. Existing resources such as these may also help instructors find and utilize software that students are familiar with, allowing them to connect with students and avoid the pitfalls of using technology ineffectively.

Communication instructors are uniquely positioned to lead the charge in teaching Gen Z online. The skill set required to teach the basic communication course and other important communication courses fall in line with the preferences and expectations of Gen Z students. The basic communication course is increasingly being taught online, and the number of online courses in general is rapidly increasing. Communication technologies evolve quickly, and Gen Z students are on the forefront of that evolution.

Finally, university administration can meet the needs of Gen Z students by helping them establish and engage with community connections. Instructors may be routinely unaware of the community leaders, organizers, and activists who may have connections to their colleges, departments, or units. The authors of this chapter were shocked to see a top local newscaster attend a college-wide meeting in preparation for a journalism class she was teaching in the upcoming semester! Gen Z students would benefit through the increased presence of leaders with community connections who can stress the relevance or course concepts or ideas in their everyday lives. Although some may argue that finding such connections are the responsibility of the instructors, we believe that an aggregated resource of community connections can help instructors stay more closely engaged with the local community to create opportunities for service-learning, internships, or community involvement.

A Note about the COVID-19 Pandemic and Online Learning

As the COVID-19 global pandemic began to spread worldwide, the shift in education could be felt almost immediately. Colleges and universities began to assess the risk of continuing to hold in-person classes, with most institutions shifting to a distance-learning model for public health reasons. Given this sudden and widespread shift in modality, all eyes became focused on best practices for learning online. Thus, the importance of online instruction became even more pronounced as schools were forced into modality shifts in the name of safety. Colleges and universities relied heavily on programs that were successful in online pedagogy and on centers for teaching and learning. And while students in Gen Z perhaps have a slight advantage in terms of exposure to online learning, this modality shift was accompanied by a range of cultural, economic, and personal shifts as well. The pandemic underscores the importance of online learning and demonstrates the hard work that goes into making online pedagogy successful. As universities continue to grapple with the effects of the pandemic and the accompanying pedagogical considerations, online instruction will remain an important area of study. Gen Z is likely to be remembered as the generation who survived a global pandemic and educators' roles in facilitating this generation's academic studies is crucial.

REFERENCES

Asikainen, Henna, Jaanika Blomster, and Viivi Virtanen. 2018. "From Functioning Communality to Hostile Behaviour: Students' and Teachers' Experiences of the Teacher-student Relationship in the Academic Community." *Journal of Further and Higher Education* 42: 633–648. DOI: 10.1080/0309877X.2017.1302566.

Chang, Bo. 2019. "Reflection in Learning." *Online Learning* 23 (1): 95–110.

Chicca, Jennifer, and Teresa Shellenbarger. 2018. "Connecting with Generation Z: Approaches in Nursing Education." *Teaching and Learning in Nursing* 13 (3): 180–184. DOI: 10.1016/j.teln.2018.03.008.

Deep Focus. 2015. "Deep Focus Cassandra Report: Gen Z Uncovers Massive Attitude Shifts Toward Money, Work and Communication Preferences." Accessed June 30, 2020. http://www.marketwired.com/press-release/deep-focus-cassandra-reprot-gen-z-uncovers-massisve-attitude-shifts-toward-money-work-2004889.htm.

Dixson, Marcia, Mackenzie Greenwell, Christie Rogers-Stacy, Tyson Weister, and Sara Lauer. 2016. "Nonverbal Immediacy Behaviors and Online Student Engagement: Bringing Past Instructional Research into the Present Virtual Classroom." *Communication Education* 66: 37–53. DOI: 10.1080/03634523.2016.1209222.

Fry, Richard, and Kim Parker. 2018. Early Benchmarks Show "Post-Millennials" on Track to be Most Diverse, Best-Educated Generation Yet. *Pew Research Center.* Last Modified November 15, 2018. Washington, D.C. https://www.pewsocialtrends.org/2018/11/15/early-benchmarks-show-post-millennials-on-track-to-be-most-diverse-best-educated-generation-yet/.

Gardner, Jolynn, Cynthia Ronzio, and Anastasia Snelling. 2018. "Transformational Learning in Undergraduate Public Health Education: Course Design for Generation Z." *Pedagogy in Health Promotion* 4 (2): 95–100. DOI: 10.1177/2373379917721722.

Genota, Lauraine. 2018. "Why Generation Z Learners Prefer YouTube Lessons Over Printed Books; Video Learning Outranks Printed Books in Survey." *Education Week.* Last Modified September 11, 2018. https://www.edweek.org/ew/articles/2018/09/12/why-generation-z-learners-prefer-youtube-lessons.html.

Guthrie, Kathy, and Holly McCracken. 2010. "Making a Difference Online: Facilitating Service-Learning Through Distance Education." *The Internet and Higher Education* 13: 153–157. DOI: 10.1016/j.iheduc.2010.02.006.

Hartman, Rita, Mary Townsend, and Marlo Jackson. 2019. "Educators' Perceptions of Technology Integration into the Classroom: A Descriptive Case Study." *Journal of Research in Innovative Teaching & Learning* 12: 236–249. DOI: 10.1108/JRIT-03-2019-0044.

Lehmann, Thomas, Inka Haehnlein, and Dirk Ifenthaler. 2014. "Cognitive, Metacognitive and Motivational Perspectives on Preflection in Self-regulated Online Learning." *Computers in Human Behavior* 32: 313–323. DOI: 10.1016/j.chb.2013.07.051.

Mintz, Steven. 2019. "Are Colleges Ready for Generation Z?" *Higher Ed Gamma* [Blog]. Last Modified March 18, 2019. https://www.insidehighered.com/blogs/higher-ed-gamma/are-colleges-ready-generation-z.

Molnar, Alex, G. Miron, N. Elgeberi, M. K. Barbour, L. Huerta, S. R. Shafer, and J. K. Rice. 2019. "Virtual Schools in the U.S. 2019." *National Education Policy Center.* https://nepc.colorado.edu/publication/virtual-schools-annual-2019.

National Center for Education Statistics, U.S. Department of Education. 2019. "Number and Percentage Distribution of Students Enrolled at Title IV Institutions, by Control of Institution, Student Level, Level of Institution, Distance Education Status of Student, and Distance Education Status of Institution: United States, Fall 2018." In *Integrated Postsecondary Education Data System*, edited by U.S. Department of Education, National Center for Education Statistics. https://nces.ed.gov/ipeds/Search/ViewTable?tableId=26394&returnUrl=%2Fipeds%2FSearch.

O'Sullivan, Patrick, Steven Hunt, and Lance Lippert. "Mediated Immediacy: A Language of Affiliation in a Technological Age." *Journal of Language and Social Psychology* 23: 464–490. DOI: 10.1177%2F0261927X04269588.

Pearson. 2018. "Beyond Millennials: The Next Generation Learners." https://www.pearson.com/content/dam/one-dot-com/one-dot-com/global/Files/news/news-announcements/2018/The-Next-Generation-of-Learners_final.pdf.

Plochocki, Jeffrey. 2019. "Several Ways Generation Z May Shape the Medical School Landscape." *Journal of Medical Education and Curricular Development.* DOI: 10.1177/2382120519884325.

Pousson, J. Mark, and Karen Myers. 2018. "Ignatian Pedagogy as a Frame for Universal Design in College: Meeting Learning Needs of Generation Z." *Education Sciences* 8 (4): 1–10. DOI: 10.3390/educsci8040193.

Schwieger, Dana, and Christine Ladwig. 2018. "Reaching and Retaining the Next Generation: Adapting to the Expectations of Gen Z in the Classroom." *Information Systems Education Journal* 16(3): 45–54.

Seemiller, Corey, and Jason Clayton. 2019. "Developing the Strengths of Generation Z College Students." *Journal of College and Character* 20: 268–275. DOI: 10.1080/2194587X.2019.1631187.

Seemiller, Corey, and Meghan Grace. 2017. "Generation Z: Educating and Engaging the Next Generation of Students." *About Campus: Enriching the Student Learning Experience* 22 (3): 21–26. DOI: 10.1002/abc.21293.

Sellnow, Deanna, and Renee Kaufmann. 2018. "Instructional Communication and the Online Learning Environment: Then, Now, Next." In *The Handbook of Instructional Communication: Rhetorical and Relational Perspectives* (2nd Ed.), edited by M. L. Houser and A. M. Hosek, 195–206. London: Taylor and Francis.

Shatto, Bobbi, and Kelly Erwin. 2016. "Moving on From Millennials: Preparing for Generation Z." *The Journal of Continuing Education in Nursing* 47 (6): 253–254. DOI: 10.3928/00220124-20160518-05.

Shearer, Rick, Tugce Aldemir, Jann Hitchcock, Jessie Resig, Jessica Driver, and Megan Kohler. 2020. "What Students Want: A Vision of a Future Online Learning Experience Grounded in Distance Education Theory." *American Journal of Distance Education* 34 (1): 36–52. DOI: 10.1080/08923647.2019.1706019.

Sherblom, John. 2010. "The Computer-Mediated Communication (CMC) Classroom: A Challenge of Medium, Presence, Interaction, Identity, and Relationship." *Communication Education* 59: 497–523. DOI: 10.1080/03634523.2010.486440.

Strait, Jean, and Tim Sauer. 2004. "Constructing Experiential Learning for Online Courses: The Birth of E-service." *Educause Quarterly* 1: 62–65.
Strelan, Peter, Amanda Osborn, and Edward Palmer. 2020. "The Flipped Classroom: A Meta-Analysis of Effects on Student Performance Across Disciplines and Education Levels." *Educational Research Review* 30: 100314. DOI: 10.1016/j.edurev.2020.100314.
Vallade, Jessalyn, and Renee Kaufmann. 2018. "Investigating Instructor Misbehaviors in the Online Classroom." *Communication Education* 67: 363–381. DOI: 10.1080/03634523.2018.1467027.
Wombacher, Kevin, Christina Harris, Marjorie Buckner, Brandi Frisby, and Anthondy Limperos. 2017. "The Effects of Computer-mediated Communication Anxiety on Student Perceptions of Instructor Behaviors, Perceived Learning, and Quiz Performance." *Communication Education* 66: 299–312. DOI: 10.1080/03634523.2015.1221511.

Chapter 7

The Applied Case Study as a Pedagogical Tool for Educating Today's Generation Z Student Population

Corey Jay Liberman

INTRODUCTION

As educators, we are perpetually attempting to, through reflective processes, determine what succeeds, and what does not, within the confines of the classroom. In so doing, we look at the educational process unwinding through the lens of the student, manifesting the looking glass self about which Charles Horton Coley (1902) once wrote. I still remember, over two decades later, what made Mrs. Patton (my high school journalism teacher), Mr. Brown (my high school English teacher), and Mr. Zwibek (my middle school mathematics teacher) such effective and memorable instructors. Was it their mere intellect that, retrospectively, made them such high-impact teachers? Probably. However, there is an even more important independent variable at play here. They were able to make the material come to life. Mrs. Patton was able to show us how one could write a musical review after our class chose to watch a recorded taping of a James Taylor concert. Mr. Brown was able to illustrate the relationship between George Milton and Lennie Small (from the book *Of Mice and Men*) by linking it to familial relationships of which he had been a part. Mr. Zwibek was able to teach us the properties of algebra when we, as a class, became a fictional casino. These effective instructors left a lasting impression on me because they had this insatiable desire to have information become applicable to and for the learner. Quoting Raju and Sankar (1999, 501), "real-world problems allow . . . students to vicariously experience situations in the classroom that they may face in the future and thus help bridge the gap between theory and practice."

However, over the past 25 years, the very definition of an effective instructor, and what it means for class material to come alive, have both changed. I often think to myself: what is effective pedagogy in today's world of higher education? While this is a rhetorical question, which, by definition, ought to have *no* answer, I fear that this question has *too many*. What the data indicate is that today's college student requires a different type of educational experience, due, at least in part, to a decreased ability to pay attention, an increased desire for multidisciplinary education, the hope for place-based learning, and an overall change in the psychosocial characteristics of students (Strawser 2018). From a teacher's perspective, then, it is important to underscore Seemiller and Grace's (2017) dialectical tension wherein "higher education can either adopt philosophies and practices that educate, mobilize, empower, and prepare Generation Z to solve our world's problems or miss the opportunity to influence significantly the great minds of our next great generation" (25). Given the foregoing conundrum, one effective pedagogical approach to education, which is the focal point of this chapter, is the implementation of a case study approach. That is, providing the student with immediate, practical examples of ideas, concepts, models, theories, and paradigms in action, so that course information seems to come alive. In his own casebook, Wrench (2012, vii–viii) writes that "showing students how to apply the theoretical content of organizational communication, or how to employ the skills discussed in organizational communication, is quite difficult because they do not immediately see the utility." He continues, however, by saying that "thankfully . . . a method has been devised . . . to help students see the applicability and utility of course content. This method is called the case method."

This chapter will showcase why and how case studies are useful, pedagogical tools for today's learners. The chapter will first introduce research that has focused on the independent variables that have produced the new educational landscape for Generation Z, within which new benchmarks and outcomes are evaluated, inclusive of the very learning goals that currently exist across institutions of higher education, and how these are to be achieved given the mindset of today's student. This will be followed by a section detailing both the nature and role of the case study approach and how this can be incorporated into new, and existing, course structures. The chapter will conclude with a final discussion regarding best practices associated with the case study method/approach, providing today's Generation Z learner with, as Seemiller and Grace (2016) speak, a pedagogical approach aligned with a new type of learning style. Especially within the media-saturated pedagogical world in which instructors currently find themselves embedded, due to the COVID-19 pandemic, the use of the case study method becomes an exponentially more important tool for assessment than ever before, as teachers are attempting to determine how to best assess students in a geographically dispersed, non-collocated "classroom." Regardless of the course, and even the department within which the course is housed, you will learn that there is perhaps no better, more effective, way of teaching the Generation Z cohort than by employing this case study approach, applying Lewin's (1951, 169) age-old adage that "there is nothing so practical as a good theory."

The New Educational Landscape

According to Rickes (2016, 21), students within the Generation Z cohort "are being perceived as a 'new' generation precisely because they have begun to exhibit notably different characteristics, values, and attitudes." This section will highlight these characteristics, values, and attitudes, and showcase how they have come to shape the new normal within the world of higher education. When academics first began to think about the changing educational landscape within the context of higher education, as the Generation Z population began to fill the seats within the college classroom, it was common for their minds to jump, almost automatically, to the role that technology would play during the educational process. Whether it be the introduction of a mediated guest lecture, the use of online group decision support systems (which allow students to anonymously engage in group dialogue about a class project via an online platform), or an entire course offered online, college professors were plagued with that important question: will technology work for us? Although much research has examined the relationship between computer-mediated technologies and the role of higher education, with not much consensus about whether such technology use within the classroom has increased or decreased such variables as student focus, writing abilities, comprehension, self-esteem, and overall student achievement (Lei 2010), the literature does point out that understanding the new educational landscape extends far beyond technology. As Giunta (2017) clearly argues, understanding this new educational landscape first requires an understanding of the Generation Z student population.

According to Singh (2014, 59), the Generation Z student population comprises those born between 1995-2012, and has overarching characteristics that become challenging for the college professor, including the following: they are prematurely mature; they are pampered; they are empowered; they are risk adverse; and they are protected. Each of these cohort traits, by and large, presents the higher education instructor with obstacles. Using the trait that Singh (2014) called risk adverse, which has implications for everything from one's strategy of notetaking in the classroom (perhaps the students asks herself if she needs to write down everything about which the said instructor is speaking) to class participation (there is an inverse, psychosocial relationship between one's avoidance to risk and her inclination to participate during class discussion or debate), the professor in question is forced to reconsider his/her strategies of educational design. How is he/she to impart information and assess pedagogical effectiveness and student success?

Iorgulescu (2016) notes, despite some of her study's results, that while Generation Z students are likely to be more creative and innovative, they are also less likely to desire to work in groups or teams (despite an increased comfort in them), less likely to be able to develop effective writing skills (in large part due to their propensity toward social media and the abbreviated rhetoric developed as a result), and more likely to desire pedagogical practices that hone a student's soft (e.g., communication, leadership, time management), as compared to hard (e.g., computer skills, mathematical skills, programming skills), skills. This, again, has huge implications for higher education pedagogy. How, for example, does a professor of chemistry teach to an audience who, predominantly, is less interested in the elements within the periodic table and more interested in the effects of opioids on those considered addicted? How does a professor of composition teach to students who are less interested in the skill of writing well and more interested in the skill of developing creative ideas? How does the professor of political science, who sees the true merit of class discussion and, more importantly, class debate, teach to a population of students who would prefer working in isolation as compared to working in groups? This, again, forces the professor to question whether or not instructional techniques need to be edited and how a new pedagogical strategy could be assessed.

From a neurological perspective, the arousal created by the mere quantity of things to which today's Generation Z will pay attention both affects, and is affected by, the new educational landscape (Turner 2015). That is, if a student is going to multitask, attempting to listen to her instructor, respond to a series of text messages, check her Twitter feed, and post a reaction to Instagram, not only is her attention going to be dispersed in a multitude of different directions, but her course instructor will be forced to rethink how to teach in a world where, according to Giunta (2017), the average student in today's classroom has the attention span of approximately eight seconds. As Turner (2015, 110) argues, "the time available for young people to sit and think, uninterrupted, has shrunk over the years, as the current culture of communication no longer allows sufficient space to ponder complicated issues." In fact, Desao and Lele (2017, 808) inform their readers that the very term Generation Z emerged from the word zappers, "characterized by quick shifts," and argue that such quick shifts have had instrumental effects on the ability of students to concentrate and pay attention. This has, unfortunately, created what Firat (2013) has called continuous partial attention: one's inability to completely focus on one, isolated thing because she is partially focusing on a multitude of different things. According to First (2013, 270), continuous partial attention occurs when students have a desire to "[monitor] and [be] engaged with everything but [stay] focuse[d] on nothing." Clearly, this has implications for, and becomes disruptive to, the learning process. What is the college professor to do?

Given the previous examples, the answer is to take, seriously, the advice of Hilcenko (2017, 380), and realize that "the class-hour system of Comenius, founded 500 years ago, with 45 minutes, is inappropriate when it comes to the attention of this generation." Once this happens, it is necessary to make pedagogical changes. And such changes have occurred, have been vast, and have revolutionized the higher education landscape as we once knew it. In short, each of these new pedagogical strategies has somehow incorporated what Rickes (2016) calls an active learning classroom, wherein students are not merely in a lecture-only-style environment. Rather, they are in a context more conducive for active involvement in the learning process (Hampton et al. 2020). They are in an educational environment that fosters interactive learning, producing the student-centered dependent variable that Rospigliosi (2019) argues is one of three necessary prerequisites for all successful institutions of higher education. This is analogous with what Raju and Sankar (1999) call teaching by telling. In such a learning environment, students no longer view their professor as she who delivers information, but as a "learning facilitator who helps [students]... develop relevant and practical skills" (Moore et al. 2017, 116). In such a learning environment, the blended classroom about which Malroutu (2017, 324) speaks allows, and in some sense forces, "students to be more active participants in the learning process."

A prime example of such a new learning environment, aligned with the needs, wants, and desires of Generation Z students, is the escape room (Healy 2019). An escape room is loosely defined as a locked workspace where individuals are required to engage in collective dialogue about some problem (with either an objective solution or an answer rife with ambiguity and requiring creativity) and are only allowed exit upon completion of the task. This requires, of course, group interaction, inductive and deductive reasoning, and critical thinking, which are variables emblematic of the hands-on learning approach mentioned by Seemiller and Grace (2007, 22), where "[students] can immediately apply what they learn to real life." These very ideas are underscored by Popil (2011), who argues that "... cases present situations and 'food for thought,' making students think, ask questions, and use their knowledge to answer those questions ... [and] thus they elicit critical thinking" (p. 206).

What is gained by such an approach to learning? As an undergraduate student matriculating just prior to the mass inculcation of mediated technologies, I sat in many required, general education courses, thinking to myself "when am I ever going to have to use this?" I wondered whether I would ever use the knowledge about vectors, composite functions, and polynomials that I was learning in my precalculus course. I was skeptical that I would never be able to use the information about the cultural practices of the fish farmers in Belize, the forest dwellers of the Southern Maya Lowlands, and the rain forest inhabitants in the Amazon that I was required to read in my introductory anthropology course. Over two decades later, however, I realize, which is highlighted in a recent piece by Safronova et al. (2019), that it was not a question of *will* I ever use this information, but rather a question of *how*. How could I use composite functions to strategize and negotiate the pricing for a new promotional product used to endorse a company's newest innovation? How could I use information about fish farmers to anticipate how others would respond to a joke told about Jewish stereotypes and traditions? I realize, over 20 years later, that it was applying these data that was most important.

In brief, among the salient independent variables predicting this applicability is a course's learning goals and learning outcomes. The very learning goals and learning outcomes of the new educational landscape, and which comes to define the overarching nature of the escape room, are emblematic of the shift from "information storage" to "critical thinking and problem solving" (Hilcenko 2017, 370). This new style of education radically decreases the likelihood of the boredom and perceived monotony and repetition about which Chicca and Shellenbarger (2018) speak in relation to the Generation Z cohort. Such a new learning strategy also provides the Generation Z student with the instant gratification that much of the scholarly literature argues this population desires (Giunta 2017). They will, immediately, know the extent to which their application of key course material was effective or ineffective; right or wrong; on track or skewed; creative or mundane. This new style of learning also becomes a prime example of the learning communities about which Spears et al. (2015) speak, providing students with the face-to-face interaction that they found to be a necessary requisite for student success. This form of experiential learning has completely revolutionized the once lecture-laden landscape of higher education that might very well have worked for the students of yesteryear, but needs to be altered for Generation Z students.

It is important to note something before moving forward. While one might question the extent to which most of those part of the Generation Z cohort exhibit all (or even most) of the foregoing characteristics and traits, especially Shatto and Erwin (2017, 24), who argue that this generation is "projected to be the most diverse generation in the history of the United States," research does demonstrate that they do share much in common. This is underscored by Seemiller and Grace's (2017, 21) claim that "although not everyone born in a generational period shares the same values or experiences, they do share a common context that shapes their worldview" and Desai and Lele's (2017, 804) argument that "all agree that students in Generation Z display shared characteristics." As such, attitudinal, behavioral, and cognitive similarities among those in this cohort do exist and must be taken into account when redesigning such things as course objectives, general education learning goals, and overall course design. The foregoing characteristics and traits do have real consequences for both pedagogical practices and student learning, and must be incorporated into college-wide policies, practices, and initiatives: namely in the form of learning goals, institutional learning objectives, and student learning outcomes.

The Case Study Method

What, specially, is a case study? First and foremost, it is important to note that there are numerous ways that one can refer to a case study. For example, Townend (2001, 205) refers to the foregoing as an integrated case study (ICS), highlighting that they are not merely assignments that students do as part of a syllabus requirement, but rather are "an integral part of [a course's] module." Popil (2011, 206) refers to the case study approach as case-based instruction (CBI), which "promot[es] critical thinking and connect[s] theory to practice." Carder et al. (2001, 181) speak of case-based, problem-based learning (CBPBL), which uses "an active, student-centered approach to learning, encourag[ing] the development of critical thinking and lifelong learning skills."

Richards et al. (1995) goes even further by differentiating among a case history (a recount of the decision-making processes of some individual, or collection of individuals, which requires students to assess the extent to which the decision was effective), a case problem (the decision or solution is entirely dependent on student interaction, decision-making, and rationality), and a case study (an example of best practices regarding a decision that needed to be made between and among individuals). They conclude that "a case is a narrative account of a situation, problem, or decision . . . [and is] written to engage a student in a problem situation" (Richards et al. 1995, 375). All of the foregoing become illustrative of what Ilguy et al. (2014, 1525) call case-based learning (CBL), which involves teaching that is learner-centered, not lecture-based, and which has been found to be linked to both deeper learning and the retainment of information (Ilguy et al. 2014, 1526).

Spackman and Camacho (2009, 548) perhaps provide the most succinct and informative definition when they argue that "the case method of instruction is a Socratic approach . . . [which] consists of placing students in the context of real-life scenarios, and, through discussion, encouraging them to see the full complexity of those situations and apply their own analysis in deriving a solution." In fact, Mustoe and Croft (1999, 469) noted this over two decades ago when they argued that "a carefully-chosen case study can act as a real motivator to students and help to convince them [that such information] is relevant to their . . . world." Adding to this, Crowther and Baillie (2016) argue that the case study can be employed using various approaches, including being part of a class session, occupying the entirety of a class session, or used as a more ancillary assignment to be completed in teams of students.

The case study method, while more embedded within curricula today than ever before, has been part of the higher education landscape for some time. As such, much research has been conducted to determine not only the academic fields for which case studies are most conducive, but also how case studies should be written and introduced into pedagogical practices. In fact, a special issue of *International Studies Notes* from 1994 (Volume 19, Number 2) was entirely devoted to these issues and, as such, was titled *Case Teaching in International Relations*. I, myself, remember, clear as day, the first time that I had ever been exposed, in the classroom, to a case study. It was during my first graduate-level course in organizational communication, and we were assigned the second edition of Beverly Davenport Sypher's (1997) text, entitled *Case Studies in Organizational Communication 2: Perspectives on Contemporary Work Life*. These cases ranged, in nature and scope, from employee conflict strategies to teamwork to communication networks to culture to organizational gossip. These case studies provided our class with a phenomenal way of complementing, not replacing, the ideas and theories about which we were learning in the aforementioned course.

As Rickes (2016, 30) reminds us, as college instructors, "students learn best when they work with course materials within the context of what is important in their lives." While the word important is difficult to define, suffice it to say that, within the confines of this chapter, it refers to something necessary for a student's future career or general information base. Rickes (2016) continues by providing an example of makerspaces: campus spaces designed to teach students, mainly in the industrial and creative arts, using a learn-by-doing pedagogical philosophy. Rickes (2016, 32) defines a makerspace as "a learner-driven environment that revolves around hands-on experimentation . . . encourag[ing] individuals to work individually or collaboratively on projects, sharing resources and knowledge." While it is perhaps easier to see the implementation of a makerspace in a course dealing with photography, drawing, or dance, it is equally as important for such courses as marketing, anatomy, and group communication. It is through the use of the case study approach that such makerspaces can be employed regardless of the field or discipline in which a course is housed. Relating this back to Generation Z students, Kantorova et al. (2017, 86) claim that "above all, they believe in their own ability to solve all problems in their own way." The case study approach allows them to showcase this ability, while, concomitantly, providing them with the "practical, real life experience" (Loveland 2017, 36) that they clearly desire.

The case study approach can be envisioned as a bridge that connects the chasm between the small, albeit noticeable, disconnect between what Moore et al. (2017) call active learning (e.g., activities) and problem-based learning (e.g., using critical thinking to propose solutions and explanations for some social, physical, mathematical phenomenon). This relates well to Grant and Grace's (2019, 198) argument that "the case-based approach is positively viewed by students and educators as a motivating and engaging gateway between surface and deep-level learning experiences." As Grant and Grace (2019) explain, students working on case studies are required to interpret information, develop arguments, and analyze data, all within the confines of a new and exciting educational environment. They conclude by arguing that, with the introduction of case studies into the curriculum, "the most recent cohort reported 98% agreement with the statement that this course would help them achieve their personal, professional, or educational goals" (Grant and Grace 2019, 209). Why is this so likely the case? Herreid and Schiller (2013) provide a rational answer when they claim that:

> Case study teaching has been extolled for its ability to engage students and develop critical thinking skills, among other benefits. A central theme in all of this . . . is the idea that active learning works best. Telling doesn't work very well. Doing is the secret. (62–65)

This engagement and development of critical thinking skills is perhaps more important today than ever before, as Zoom-based instruction has both facilitated online pedagogy, but also complicated the processes and practices linked to education of yesteryear. The case study approach to learning has become the missing link necessary to connect the ascertainment of information with any (and all) student learning outcomes linked to an instructor's course.

In speaking about the role of the case study connecting what he calls shallow learning and deep learning, Townend (2001, 212) concluded that "shallow learning [is] equated to procedural competence only, whereas deep learning implies conceptual understanding, too." Even a cursory review of the literature on Generation Z learners showcases their desire, through both empirical data and informal testimony, to engage in deep learning: something that the case approach is able to accomplish. What does this accomplish? Dori et al. (2003, 768) found that not only did the use of case studies "result in improving students' knowledge, understanding, and higher order thinking skills," but it also lessened "the achievement gap that had existed between low and high academic level students." Among the implications of this is that the case study approach not only introduces a new form of instruction, conducive for Generation Z students, but it also provides a new form of assessment, inclusive of critical thinking, written and oral communication skills, classroom engagement, and overall motivation (Bonney 2015), problem-solving abilities (Yoo and Park 2015), and inference and judgement (Dori et al. 2003).

But why, specifically, does the case study approach about which Grant and Grace (2019) speak seem to be so effective for today's Generation Z learner? In an attempt to answer this query, Rawal and Pandey (2013) discuss a model of learning that focuses on whether students remember, most, what they do, what they say/write, what they hear/see, or what they read. Unsurprising, students remember *least* from what they read and *most* from what they do. Consequently, case studies become the educational, pedagogical tool for bringing the two variables mentioned by Grant and Grace (2019) together (active learning and problem-based learning), ultimately increasing the attainment of information. Corroborating this idea is Malroutu (2017, 325), who found that "more than 50% of students surveyed indicated that they learn best by doing and tend to enjoy . . . interactive classroom environments over traditional teaching methodologies," further providing evidence of the positive impact produced by the "student-centered, problem-based" (Malroutu 2017, 330) college classroom about which she speaks.

The case study seems to work for the Generation Z student because, as pointed out by Kreber (2001, 217), "case studies are seen to be particularly appropriate if the goal is to provoke a student's involvement and active experimentation with an issue." It is exactly this mentality, the desire to learn-by-doing and learn-by-applying, rather than learn-by-lecturing, that currently dominates the Generation Z educational landscape, and why case studies are so commensurate with the new cohort of higher education student. As Kreber (2001, 220) further explicates, "learning becomes experiential only after experiences or events have been transformed by either reflection or action, or preferably both." This strategy of education "extends the learning experience beyond classroom exercises and laboratory experiments . . . [and is] one solution to the purported discrepancy between what is taught at the university and what really goes on in industry" (Richards et al. 1995, 375). This is not only emblematic of the case approach, but also representative of the new learning goals and learning outcomes of students embedded within the Generation Z population: those that highlight the link between academia and future employment.

The case study also seems to be an effective pedagogical approach to higher education, today, because, as Arseven (2018, 112), using experiential learning theory (which Elam and Spotts 2004, argue produces realism and increases learning effectiveness), claims, "learning is an ongoing process based on experience . . . [and] requires a resolution of the dialectical conflict between opposing modes in the adaptation to the world." Learning, as Arseven (2018, 112) continues, "involves processes between individuals and the environment . . . [and] is the process of creating information." These, collectively, are learning outcomes: to illustrate the link between course material and some applied situation; to produce a collective decision about a particular domain that, in and of itself, has [potentially] no objective answer; to engage with others about best practices; and ultimately produce, rather than be provided, data or results.

This type of learning is what today's student wants. This is the type of learning that today's student needs. This approach to teaching and learning is amazingly conducive given the characteristics of Generation Z mentioned earlier in the chapter. In fact, Schonell and Macklin (2019) speak about what they call the live case study (LCS), where students are provided with a case study and then actually help organizations dealing with the very issues manifested in the case with their critically examined, and collectively dialogued, advice. This approach has been linked to positively-valenced student outcomes, especially since they "usually include active participation by key decision makers in the company and immediate accessibility of the company to students" (Elam and Spotts 2004, 52). In this same study, students commented that "as a result of participating in this [live case study], they had gained confidence in their own ability to apply what they learned in a company setting" (Elam and Spotts 2004, 59). As Arseven (2018) notes, the case study approach is representative of the experiential learning cycle, wherein abstract ideas become concrete experiences as a result of active experimentation (with the case itself) and reflective observation (determining not whether, but how, the case results can be fruitfully applied to some real world problem) (p. 113). Such occurs when students actively engage with the live case study about which Schonell and Macklin (2019), and Elam and Spotts (2004), write. This all, again, relates quite well to the new educational landscape in which we currently find ourselves embedded as a result of the COVID-19 pandemic. When instructors strut and fret to find assessment tools that mirror both the advantages and weaknesses of this new educational landscape, the case study approach produces the engagement, collaboration, and application that is needed.

The case study approach also, by its very nature, encourages teamwork and, hence, team interaction. It requires students to apply course information to a *real* situation that has *real* consequences for *real* people. It fulfills the Generation Z student's desire to engage with "solo work [that is practical] that leads to group work" (Hope 2016, 7). In so doing, as Richards et al. (1995) claim, judgment of key arguments comes into play as a result of such group communication. That is, decisions are made based on such variables as rationality, collective thought processing, and shared engagement. The case study also reduces (eliminates being foolishly optimistic) the global inability for Generation Z students to critically analyze, and think about, information (Hampton et al. 2020), requiring that students apply links between a problem and the course information ascertained, and frames higher education as a way of combining active learning, experiential learning, and multidisciplinary learning (Hampton et al. 2020). Students are required, as per the research of Kreber (2001, 224), "to use their logical reasoning skills in some phases, and their intuitive and creative skills in others," which will increase the role of "self-direction in learning" (Kreber 2001, 225). In other words, students need to use their critical thinking skills during case reflection as they transform from learner to teacher and back to learner. Unsurprisingly, Spackman and Camacho (2009, 553) not only found that there is a correlation between the employment of a case study and overall student learning and satisfaction, but also that there is causation. In other words, not only are the two related to one another (an increase in the use of a case study approach to course design is met with an increase in learning and satisfaction), but the former is the independent variable responsible for producing such effects. The key takeaway here is that case studies should certainly be incorporated into today's higher education curricula.

CONCLUSION

As Hilcenko (2017, 379) writes in his article about the need to better understand the link between pedagogical practices and the changing nature of today's higher education student, "traditional methods of teaching are not compatible with the new generation of young people born in the digital era." If among the goals of today's educators is to graduate a student who has strong analytical skills, practical ingenuity, creativity, good communication skills, and who is adaptable to change (Moore et al. 2017), a new educational landscape, rife with new pedagogical approaches to teaching, is necessary. Shatto and Erwin (2017, 26) underscore this claim when they argue that "mixed method teaching . . . such as flipped classrooms and active learning . . . will maximize the extent to which younger generations feel engaged." Engagement, clearly, is among the key independent variables predictive of student satisfaction among the Generation Z cohort. Among such active learning strategies mentioned by Shatto and Erwin (2017) is the use of case studies. While not community-based, the case study does mirror the transformational learning model proposed by Gardner et al. (2018), where the result of education is not the memorization of facts, but rather collaboration, critical thinking, application, and overall engagement with the course material.

It not only "enhances [students'] research skills and thinking abilities," but also makes learning easier, creates the context for more effective learning, increases active participation and engagement in class, and leads to an increase in the accruement of knowledge" (Safapour et al. 2019, 9–10).

Case studies, according to Popil (2011, 205), "are based on real life scenarios [and] they provide supporting data and documents to be analyzed, and an open-ended question or problem is presented for possible solution." That said, however, there are best practices regarding the implementation of the case study approach itself. For example, Davis (2009, 222–229) mentions that all case studies must have the following in order to be effective pedagogical tools: they must raise a thought-provoking issue; they must tell a story; they must have elements of conflict; they must encourage students to think and take a position; and they must lack an obvious or clear-cut right answer. In addition to these best practices, Knoop's (1984) pragmatic problem-solving model, too, recommends that students completing a case study must engage in the following six steps of deductive reasoning: identify the problem; distinguish the problem from its underlying causes and overt symptoms; generate alternative problem-solving strategies; evaluate each alternative; select the best strategy; and develop a plan for implementing the preferred strategy. Case studies must also, as Carder et al. (2001, 188) conclude, somehow relate to a real-world problem, garner student interest, and incorporate key course learning objectives.

In speaking about best practices, Richards et al. (1995, 375–376) note that all case studies must illustrate/exhibit the following: have relevance (a clear link between the case and some career-based outcome); produce motivation (there must be some desire for students to become immersed within them); foster active involvement (students must be willing to collectively discuss the case study in question); produce integration (assess and dissect the case study using a multitude of academic resources); and create transfer (students must be able to see the applicability of the study's analysis to other real world phenomena). Hoffer (2020, 75) contends that all case studies need to "present problems with societal stakes." In other words, case-based learning (CBL) must provide today's student with examples and situations that not only matter, but also have grave consequences (if actually applied to the situation that the case in question examines). As Arseven (2018, 111) argues, "knowledge and experience are two fundamental concepts, the combination of which constitutes learning." It is exactly this combination that is offered as a result of the case study in an educational landscape permeated with Generation Z students. Interestingly, Wrage (1994, 22) likens a good case study to a bad lecture, insofar as it leaves issues left unresolved, is ambiguous (opening the opportunity for group dialogue), is open to several [likely conflicting] interpretations. This is, on one hand, humorous, yet, on the other hand, a reality to which today's higher education instructor must adapt. The solution? Employ the advice offered by Boehrer (1994, 14) and make sure that the case "offers students . . . issues, problems, dilemmas, puzzles, [and] something to grapple with."

Finally, case studies need to, by their very nature, introduce a new (and different) role for the college instructor: what Raju and Sankar (1999, 502) call a nontraditional role, whereby "the instructor's role is not so much to teach students as to encourage learning." This forces the instructor in question to completely revolutionize her pedagogical and assessment strategies. As Elam and Spotts (2004) point out, students, in essence, become the teacher and, by default, the instructor becomes the student. Wrage (1994, 21) argues that the student adopts the role of instructor since they engage in the academic pursuits representative of one: "sifting evidence, constructing theories or testing them, making distinctions, and forming judgments." One might question the extent to which this would seem to work in the classroom, though, as Fratantuono (1994) points out, when students seem to take control of, and become responsible for, their own learning, they, by and large, are successful. Results from the same study indicate that such student-centered, student-led learning leads to increased retention of information, better preparation for class discussion, and increased student collaboration and connection. This type of education, where, as Carder et al. (2001, 182) argue, "the instructor serves as a facilitator rather than as the group leader," is largely effective given today's student population, where the teacher becomes the liaison between the group engaged in the case study and the material used to produce key arguments and decisions. According to Grant (1997, 172), "the teacher's role is not to profess, diagnose, analyze, and interpret, but to act as a facilitator, posing open-ended questions that invite students to explore and interpret the material for themselves and to allow students to benefit from the group's work."

As Moore et al. (2017) make poignantly clear, "Generation Z students will certainly come to the university with different experiences and skill sets than the Generation X and Baby Boomer instructors teaching the majority of their classes" (p. 111). They continue by claiming that "new educational techniques will seek to address these differences, but they will also simply be grounded in good pedagogy" (Moore et al. 2017, 111). If, as Hampton et al. (2020, 161) claim, "student engagement is one of the best predictors of learning and personal development," especially given the differences about which Moore et al. (2017) speak, the case study is a key educational vehicle for student success, student satisfaction, and student drive. Not only does it increase information literacy skills and perceived engagement on behalf of the student, but it also improves the overall teaching experience for instructors, as they are likely to "feel more energized" (Milczarski and Maynard 2015, 41).

Milczarski and Maynard (2015, 43) summarize their findings well when they claim that:

> It is expected that by employing this case study technique to teach information literacy skills, students will be better able to apply these skills to their professional and personal lives. Rather than simply measuring student's attitudes toward information literacy skills or their knowledge of information literacy concepts, our technique requires students to directly demonstrate the actual skills of information literacy.

This is, with little question, representative of the learning goals necessary for today's student. Whether in a freshman seminar or a senior capstone course (Holsti 1994), when students are able to take information from class and apply it to real world situations, as well as synthesize such information and engage in the process of "choosing the most appropriate solution" (Harper et al. 2008, 414), the world of higher education brings its collective curricular design one step closer to the needs, wants, and desires of the student population in today's college classroom: those part of the Generation Z cohort. Using a case study approach, student skills related to writing, listening, and speaking are improved (Mingst 1994). When employed successfully, the case study does exactly that which Grant (1997, 171) recommends: "shifting the core concept of education from teaching to learning."

REFERENCES

Arseven, Ilami. 2018. "The Use of Qualitative Case Studies as an Experiential Teaching Method in the Training of Pre-Service Teachers." *International Journal of Higher Education* 7 (1): 111–125.

Boehrer, John. 1994. "On Teaching a Case." *International Studies Notes* 19 (2): 14–20.

Bonney, Kevin. 2015. "Case Study Teaching Method Improves Performance and Perceptions of Learning Gains." *Journal of Microbiology & Biology Education* 16 (1): 21–28.

Carder, Linda, Patricia Willingham, and David Bibb. 2001. "Case-Based, Problem-Based Learning: Information Literacy for the Real World." *Research Strategies* 18 (3): 181–190.

Chicca, Jennifer, and Teresa Shellenbarger. 2018. "Connecting with Generation Z: Approaches in Nursing Education." *Teaching and Learning in Nursing* 13 (3): 180–184. DOI: 10.1016/j.teln.2018.03.008.

Crowther, Emma, and Sarah Balliee. 2016. "A Method of Developing and Introducing Case-Based Learning to a Preclinical Veterinary Curriculum." *Anatomical Sciences Education* 9 (1): 80–89.

Davis, Barbara. 2009. *Tools for Teaching* (2nd Ed.). San Francisco: Jossey-Bass.

Desai, Supriya, and Vishwanath Lele. 2017. "Correlating Internet, Social Networks and Workplace: A Case of Generation Z Students." *Journal of Commerce & Management Thought* 8 (4): 802–815.

Dori, Yehudit, Revital Tal, and Masha Tsaushu. 2003. "Teaching Biotechnology Through Case Studies: Can We Improve Higher Order Thinking Skills of Nonscience Majors?" *Science Education* 87 (6): 767–793.

Elam, Elizabeth, and Harlan Spotts. 2004. "Achieving Marketing Curriculum Integration: A Live Case Study Approach." *Journal of Marketing Education* 26 (1): 50–65.

Firat, Mehmet. 2013. "Multitasking or Continuous Partial Attention: A Critical Bottleneck for Digital Natives." *Turkish Online Journal of Distance Education* 14 (1): Article 23. DOI: 10.17718/tojde.52102.

Fratantuono, Michael. 1994. "Evaluating the Case Method." *International Studies Notes* 19 (2): 34–44.

Gardner, Jolynn, Cynthia Ronzio, and Anastasia Snelling. 2018. "Transformational Learning in Undergraduate Public Health Education: Course Design for Generation Z." *Pedagogy in Health Promotion* 4 (2): 95–100. DOI: 10.1177/2373379917721722.

Giunta, Catherine. 2017. "An Emerging Awareness of Generation Z Students for Higher Education Professors." *Archives of Business Research* 5 (4): 90–104. DOI: 10.14738/abr.54.2962.

Grant, Janie, and Tim Grace. 2019. "Use of Diverse Case Studies in an Undergraduate Research Methods and Statistics Course." *Psychology Learning & Teaching* 18 (2): 197–211.

Grant, Richard. 1997. "A Claim for the Case Method in the Teaching of Geography." *Journal of Geography in Higher Education* 21 (2): 171–185.

Hampton, Debra, Darlene Welsh, and Amanda Wiggins. 2019. "Learning Preferences and Engagement Level of Generation Z Nursing Students." *Nurse Educator* 45 (3): 160–164.

Harper, Jeffrey, Steven Lamb, and James Buffington. 2008. "Effective Use of Case Studies in the MIS Capstone Course Through Semi-Formal Collaborative Teaching." *Journal of Information Systems Education* 19 (4): 411–418.

Healy, Kristen. 2019. "Using an Escape-Room-Themed Curriculum to Engage and Educate Generation Z Students About Entomology." *American Entomologist* 65 (1): 24–28.

Herreid, Clyde, and Nancy Schiller. 2013. "Case Studies and the Flipped Classroom." *Journal of College Science Teaching* 42 (5): 62–66.

Hilcenko, Slavoljub. 2017. "How Generation Z Learns Better." *European Journal of Social Sciences Education and Research* 11 (2): 379–389.

Hoffer, Erin. 2020. "Case-Based Teaching: Using Stories for Engagement and Inclusion." *International Journal on Social and Educational Sciences* 2 (2): 75–80.

Holsti, Ole. 1994. "Case Teaching: Transforming Foreign Policy Courses with Cases." *International Studies Notes* 19 (2): 7–13.

Hope, Joan. 2016. "Get Your Campus Ready for Generation Z." *Student Affairs Today* 19 (7): 1–7. DOI: 10.1002/say.30253.

Horton, Charles. 1902. *Human Nature and Social Order*. New York: Scribner.

Ilguy, Mehmet, Dilhan Ilguy, Erdogan Fisekcioglu, and Inci Oktay. 2014. "Comparison of Case-Based and Lecture-Based Learning in Dental Education Using the SOLO Taxonomy." *Journal of Dental Education* 78 (11): 1521–1527.

Iorgulescu, Maria-Cristina. 2016. "Generation Z and Its Perception of Work." *Cross-Cultural Management Journal* 18 (1): 47–54.

Kantorova, Katerina, Hana Jonasova, Jan Panus, and Roman Lipka. 2017. "A Study of Generation Z from the Communication Perspective of Universities." *Scientific Papers of the University of Pardubice* 24 (1): 83–94.

Knoop, R. 1984. *Case Studies in Education*. Ontario: Praise Publishing.

Kreber, Carolin. 2001. "Learning Experientially Through Case Studies? A Conceptual Analysis." *Teaching in Higher Education* 6 (2): 217–228.

Lei, Jing. 2010. "Quantity Versus Quality: A New Approach to Examine the Relationship Between Technology Use and Student Outcomes." *British Journal of Educational Technology* 41 (3): 455–472.

Lewin, Kurt. 1951. "Problems of Research in Social Psychology." In *Field Theory in Social Science: Selected Theoretical Papers*, edited by Dorwin Cartwright, 155–169. New York: Harper & Row.

Loveland, Elaina. 2017. "Instant Generation." *The Journal of College Admission* 234: 34–38.

Malroutu, Y. 2017. "Enhancing Student Learning Experience in Blended Classroom Teaching." *Journal of Advances in Humanities and Social Sciences* 3 (6): 324–331.

Milczarski, Vivian, and Amanda Maynard. 2015. "Improving Information Literacy Skills for Psychology Majors: The Development of a Case Study Technique." *College & Undergraduate Libraries* 22 (1): 35–44.

Mingst, Karen. 1994. "Cases and the Interactive Classroom." *International Studies Notes* 19 (2): 1–6.

Moore, Kevin, Carol Jones, and Robert Frazier. 2017. "Engineering Education for Generation Z." *American Journal of Engineering Education* 8 (2): 111–126.

Mustoe, L. R., and A. C. Croft. 1999. "Motivating Engineering Students by Using Modern Case Studies." *International Journal of Engineering Education* 15 (6): 469–476.

Popil, Inna. 2011. "Promotion of Critical Thinking by Using Case Studies as Teaching Method." *Nurse Education Today* 31 (2): 204–207.

Raju, P. K., and Chetan Sankar. 1999. "Teaching Real-World Issues Through Case Studies." *Journal of Engineering Education* 88 (4): 501–508.

Rawal, Sangtia, and U. S. Pandey. 2013. "E-Learning: Learning from Smart Generation Z." *International Journal of Scientific and Research Publications* 3 (5): 564–568.

Richards, Larry, Michael Gorman, William Scherer, and Robert Landel. 1995. "Promoting Active Learning with Cases and Instructional Modules." *Journal of Engineering Education* 84 (4): 375–381.

Rickes, Persis C. 2016. "Generations in Flux: How Gen Z Will Continue to Transform Higher Education Space." *Planning for Higher Education* 44 (4): 21–45. http://eres

.regent.edu:2048/login?url=https://search-proquest-com.ezproxy.regent.edu/docview/1838982286?accountid=13479.

Rospigliosi, Pericles. "The Role of Social Media as a Learning Environment in the Fully Functioning University: Preparing for Generation Z." *Interactive Learning Environments* 27 (4): 429–431.

Safapour, Elnaz, Sharareh Kermanshachi, and Piyush Taneja. 2019. "A Review of Nontraditional Teaching Methods: Flipped Classroom, Gamification, Case Study, Self-learning, and Social Media." *Education Sciences* 9 (4): 273–292.

Safranova, Margarita, Caleb Miller, and Colin Kuehl. 2019. "When Are We Ever Going to Have to Use This? Discussing Programmatic Learning Outcomes in the Classroom." *Journal of Political Science Education* 4 (4): 421–432.

Schonell, Stuart, and Rob Macklin. 2019. "Work Integrated Learning Initiatives: Live Case Studies as a Mainstream WIL Assessment." *Studies in Higher Education* 44 (7): 1197–1208.

Seemiller, Corey, and Meghan Grace. 2016. *Generation Z Goes to College*. Hoboken, NJ: John Wiley & Sons.

Seemiller, Corey, and Meghan Grace. 2017. "Generation Z: Educating and Engaging the Next Generation of Students." *About Campus: Enriching the Student Learning Experience* 22 (3): 21–26. DOI: 10.1002/abc.21293.

Shatto, Bobbi, and Kelly Erwin. 2017. "Teaching Millennials and Generation Z: Bridging the Generational Divide." *Creative Nursing* 23 (1): 24–28.

Singh, Anjali. 2014. "Challenges and Issues of Generation Z." *Journal of Business and Management* 16 (7): 59–63.

Spackman, Andy, and Leticia Camacho. 2009. "Rendering Information Literacy Relevant: A Case-Based Pedagogy." *The Journal of Academic Librarianship* 35 (6): 548–554.

Spears, Julia, Stephanie Zobac, Allison Spillane, and Shannon Thomas. 2015. "Marketing Learning Communities to Generation Z: The Importance of Face-to-Face Interaction in a Digitally Driven World." *Learning Communities Research and Practice* 3 (1): 1–10.

Strawser, Michael. 2018. *Transformative Student Experiences in Higher Education: Meeting the Needs of the Twenty-First-Century Student and Modern Workplace*. Hoboken: Lexington Books.

Sypher, Beverly. 1997. *Case Studies in Organizational Communication 2: Perspectives on Contemporary Work Life*. New York: The Guilford Press.

Townend, M. 2001. "Integrating Case Studies in Engineering Mathematics: A Response to SARTOR 3." *Teaching in Higher Education* 6 (2): 203–215.

Turner, Anthony. 2015. "Generation Z: Technology and Social Interest." *The Journal of Individual Psychology* 71 (2): 103–113. Accessed May 25, 2020. DOI: 10.1353/jip.2015.0021.

Wrage, Stephen. 1994. "Best Case Analysis: What Makes a Good Case and Where to Find the One You Need." *International Studies Notes* 19 (2): 21–27.

Wrench, Jason. 2012. *Casing Organizational Communication*. Dubuque: Kendall Hunt.

Yoo, Moon-Sook, and Hyung-Ran Park. 2015. "Effects of Case-Based Learning on Communication Skills, Problem-Solving Ability, and Learning Motivation in Nursing Students." *Nursing and Health Sciences* 17 (2): 166–172.

Chapter 8

When Learning Is Play

Using Video Games to Educate Gen Z in the Classroom

Gwendelyn S. Nisbett, Newly Paul, and Juli James

As humans, play is our first framework for learning about our world. Children play games to learn about themselves and their surroundings, to grapple with experiences in their daily lives, practice flexibility, express themselves creatively, and solve problems. This chapter argues for harnessing this natural desire for play through using digital learning games to create and aid a dynamic educational environment. Gen Z are true digital natives, having been exposed to digital technology since their early childhood. The ubiquitous presence of technology, especially gaming, affects every aspect of their life including socializing and education. This generation knows that games are social, collaborative, engaging, and that, to some extent, all games are learning games.

Video games carry a certain pejorative baggage, often associated with antisocial behavior, violence, and apathy. Despite concerns, it is advocated that the positive aspects of digital gaming be explored, and we urge educators to utilize video games in their coursework and classrooms. By their very nature, games are interactive and engaging for the player. Even simple games can encourage students to think more deeply about how concepts interconnect. Moreover, digital content has been made even more important given the COVID-19 pandemic which has forced many learners into online only learning situations.

This chapter first argues for the benefits of using video games for Gen Z learners. A practical approach to starting with easy games and expanding game tools are discussed. Finally, useful tips are offered and best practices for integrating digital learning games into the classroom.

GAMES IN THE GEN Z CLASSROOM

In the classroom, student engagement includes "active and collaborative learning, participation in challenging academic activities; formative communication with academic staff; involvement in enriching educational experiences; and feeling legitimated and supported by university learning communities" (Coates 2007, 122). Though there is an overlap in the idea of engagement in gaming and engagement in classrooms, it is far more common to hear educators complain about lack of engagement among students (Fredricks 2014).

As researchers have found, the reasons for disengagement in classrooms can range from the growth of consumer culture in higher education that values the prestige of a college over intellectual growth, to outdated teaching strategies that leave students frustrated (Fredricks 2014). With the country shifting to a knowledge economy that values higher-order thinking skills, it is essential to explore new learning techniques that will keep students motivated and engaged in classroom environments, and video games can provide a solution.

According to a 2019 report from Entertainment Software Association (Entertainment Software Association 2019), 74% of parents believe that video games are educational. The same report shows that 63% of Americans believe that video games help develop problem-solving skills, and 52% believe that video games help build teamwork and collaboration. These beliefs are well-founded--researchers in a wide variety of fields from neuroscience to health science have found beneficial effects of video games on users' learning skills. For example, video games promote knowledge of world history and geography (Squire 2006). Some games such as *World of Warcraft* help students build their reading skills (Steinkuehler 2012), and online gaming discussion boards encourage scientific reasoning (Steinkuehler and Duncan 2008), all of which help develop higher-order thinking skills.

Popularity of Video Games

In 2019, a survey conducted by Whistle (2019), a site that produces video content, found that 68% of Gen Z men think gaming is an integral part of their personal identity. About 91% of these men said they regularly play video games, while only 84% of Millennials said the same. Moreover, three in four Gen Z men surveyed by Whistle said they like to watch video games, which is 25% more than Millennials. Though 46% of all gamers in the United States tend to be women, (Entertainment Software Association 2019), there is a dearth of data examining gender differences between Gen Z gamers. A report released by Electronic Entertainment Design and Research Company

(EEDAR) in 2018, noted that though Gen Z girls were less likely to watch video games, they represented a large part of the active gamer world (The NPD Group 2017).

Gen Z uses video games and game adjacent tools—usually via streaming services such as *Twitch* and collaborative and social games like *Fortnite*—to socialize and bond with friends (Slefo 2019). These streaming services offer them a chance to create special characters and lingo, which helps them build an online community. In addition to streaming, Gen Z also likes to play via video consoles. A 2017 Neilsen survey found that 73% of people aged 2–20 have video game consoles, which is 7% more than Millennials (Molla 2017). Gen Z is also a high user of tablets, with 78% having one in their homes.

Benefits of Video Games

Though video games are often criticized for their addictive nature and connection with aggressiveness (Anderson et al. 2013), they are also known to provide beneficial effects for players, in addition to having an entertainment value. Early research on gamers showed that computer usage for gaming helped develop hand-eye coordination among children, raised players' self-esteem, and helped develop social skills, especially among special needs children (Griffiths 2002). With the passage of time, video games have become more complex, realistic, and social (Ferguson and Olson 2013), and tend to provide cognitive, motivational, emotional, and social benefits to players (Granic et al. 2014). Shooter video games help improve cognitive skills such as focus and creativity (Jackson et al. 2012), problem-solving abilities (Prensky 2012), and spatial skills necessary for success in science, technology, engineering and mathematics (STEM) fields (Uttal et al. 2013). The immediate and concrete feedback provided in video games tends to be motivational and provides players with incentives to improve their game responses. The games are challenging, but are set up to reward persistence, which breeds confidence and resilience among players (McGonigal 2011), helps promote positive emotions, and reduces anxiety. Games that involve role-playing and become progressively more difficult with each level tend to cause frustration, but are also known to help players adapt to challenges and channel anxiety in positive ways (Granic et al. 2014).

In contrast to single-player games of earlier decades, modern video games tend to be social affairs and help players develop prosocial skills and communal behavior (Ferguson and Garza 2011). The long-term effects of video games among teens include civic and political engagement (Pew Research Center 2008). According to a survey done by the Pew Research Center (2008), 12–17-year-olds who played video games with others were more likely to look up political information, raise money for charity, participate in civic activities, and persuade others to vote.

CREATING AND USING GAMES

Successful games are those that engage players rather than simply entertain them. The engagement is driven by a number of factors such as interactivity, presence of a clear goal, opportunity for growing one's skills, presence of a safe learning environment without fear of being criticized, and the ability to captivate all our senses (Karou n.d.). Though games contain obstacles that get harder as the game proceeds, they also provide rewards for successful completion of each level. In order to succeed, a player must demonstrate strategic thinking, planning, an ability to recover from errors, and resourcefulness in seeking help. The goal of this section is to give practical advice on how to utilize games and video games in instructional settings.

Why Games Work

The theoretical perspective of Entertainment-Education focuses on how content can be purposefully designed to promote learning through entertainment (Singhal and Rogers 2002). From this media effects tradition emerged the term *serious games* which focus on how educators can capitalize on the inherent enjoyment of digital games for learning purposes (Vorderer and Ritterfeld 2009). Entertainment-Education research sheds light on a number of factors that make games work as learning tools. First, students are often already acquainted with the process of playing digital games, thus the integration of educational or prosocial content is a natural fit (Wang and Singhal 2009). Moreover, many digital games use a narrative structure in which a player must work their way through a set of challenges in search of a goal. Entertainment narratives can function to persuade audiences about social issues by way of increasing absorption into the text (Slater and Rouner 2002) and lowering counter-arguments (Moyer-Gusé 2008). Moreover, better stories and better quality of digital games lead to better learning outcomes (Sanford et al. 2015).

In games a player can take on a role with meaning, play through an experience from start to finish, and while the player may not "win" every play session, the player knows that ultimately there will be a win. Achieving a win requires engagement, dedication, frustration, failure, starting again, building new skills, and finally, being rewarded with the win. Players are willing to play games that are hard, that might feel like work, but this work is challenging (versus hard), satisfying (versus punishing), and meaningful (versus pointless). Good game designers are careful to engineer the possibility for this experience and players trust when starting a journey that this is what they will find.

Game Design Models

To get started with game design as learning in the classroom it's helpful to play some games as the instructor of the course. These games can be tabletop or digital. Keep one or two games in mind as you work through the game design models in this section.

Games, at their core, are made with a beginning (start) and an end (win) and include a series of obstacles between (levels). Games give players the tools they need to overcome obstacles and potential to reach the goal (win), though this potential is not guaranteed (lose). Think of a game you have played and deconstruct it at its most basic structure using the simple game design model. See figure 8.1 for a simple game design model depiction.

Structurally, most games will fit within the simple game design model both as a whole and by level. This is enough to approach pen and paper game design fairly quickly in the classroom. Learners generally have an orientation to game design without realizing it due to having played games in their lives, whether currently or as children. To take the game design experience one step further, and to really begin to unpack meaningful games and learning, the core mechanic design model offers a next step to go deeper into game design as depicted in figure 8.2.

Game mechanics are the processes that a player will use (e.g., rules) and actions (e.g., rolling dice, running, jumping) the player will take to play the game. Games have core mechanics, a meaningful action that is repeated across the entire game, and secondary mechanics. Secondary mechanics support and augment the core mechanic of the game. For example, in the platformer genre, a player can count on jumping onto various types of platforms as the primary game mechanic to progress in the game. In a board game, the

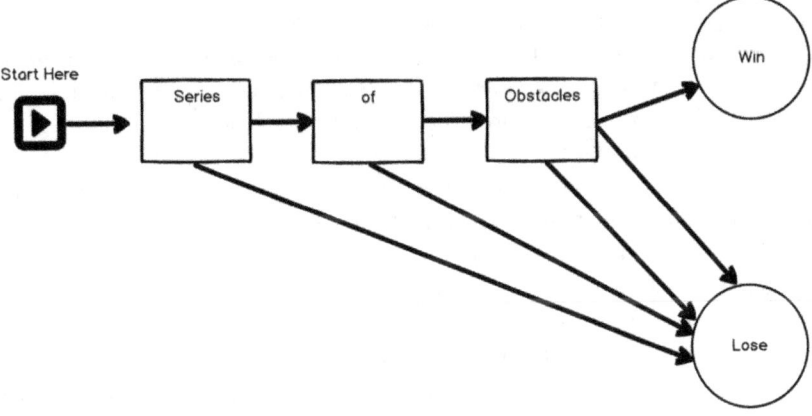

Figure 8.1 Simple Game Design Model. *Source:* James (2021).

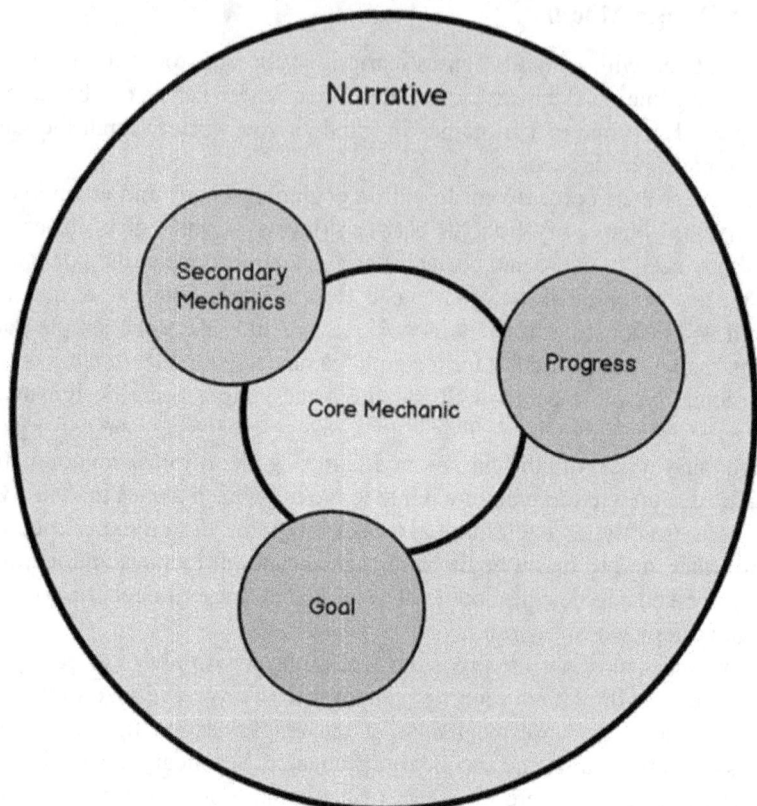

Figure 8.2 Core Mechanic Design Model. *Source:* James (2021).

player can count on a core action for navigating the game board. If a player will also skip, climb, or run, these actions are secondary mechanics.

The core mechanic design model provided shows how the core mechanic is central to the game experience. Progression, secondary mechanics, and goals revolve around the core of the game experience. Encapsulating the experience as a whole is narrative. Narrative can become a powerful tool to welcome a player into the game world. Indeed, Zhou (2020) found in a meta-analysis of narrative-based games that the presence of narrative increases message processing and learning.

Creating small, simple games with a connection between core mechanics and game narrative gives birth to meaningful play experiences and provides the possibility for engaging players in new identities, activities, and ways of thinking. A powerful example of this is the game Spent (https://playspent.org) by the Urban Ministries of Durham. This game asks the player to take the role of a person who's lost their home and job. The player has $1,000 to make it through the month. The core mechanic of the game is moral decision-making and each decision is met with an economic consequence. This game serves as a fair model for students to start thinking about the connection between a meaningful game action and narrative consequence.

Getting Started Using Tabletop Game Tools

Few tools are truly needed to get started with game design in the classroom. Challenge yourself or your students to use only tools available to them in the classroom or at home. After familiarizing yourself with the game design models and using the models to deconstruct a few of your favorite games, try downloading the Game Design Challenge[1] activity to create a small, original game in a short amount of time. Once you walk through this process, you will be able to walk your students through the same process in the classroom.

The Game Design Challenge is an exercise to teach you the basics of game design by building a small game of your own. As you get started with the activity, remember these four concepts:

1. Games need rules and a starting point.
2. Games have obstacles and tools for the player.
3. Games end levels with a goal, and the game will have an overall win/lose condition.
4. Finally, as you make your game, you will need to test it. Play and fix for a few cycles.

Starting small, and staying small, allows designers to dig deeper into their game topics. Keeping the first few games simple will help students as they practice game design. Games can be about one simple thing and still be quite complex (e.g., reaching 21 in Blackjack). Also, gather a small set of materials that you have on hand, and brainstorm ways to solve the problems that arise while game designing. Remember, constraints create conditions for innovation in game designs.

Moving on to Digital Game Design Tools

Graduating from tabletop game design, you and your students can take some aspect of the Game Design Challenge and create small digital demos with education-friendly digital tools (see this list of Free Game Design tools[2] for educators). These recommendations are all browser-based visual tools that do not require coding and supporting tutorials online to help you and your students get started.

As students learn digital tools, design will take a back-burner to technical development. Using an existing design, or staying within the same topic, will serve you and your students well as they learn how to design for digital. Creating narrative storyboards and scripts before jumping into the process is also helpful; students may have to modify the game experience as they develop and a narrative storyboard will keep the game design on track even with modifications. This Game Design Rubric[3] can also be helpful for you and your students as game design progresses.

Example Game

The Mayborn School of Journalism Play Lab designs and tests games to engage young people about serious topics. The Play Lab focuses on collaborative and project-based learning to create narrative learning games. The goal for the classroom is to utilize digital learning games to provide a psychologically safe context to explore identities, make choices, and experience the consequences in a low-stakes, high-learning environment.

A popular game called *Hoaxes & Havoc*[4] was created to teach media literacy skills, specifically differentiating between credible journalism and misinformation. The game was developed by the Mayborn's Juli James as a product of collaboration between *Playable Media* and Arizona State University. The game positions the player as a media manipulator in order to demonstrate the mechanics of spreading false messages and the social impact of this kind of activity. As the player spreads false information

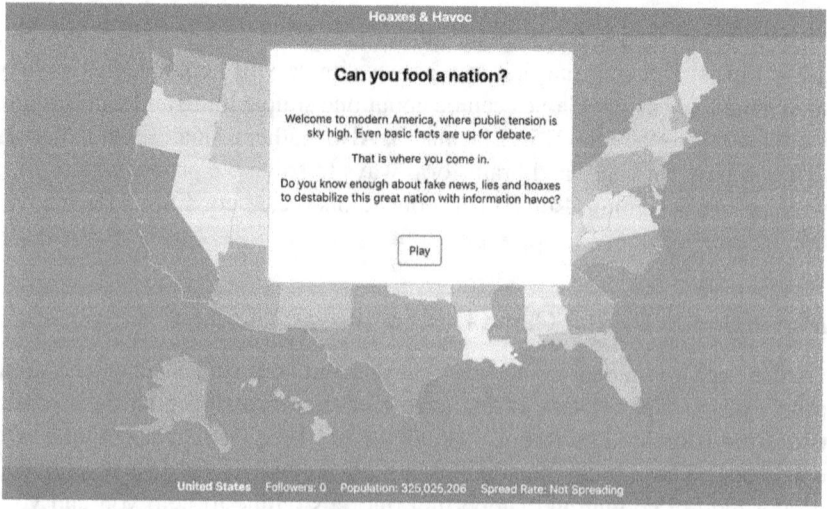

Figure 8.3 Hoaxes and Havoc by Playable Media. *Source:* James (2021).

further and further, the game displays the collateral damage of misinformation. Figure 8.3 is an image of Hoaxes and Havoc by Playable Media (2021).

TIPS AND BEST PRACTICES

1. *Even Simple Games Can Be Engaging*: Games need not be complex in order to engage players. Simple games that are interactive, have clearly defined goals, offer incentives for completion, and provide a safe learning space can be successful in encouraging players to think deeply about topics. The added advantage of simple games is that they allow players to explore a given topic in greater detail.
2. *Understand Game Flow and Narrative*: Games should have a definitive flow—they must have clear start and end points, and various levels of play that challenge players. A well thought out game flow includes tools that players need to overcome obstacles, as well as rewards for overcoming them. An overarching narrative is needed to meaningfully connect the various parts of a game and the tasks that players must complete to win.
3. *Link Game Experience with Learning Content*: Educational games must be designed around a core learning component. Games that are built around the intricacies of a topic that students are learning tend to be most successful in engaging users. Players find such games useful because of the low stakes, high-learning game environment that helps them develop their physical and cognitive skills.
4. *Don't Be Afraid of Technology*: Plenty of resources are available for educators looking to incorporate learning games in the classroom. These resources cater to people with various skill levels and do not require advanced knowledge of coding. In addition to step-by-step instructions, resources include worksheets, curriculum design suggestions, media resources, and opportunities for professional development, all of which make it easier for educators to implement game-based tools in classrooms (see notes for linked resources).
5. *Meet Students Where They Are:* In education today, while one might like to claim that teachers are engaging students in content using the best learning design, the reality is murkier. Students will often claim subjects are hard, the work is punishing, and the school experience is meaningless. It is unclear if these sentiments are due to parents, students' own apathy, or that technology has become our competition. Perhaps, if educators approach learning as game designers approach game design, teachers will more often meet students where they are with huge possibilities for good learning.

6. *Link Games to the Moment:* If 2020 taught educators anything, it's that there is a need to be flexible and adaptable to complex situations. The COVID-19 pandemic mixed with the current rise in social justice activism and political polarization creates teachable moments and the need for digital content and tech learning. Games can break down tough issues and make them easier to digest and navigate. Moreover, online games are invaluable in a world where face-to-face learning is not always available.

NOTES

1. Game Design Challenge: https://drive.google.com/file/d/1JPEgzaszC-Miw-Ka2PGX0-QuYXSBfL4z/view
2. Free Game Design Tools: https://drive.google.com/file/d/1lyZktNnX4FjmbysZ_fBhtonBkYuFcdei/view?usp=sharing
3. Game Design Rubric: https://drive.google.com/file/d/1B76WLzlq6CT4X5GF87Gh4QfsTgqbSOwr/view?usp=sharing
4. Hoaxes & Havoc can be found here: fakenewsgame.playablemedia.org/

REFERENCES

Anderson, Craig, Akiko Shibuya, Nobuko Ihori, Edward L. Swing, Brad J. Bushman, Akira Sakamoto, Hannah R. Rothstein, and Muniba Saleem. 2010. "Violent Video Game Effects on Aggression, Empathy, and Prosocial Behavior in Eastern and Western Countries: A Meta-Analytic Review." *Psychological Bulletin* 136 (2): 151–173. DOI: 10.1037/a0018251.

Coates, Hamish. 2007. "A Model of Online and General Campus-Based Student Engagement." *Assessment & Evaluation in Higher Education* 32 (2): 121–141. DOI: 10.1080/02602930600801878.

Entertainment Software Association. 2019. "Essential Facts About the Computer and Video Game Industry." Accessed June 1, 2020. https://www.theesa.com/wp-content/uploads/2019/05/ESA_Essential_facts_2019_final.pdf.

Ferguson, Christopher J., and Adolfo Garza. 2011. "Call of (Civic) Duty: Action Games and Civic Behavior in a Large Sample of Youth." *Computers in Human Behavior* 27 (2): 770–775. DOI: 10.1016/j.chb.2010.10.026.

Ferguson, Christopher J., and Cheryl K. Olson. 2013. "Friends, Fun, Frustration and Fantasy: Child Motivations for Video Game Play." *Motivation and Emotion* 37 (1): 154–164. DOI: 10.1007/s11031-012-9284-7.

Fredricks, Jennifer. 2014. *Eight Myths of Student Disengagement: Creating Classrooms of Deep Learning*. Thousand Oaks: Corwin Press.

Granic, Isabela, Adam Lobel, and Rutger CME Engels. 2014. "The Benefits of Playing Video Games." *American Psychologist* 69 (1): 66–78. DOI: 10.1037/a0034857.

Griffiths, Mark D. 2002. "The Educational Benefits of Videogames." *Education and Health* 20 (3): 47–51.

Jackson, Linda A., Edward A. Witt, Alexander Ivan Games, Hiram E. Fitzgerald, Alexander Von Eye, and Yong Zhao. 2012. "Information Technology Use and Creativity: Findings from the Children and Technology Project." *Computers in Human Behavior* 28 (2): 370–376.

Karou, Ki. n.d. "5 Video Game Principles that Motivate Endless Play and Learning." *Mind Research Institute*. Accessed June 2, 2020. https://blog.mindresearch.org/blog/video- game-principles-play-learning.

McGonigal, Jane. 2011. *Reality is Broken: Why Games Make Us Better and How They Can Change the World*. New York: Penguin Press.

Molla, Rani. 2017. "Millennials Have a Netflix Account. Gen Z is Playing Video Games." Accessed June 2, 2020. https://www.vox.com/2017/7/17/15961370/millennials-netflix- account-gen-z-video-games-mobile-phone-nielsen.

Moyer-Gusé, Emily. 2008. "Toward a Theory of Entertainment Persuasion: Explaining the Persuasive Effects of Entertainment-Education Messages." *Communication Theory* 18 (3): 407–425. DOI: 10.1111/j.1468-2885.2008.00328.x.

Pew Research Center. 2008. "Teens, Video Games, and Civics: Teens' Gaming Experiences are Diverse and Include Significant Social Interaction and Civic Engagement." Accessed May 28, 2020. https://www.pewresearch.org/internet/2008/09/16/teens-video-games-and-civics/.

Prensky, Marc R. 2012. *From Digital Natives to Digital Wisdom: Hopeful Essays for 21st Century Learning*. Thousand Oaks: Corwin Press.

Sanford, Kathy, Lisa J. Starr, Liz Merkel, and Sarah Bonsor Kurki. 2015. "Serious Games: Video Games for Good?" *E-Learning and Digital Media* 12 (1): 90–106. DOI: 10.1177/2042753014558380.

Singhal, Arvind, and Everett M. Rogers. 2002. "A Theoretical Agenda for Entertainment—Education." *Communication Theory* 12 (2): 117–135. DOI: 10.1111/j.1468- 2885.2002.tb00262.x.

Slater, Michael D., and Donna Rouner. 2002. "Entertainment—Education and Elaboration Likelihood: Understanding the Processing of Narrative Persuasion." *Communication Theory* 12 (2): 173–191.

Slefo, George. 2019. "Fortnite Emerges as a Social Media Platform for Gen Z." Accessed May 27, 2020. https://adage.com/article/digital/fortnite-emerges-social -media-platform-gen-z/2176301.

Squire, Kurt. 2006. "From Content to Context: Videogames as Designed Experience." *Educational Researcher* 35 (8): 19–29.

Steinkuehler, Constance. 2012. "The Mismeasure of Boys: Reading and Online Videogames." WCER Working Paper No. 2011-3. Madison: Wisconsin Center for Education Research, University of Wisconsin. Accessed May 28, 2020. https://wcer.wisc.edu/docs/working-papers/Working_Paper_No_2011_03.pdf.

Steinkuehler, Constance, and Sean Duncan. 2008. "Scientific Habits of Mind in Virtual Worlds." *Journal of Science Education and Technology* 17 (6): 530–543. DOI: 10.1007/s10956-008-9120-8.

The NPD Group. 2017. "Three Ways to Win Over the Thrifty Gen Z Consumer." Accessed May 27, 2020. https://www.npd.com/wps/portal/npd/us/news/thought-leadership/2019/3-ways- to-win-over-the-thrifty-gen-z-consumer/.

Uttal, David H., Nathaniel G. Meadow, Elizabeth Tipton, Linda L. Hand, Alison R. Alden, Christopher Warren, and Nora S. Newcombe. 2013. "The Malleability of Spatial Skills: A Meta-Analysis of Training Studies." *Psychological Bulletin* 139 (2): 352–402. DOI: 10.1037/a0028446.

Vorderer, Peter, and Ute Ritterfeld. 2009. "Digital Games." In *The SAGE Handbook of Media Processes and Effects*, edited by Robin L. Nabi and Mary Beth Oliver, 455–468. Los Angeles: Sage.

Wang, Hua, and Arvind Singhal. 2009. "Entertainment-Education Through Digital Games." In *Serious Games: Mechanisms and Effects*, edited by Ute Ritterfeld, Michael Cody, and Peter Vorderer, 271–292. New York: Routledge.

Whistle. 2019. "Two-Thirds of Gen Z Males Say Gaming is a Core Component of Who They Are." Accessed May 26, 2020. https://www.aaaa.org/gen-z-males-say-gaming-core- component-who-they-are/.

Zhou, Chun, Aurora Occa, Soyoon Kim, and Susan Morgan. 2020. "A Meta-Analysis of Narrative Game-Based Interventions for Promoting Healthy Behaviors." *Journal of Health Communication* 25 (1): 54–65. DOI: 10.1080/10810730.2019.1701586.

Chapter 9

Getting Outside of the Norm

Adopting Outdoor Adventure Education Pedagogy to Engage Generation Z

R. Tyler Spradley

Given the challenges of civil unrest, pandemics, and mandated teleteaching, considering how students are enabled or constrained by macro influences, such as social structures and crises, and micro influences, such as problem-solving and critical thinking, is a significant pedagogical undertaking (Giddens 1984). Education is facing unexpected hurdles in the black hole of these tensions and questions. As the methods of pedagogical tools such as lecturing, learning activities, testing, and writing are evolving to meet the hurdles, it remains paramount that instruction includes 1) learning about the learner and 2) adapting to the learner. In these increasingly high stakes times, faculty find themselves in discover mode. How will upcoming generations be taught?

With limited focus on the college years of Generation Z, much is to be unearthed and surmised about Generation Z as college students (Seemiller and Grace 2016). Because Generation Z's moniker is *digital natives,* the limited research focusing on Generation Z seems to privilege technology and how to use technology in higher education to appeal to them (see Thurston 2018; Turner 2015). Much of the literature bends toward technology, for example digital gamification, even when faculty recognize and value the need for collaboration and adaptivity (Barak 2018). In light of the pandemic, the emphasis on technology has only increased, as Zoom becomes a method and a verb. Nonetheless, technological privileging may negatively impact the classroom and learners.

Much is assumed about Generation Z as digital natives and their preferences for digital pedagogy, instructional practices, and communication (Thurston 2018), which could generate tensions between face-to-face and digital instructional practices with Generation Z. Putting face-to-face in tension with digital pedagogy creates a false dichotomy for both faculty and students. The real question facing faculty is: how to adapt instructional practices for Generation Z based on researched characteristics and needs? Such a generally worded question opens doors to a broader set of instructional practices from various disciplines, methodologies, and theoretical backgrounds. Faculty or programs may avail themselves of high and low technological pedagogy to engage students with content and make relevant personal, professional, and academic applications. This chapter decidedly errs on the low-tech side by exploring how to use outdoor adventure education (OAE) for instructing Generation Z despite this generation being characterized by the technology shaping it. Breaking with some recommendations to design curriculum using the mobile technology familiar to Generation Z, this chapter recommends creative, interactive, and technology-free group-based outdoor activities to engage students with content, promote critical thinking, enable appreciation of the environment, and flip learning by *doing, reflecting,* and *integrating.* Additionally, prior to the COVID-19 pandemic, OAE activities were more easily applied alternatives within in-person pedagogical repertoire. Arguably, OAE is more challenging to implement, but maybe more needed than ever in a digitally saturated and bifurcated environment. To begin, let's stop and think about techno-centric assumptions and their consequences.

(RE)THINKING ASSUMPTIONS ABOUT *DIGITAL NATIVES*

Neil Postman (1993), in his work *Technolopy: The Surrender of Culture to Technology*, critiques the consequences from the transformation of technology as a tool of members of a society to the primary *thing* that shapes society. The material consequences of such a transformation impacts the pillar institutions of a culture like education. In turn, education, for example, is transformed by its dependency on the technology's strengths and weaknesses. Education becomes limited by the entertainment characteristics and expectations of technology, limited interaction with the environment and humans, and the instant gratification afforded through the technology. Despite the transformative nature of technology to culture, more generally, and education, more specifically, there is caution to resist technology's talons and complicate assumptions about Generation Z's digital dependence and bifurcated environment.

Not challenging our students, even *digital natives,* to move outside of their technological dependencies limits faculty from adequately engaging Generation Z with our complex world. While not all educators will agree with the total takeover of culture by technology that Postman argues, it should be noted that new technologies we cannot conceive will most likely be an instrumental part of these digital natives' lives in the near future. Zoom has certainly risen as an impactful actor in the social distancing world Generation Z finds itself. They, like generations before, need skills that will enable them to adapt to changing work environments, relationships, and technologies. To educate by maintaining technological dependency in the digital generation may neglect Generation Z's relational, critical thinking and collaborative problem-solving skill development in addition to the increasing importance of environmental conservation.

This chapter argues that learning through face-to-face teamwork for digital natives can be enhanced through OAE. In a world where chaos and crisis are constant, digital natives need to be trained to navigate complex situations as teams to make sense of complex environments, confront their own assumptions and habits, and react resiliently as a team, not just as an individual (Weick 1995; Weick and Ashford 2001; Weick and Roberts 1993; Weick and Sutcliffe 2007). Such collaborative, resilience is not accomplished through technical skill alone, and as such, digital natives need relational skills to build trust and high performing teams that can respond and adapt.

(RE)INTRODUCING SOFT SKILLS TO HIGHER LEARNING

Given technological, economic, and social shifts within employability, soft skills of college graduates have received attention (Andrews and Higson 2008; Robles 2012). Often defined by contrasting them with hard skills, soft skills are typically delineated by a subset of skills including interpersonal or people skills (e.g., customer service, respectful interaction, teamwork, leadership, conflict management) and personal attributes (e.g., integrity, responsibility, motivation, time management) (Robles 2012). Surveys like the National Association of Colleges and Employers Job Outlook Survey 2016 underscore the need for soft skills. In this survey, employers looked for the following skills on resumes, which are listed in order of most sought after: leadership, ability to work in a team, written communication skills, problem-solving, verbal communication, strong work ethic, initiative, and several more. Soft skills are attractive and necessary for employability and professional advancement for Generation Z because they enable workers to adapt to new jobs and changes in the workplace, overcome challenges, manage collegial relationships across the organizational hierarchy, and fulfill collective goals (Appleby 2017).

Unfortunately, some of the research out there indicates that employers find college graduates lacking in soft skills (Bauer-Wolf 2019). Faculty, regardless of what they are teaching, are positioned to model, teach, and reinforce soft skills in a variety of ways through human interaction. From team-based learning in a science lab to students organizing a health fair in a health science seminar, faculty, like employers, often expect students to employ soft skills to fulfill course-related expectations. So, consider the following questions. We may expect soft skills, but are we teaching soft skills? If we are teaching soft skills, how are we teaching soft skills? If we are expecting and teaching soft skills, are we considering how to engage Generation Z? In reflecting on pedagogy and considering how to teach soft skills to Generation Z, this chapter focuses on the specific branch of active learning pedagogy, outdoor adventure education, and teamwork.

(Re)Learning Teamwork Generation Z through Outdoor Adventure Education (OAE)

Moving from the classroom to the outdoors is quite a change. In some cases, our frames of reference, most likely built on more traditional models of pedagogy from inside the classroom, may contest the space of the outdoors as a viable option for engaging students, especially Generation Z students. Subsequently, as the COVID-19 pandemic rages, research shows that outdoor environments decrease the threat of contagions (Coyle and Bodor 2020; CDC 2021). While masking is necessary, interacting outdoors provides a safer space to educate. Thus, as faculty move teamwork outdoors and relinquish their smart boards and high-tech classrooms, faculty are freed to focus on their student-faculty and student-student interactions in team-based adventure education exercises. Marsi (2019) points out the importance of teamwork being an interpersonal exercise that puts into practice concepts about team dynamics. Building teamwork skills requires group communication processes developed through interrelating. Conveying information about teamwork didactically is not enough to move students from knowledge to practice. Given the importance of effective teamwork in organizational and educational life, students need to have opportunities built into postsecondary learning that enable them to work in teams to make decisions, manage conflict, lead, and collaborate.

Transformative Learning Theory in Outdoor Adventure Education

At its core, Transformative Learning Theory (TLT) moves students through stages of action, reflection, revision, and application aimed at perspective transformation to shift the learners' perspectives and/or behaviors (Meerts-Brandsma et al. 2019). To use TLT in OAE, the activity must follow these aforementioned stages of TLT and meet OAE criteria (Williams and Wainwright 2016), which are:

1. The activity must be outdoors.
2. Experiential learning processes must be followed with reflection that allows learners to take ownership for what they have learned.
3. The activity must present learners with choices.
4. Risks should be managed to ensure that learners can meet the challenge set before them in the activity.

For the purposes of this chapter, the stages of TLT will be reconceptualized into three primary stages of: 1) *doing*, which includes the briefing with instructions and outdoor team-based activity, 2) *reflecting*, which is accomplished through professor guided debriefing, and 3) *integrating*, which fulfills both revision and application as students experience perspective transformations that shape how they approach future collaborative work.

TEAM-BUILDING THROUGH OUTDOOR ADVENTURE EDUCATION WITH TLT DESIGN

Given Generation Z's desire for interactivity and professional development (Mohr and Mohr 2017; Seemiller and Grace 2016), team-building OAE instructional practices fulfill the need to customize pedagogy to the current generation and to prepare them for soft skills needed post-graduation (Marasi 2019). If the professor is going to use teams for course projects, research suggests that conducting an in-class team-building activity should be done prior to the class project to enhance skills and cohesion needed for success (Marasi 2019). Therefore, team-building has broad appeal as an instructional practice, and this chapter, in particular, clarifies how to design and implement team-building activities by using TLT processes with OAE. This section is broken-down into four sub-sections drawing heavily on the team OAE activities that place an emphasis on teamwork, leadership, and organizational culture: 1) doing, 2) reflecting, 3) integrating, and 4) best practices for TLT designed team OAE activities for Generation Z.

Doing Stage of TLT Design of OAE

Doing includes planning, designing, and briefing OAE teamwork activities. Action-based learning places emphasis on activities students perform, which can be as extensive as high and low ropes courses, camping trips, or canoeing expeditions, or as limited as a brief exercise conducted outside during class time. Using OAE can be as easy as consulting published resource guides available online, your library, or, if available, the outdoor education center on your campus. OAE is not a new form of learning, so resources are plentiful. To get started, here are a few resources by Karl Rohnke that include collaborative problem-solving activities, team development, relationship building, trust development, and other activities:

1) Rohnke, Karl. *Silver Bullets: A Guide to Initiative Problems, Adventure Games, Stunts and Trust Activities.* Project Adventure, Inc., PO Box 100, Hamilton, MA 01936, 1984.
2) Rohnke, Karl. "Cowstails and Cobras II: A Guide to Games, Initiatives, Ropes Courses & Adventure Curriculum." (1989).
3) Rohnke, Karl, and Steve Butler. *Quicksilver: Adventure Games, Initiative Problems, Trust Activities, and a Guide to Effective Leadership.* SAGE Publications, 1995.

Resources from Rohnke are not the end all, but his works are foundational and time tested. If you have an outdoor adventure education center on your campus, check with them to see what resources are available. Some campuses have ropes courses, canoes, camping equipment, and other adventure gear that can be used or rented. These types of programs on college campuses can be structured enough that they offer services for faculty, including leading the activities themselves. Importantly, know the safety guidelines and risk factors for any activity you choose. For example, here is a resource containing objectives, explanations, briefing information, and challenges that can be used in courses to challenge students to perform and see the value of collaborative problem-solving and teamwork: island hopping survival, which is adapted from Rohnke's work.

Island Hopping Survival

Objective

Teams must use collaborative problem-solving and conflict management skills to cross four "islands" for survival.

Explanation

Divide the class into teams of 10–15 members. Make each team an equal size within that window. Each team must meet the challenge of using three 2'x 6' boards of three different lengths to cross from four 3'x 3' platforms, islands, in the order provided by the instructor. Team members must cross from each island to the next as a whole team before moving to the following island. All four islands are labeled 1, 2, 3, and 4, and must be followed in order. No team member can step off the islands or boards at any time. If a team member does step off, then the whole team must start from the first island. Island 4 is the safe island. All members of the team must be present on Island 4 for the activity to be over.

Required Resources

1. Three 2'x 6' boards. One board must be the 6', one 4', and one 2'.
2. Four 3'x 3' square platforms should be made from 2'x 6' boards. The platforms should be a box the height of a 2' x 6' board. There should be a support beam in the middle of the platform to provide bracing.
3. Choose an outdoor space large enough and level enough to place the four platforms far enough apart that two boards must always be used to cross from one platform to the other. Spaces measuring 5', 7', 9', and 11' in any order are ideal.
4. Members of other teams in the class should assist with monitoring when the team participating has a member step off the platforms or boards and with providing spotting. Spotting is a safety act where classmates stand with their dominant foot forward and arms out straight to help students that step off to prevent them from falling.
5. Students should be aware of functional problem-solving steps before performing this activity.

Briefing/Instructions for Students

Today, we are going to put your team problem-solving and conflict management skills into practice by placing your team in a life or death situation where you must work together in a trial of island survival. You will have to collaborate to solve the challenge of moving from island to island to reach the final safe island. Each island has been given a number. Your team must move completely from each island in order using the boards provided without stepping or falling off the island or the boards. Each island must be fully populated by the team before moving to the next island. If a team member steps off a board or an island, then the whole team must start over. Can you work together to solve this challenge? Can you beat the other teams' best times? Is your team a survivor?

Challenges

As the instructor, work hard to not give hints or ideas. Let the teams find answers themselves. Before implementing an OAE that requires close interaction, it is important to make sure students know each other. Using icebreakers for several class periods before the activity is important to build familiarity. Also, you will need to set up your islands before class begins to be ready when students arrive. Inform students across several class sessions where the outdoor class will be meeting on the scheduled day. Starting class and moving to the location takes away crucial time needed to complete the activity during a class session. Following the activity, you will likely serve as the facilitator to stimulate team-based reflection.

Reflecting Stage of TLT Design of OAE

The *reflecting* stage of TLT in OAE follows the doing stage and features a systematic debriefing guided by a trained student, OAE professional, or you, the professor. In much the same way reflective learning is conceived of as a social accomplishment to avoid self-deception and unawareness (Brockbank and McGill 1998), debriefing is socially accomplished. In its simplest definition, debriefing is defined in the *Handbook of Experiential Learning* as "the facilitation of learning from experience" (Greenaway 2007, 60). Debriefing is an organized, goal-oriented group discussion lead by a facilitator following an activity, and systematic debriefing is an essential reflection activity associated with experiential, active learning used in a variety of academic disciplines and corporate/organizational trainings (Dismukes et al. 2006; Waxman 2010). To prepare for and enact reflecting, a variety of factors should be considered.

Debriefing Preparation and Enactment

1. *Adequate time should be allocated to the debriefing period.* For a 1-hour and 15-minute class, plan for a 40-20-minute OAE activity and a 15-20-minute debriefing.
2. *Questions should be pre-planned in order to relate to the soft skills or concepts associated with the OAE activity objectives and course content.* To assist, there is a set of general debriefing questions related to the top soft skills adapted from the National Association of Colleges and Employers' *Job Outlook 2016 Survey*. Additionally, questions should be open-ended to prompt discussion.
3. *Facilitators should encourage full participation in discussion.* To do so, the facilitator cannot answer the questions or fear silence, but the facilitator may need to rephrase a question, move to a different question, or call on students by name to increase participation.

The following set of debriefing questions for reflection and skill-building are designed to assist and initiate discussion related to specific soft skills (See table 9.1: Debriefing Questions to Enhance Soft Skills).

Table 9.1 Debriefing Questions to Enhance Soft Skills

Soft Skill	Questions for Reflection	Questions for Skill-Building
Leadership	• Who emerged as a leader during the activity? • What caused teammates to defer to the leader? • What did team leaders do during the activity?	• How could the leader help your team with understanding the activity goal? • How could the leader help the team consider a greater number of alternative actions or solutions? • How could the team leader encourage greater participation of each team member?
Teamwork	• How did the team accomplish the goal? • In what ways do you feel the team worked together? • In what ways do you feel like the team struggled to come together? • What were diverse contributions to the team?	• How can you motivate one another toward the team's goal? • How can the team discourage social loafing and encourage full participation?
Communication	• How did the team communicate the goal to create shared understanding? • How did the team communicate to prevent misunderstandings? • How did the team communicate to enhance coordination of the individual members?	• How could the team enhance shared understanding of the team's goals and activities? • How could the team avoid misunderstandings?
Problem-Solving	• What ideas did the team come up with to resolve the problem? • How many different ideas did the team generate before choosing one? • How did the team use multiple ideas or associations to generate the solution?	• How could the team generate more ideas? • How could group think prevent the team from generating the best ideas? • How could the team avoid group think?
Decision-Making	• What process did the team use to make a decision? • How did team members feel about the decision? • If someone had a different idea, how did you feel when your idea was not selected by the team? • If someone's idea was selected by the team, how did that feel? • How did the team evaluate the outcome of decision making? • How did timing, location, or other factors impact the team's decision?	• How can team decision-making be more inclusive? • How can team decision-making prevent dissatisfaction of teammates needed to carry out the decision? • How can the team build consensus?

(Continued)

Table 9.1 Debriefing Questions to Enhance Soft Skills (Continued)

Soft Skill	Questions for Reflection	Questions for Skill-Building
Conflict Management	• What did the group disagree about during the activity? • How did the team manage disagreements? • What were team conflicts related to? Were the team disagreements more about the activity, decision-making, leadership, or interpersonal differences?	• How can the team avoid win/loose resolutions? • How can the team promote win/win resolutions? • How could the team uncover what the conflict is really about? • How can the team make the conflict a team-builder rather than a team-destroyer?
Interpersonal Skills	• How did teammates communicate mutual respect for each other? • How did teammates make one another feel included as a member?	• What can teammates say or do to help communicate mutual respect? • How could teammates demonstrate value for one another? • How could teammates increase inclusion?

Source: Spradley (2021).

Anticipating the OAE activity is perceived as entertaining, active, valuable, and relevant, there are some students and teams that will not have a positive impression of the OAE. Nevertheless, the debriefing is an opportunity to re-frame the activity and possibly shift negative impressions. In other words, "The experience of debriefing is as important as the debriefing of experience. What participants experience during the debriefing will influence their whole attitude toward learning from experience, both in the present and in the future" (Greenaway 2007, 66). Additionally, facilitation may take on a particular theoretical approach. For example, the OAE may use a critical pedagogy design and use debriefing, in part, to help students question and challenge structures, values, and roles in the activity (Payne 2002). Or in another example, appreciative inquiry (Ricketts and Willis 2001) or strength-based education (Passarelli et al. 2010) could be used to help students focus on positive impressions and outcomes of the activity. As the instructor and facilitator this will be a judgment call, but it is worth considering.

In sum, reflection through a systematic, guided debriefing is designed to actively engage students' participation in the learning process and facilitate connections between activity and learning. While some OAE activities stop at this stage, transformational learning approaches emphasize the next stage in learning: *integrating*.

Integrating Stage of TLT Design of OAE

Given survey data indicating Generation Z's preference for independent, non-creative work (Seemiller and Grace 2014) and literature questioning students' preparation for effective teamwork in college classrooms (Cooley et al. 2015), team-based OAE activities are poised to be transformative learning experiences for Generation Z students, possibly the very activities they need to experiment, practice, and hone soft skills required for employability and professional success. To facilitate the *integrating* stage of TLT, I have embedded repetitive use of OAE in my classes and team projects. For example, in my course on teamwork and group communication, teams must work together to create and lead their own, unique OAE activity and debriefing for the class. In a different example, using OAE as a part of an organizational communication course, preceding a team-based qualitative, service-learning research project with OAE can transform how students implement teamwork processes as they complete the research project. OAE develops trust and relational bonds that help the team cohere. As students develop soft skills and connections through these transformative experiences, it is important to explore a set of best practices.

Best Practices for TLT Designed Team OAE Activities for Generation Z

1. Begin small with a brief, easy to execute OAE activity during class by taking an icebreaker activity outdoors. Then, you can transition to a class-length OAE activity like island hopping.
2. Time an OAE activity prior to course team-based projects or ongoing discussion groups for the best results for integration. The OAE with TLT design can transform Generation Z's capacity for teamwork and communication skills prior to graded projects and discussions to enhance academic performance.
3. Communicate the objectives of the OAE to students as you introduce the activity and provide instruction.
4. Use open-ended, soft skill-specific questions to facilitate a structured debriefing period.
5. Provide opportunities for students to use the soft skills that they have integrated as teams in predetermined teamwork.

CONCLUSION

This chapter uses an experiential learning theory, Transformative Learning Theory, to design and implement outdoor adventure education instructional strategies in higher education to embrace Generation Z's preferences for facilitated, reflective, and practical learning while challenging them to put down their technology, communicate effectively with others, think creatively to problem solve, and collaborate in teams (Hope 2016; Seemiller and Grace 2014). The collaborative learning process for students, subsequently, resembles *doing, reflecting,* and *integrating* to achieve perspective transformation. While the examples used in this chapter are not exhaustive means to achieve OAE with Generation Z, they aptly illustrate how to appeal to Generation Z's desire for interactivity and impact and, also, frame these activities as a means to build capacity for team problem-solving, collaborative decision-making, appreciating diversity, leadership, and conflict management for future academic and professional performances that can make a difference (Mohr and Mohr 2017). Engaging "outspoken, idealistic and action-oriented" students of Generation Z need not be high tech (Giunta 2017, 91). Lastly, COVID-19 has amplified green educational spaces as viable alternatives for the classroom. These spaces afford greater degrees of social distancing, natural airflow, and movement. Strategies like the *National COVID-19 Outdoor Learning Initiative* (2020) evince the importance of OAE. Subsequently, instructional practices can unplug the digital natives to provide transformative learning experiences by getting outside of the norm.

REFERENCES

Andrews, Jane, and Higson, Helen. 2008. "Graduate Employability, 'Soft Skills' Versus 'Hard' Business Knowledge: A European Study." *Higher Education in Europe* 33 (4): 411–422. DOI: 10.1080/03797720080252267.

Appleby, Drew. "The Soft Skills College Students Need to Succeed Now and in the Future: Transferable Skills for Success in College and the Workplace." *American Psychological Association*, September 2017. https://www.apa.org/ed/precollege/psn/2017/09/soft-skills.

Barak, Miri. 2018. "Are Digital Natives Open to Change? Examining Flexible Thinking and Resistance to Change," *Computer & Education* 121: 115–123. DOI: 10.1016/j.compedu.2018.01.016.

Bauer-Wolf, Jeremy. 2019. "Survey: Employers Want 'Soft Skills' from Graduates." *Inside Higher Ed*. https://www.insidehighered.com/quicktakes/2019/01/17/survey-employers-want-soft-skills-graduates.

Brockbank, Anne, and McGill, Ian. 1998. *Facilitating Reflective Learning in Higher Education*. Philadelphia, PA: Society for Research into Higher Education & Open University Press.

CDC. 2021. "Operational Considerations for Schools." https://www.cdc.gov/coronavirus/2019-ncov/global-covid-19/schools.html.

Cooley, Sam, Victoria Burns, and Jennifer Cumming. 2015. "The Role of Outdoor Adventure Education in Facilitating Groupwork in Higher Education," *Higher Education* 69: 567–582. DOI: 10.1007/s10734-014-9791-4.

Coyle, K. J., and S. Bodor. 2020. "North American Association for Environmental Education and National Wildlife Federation: Guide to Advocating for Outdoor Classrooms in Coronavirus-Era School Reopening." https://www.nwf.org/-/media/Documents/PDFs/NWF-Reports/2020/COVID-19-Outdoor-Classroom-Policy-Guide.

Dismukes, R. Key, David Gaba, and Steven Howard. 2006. "So Many Roads: Facilitated Debriefing in Healthcare." *Simulation in Healthcare* 1 (1): 23–25.

Giddens, A. 1984. *The Constitution of Society: Outline of the Theory of Structuration.* Berkley, CA: University of California Press.

Giunta, Catherine. 2017. "An Emerging Awareness of Generation Z Students for Higher Education Professors." *Archives of Business Research* 5 (4): 90–104. DOI: 10.14738/abr.54.2962.

Greenaway, Roger. 2007. "Dynamic Debriefing." In *The Handbook of Experiential Learning*, edited by Mel Silberman, 59–80. San Francisco, CA: John Wiley & Sons.

Hope, Joan. 2016. "Get Your Campus Ready for Generation Z." *Student Affairs Today* 19 (7): 1–7. DOI: 10.1002/say.30253.

Meerts-Brandsma, Lisa, Jim Sibthorp, and Shannon Rochelle. 2019. "Using Transformative Learning Theory to Understand Outdoor Adventure Education." *Journal of Adventure Education and Outdoor Learning* 1–14. DOI: 10.1080/14729679.2019.1686040.

Mohr, Kathleen, and Eric Mohr. 2017. "Understanding Generation Z Students to Promote a Contemporary Learning Environment." *Journal on Empowering Teaching Excellence* 1 (1): 84–94. DOI: 10.15142/T3M05T.

National Association of Colleges and Employers. n.d. "Job Outlook 2016: The Attributes Employers Want to See on New College Graduates' Resumes." Accessed June 30, 2020. https://www.naceweb.org/career-development/trends-and-predictions/job-outlook-2016-attributes-employers-want-to-see-on-new-college-graduates-resumes/.

"National COVID-19 Outdoor Learning Initiative." 2020. https://www.greenschoolyards.org/covid-learn-outside.

Passarelli, Angela, Eric Hall, and Mallory Anderson. 2010. "A Strengths-Based Approach to Outdoor and Adventure Education: Possibilities for personal growth." *Journal of Experiential Education* 33 (2): 120–135.

Payne, Phillip. 2002. "On the Construction, Deconstruction and Reconstruction of Experience in 'Critical' Outdoor Education." *Australian journal of Outdoor Education* 6 (2): 4–21.

Postman, Neil. 2011. *Technopoly: The Surrender of Culture to Technology.* New York: Vintage.

Ricketts, Miriam, and Willis, James. 2001. *Experience AI: A Practitioner's Guide to Integrating Appreciative Inquiry with Experiential Learning.* Chagrin Falls, OH: Taos Institute.

Robles, Marcel. 2012. "Executive Perceptions of the Top 10 Soft Skills Needed in Today's Workplace." *Business Communication Quarterly* 75 (4): 453–465. DOI: 10.1177/1080569912460400.

Rohnke, Karl. 1984. *Silver Bullets: A Guide to Initiative Problems, Adventure Games, Stunts and Trust Activities*. Hamilton, MA: Project Adventure, Inc.

Rohnke, Karl. 1989. *Cowstails and Cobras II: A Guide to Games, Initiatives, Ropes Courses & Adventure Curriculum*.

Rohnke, Karl, and Steve Butler. 1995. *Quicksilver: Adventure Games, Initiative Problems, Trust Activities, and a Guide to Effective Leadership*. Thousand Oaks: SAGE Publications.

Seemiller, Corey, and Meghan Grace. 2016. *Generation Z Goes to College*. Hoboken, NJ: John Wiley & Sons.

Thurston, Travis. 2018. "Design Case: Implementing Gamification with ARCS to Engage Digital Natives." *Journal on Empowering Teaching Excellence* 2 (1): 23–52. DOI: 10.26077/vsk-5613.

Turner, Anthony. 2015. "Generation Z: Technology and Social Interest." *The Journal of Individual Psychology* 71 (2): 103–113. Accessed May 25, 2020. DOI: 10.1353/jip.2015.0021.

Waxman, K.T. 2010. "The Development of Evidence-Based Clinical Simulation Scenarios: Guidelines for Nurse Educators." *Journal of Nursing Education* 49 (1): 29–35. DOI: 10.3928/01484834-20090916-07.

Weick, Karl, and Kathleen Sutcliffe. 2007. *Managing the Unexpected: Resilient Performance in an Age of Uncertainty* (2nd Ed.). San Francisco, CA: Jossey-Bass.

Weick, Karl E. 1995. *Sensemaking in Organizations* (Vol. 3). Thousand Oaks, CA: Sage.

Weick, Karl E., and Karlene H. Roberts. 1993. "Collective Mind in Organizations: Heedful Interrelating on Flight Decks." *Administrative Science Quarterly*: 357–381.

Weick, Karl E., and Susan J. Ashford. 2001. "Learning in Organizations." In *The New Handbook of Organizational Communication: Advances in Theory, Research, and Methods* 704: 731.

Williams, Andy, and Nalda Wainwright. 2016. "A New Pedagogical Model for Adventure in the Curriculum: Part Two – Outlining the Model." *Physical Education and Sport Pedagogy* 21 (6): 589–602. DOI: 10.1080/17408989.2015.1048212.

Chapter 10

Engaging Generation Z with Communication's Civic Commitments

Spoma Jovanovic, Cristiane S. Damasceno,
and Roy Schwartzman

When James Baldwin famously said to teachers a half-century ago, "It is your responsibility to change society if you think of yourself as an educated person" (1963, 44), he urged them to instruct students on how to question the persistent inequalities that have disadvantaged an increasing number of people in our communities. Baldwin claimed that teachers and their students shared a responsibility to critically examine society and take the necessary risks to change it. In the hallowed halls of higher education, those risks run deep, as they do in the communities we hope to change. Policies, governing bodies, and department politics may sideline attempts at political engagement, social justice research, and teaching about controversial topics. Taking Baldwin's challenge to heart requires offering instruction to Generation Z students that matters to them about the world in which they live.

Communication instruction plays a strategic role in preparing this new generation of learners for twenty-first century challenges. The discipline has deep roots with and connections to civic engagement, dating back to ancient times. Free speech, ethics, and rhetorical studies shed light on efforts to initiate social change through dialogue, communication activism, and the study of social movements (Tedford and Herbeck 2017; Frey and Carragee 2007; Morris and Browne 2013). To cultivate responsible citizenship, when polarized discourse and seemingly intractable differences abound, requires reliance on both tested and innovative means to engage an increasingly diverse student population. Technology's influence plays an ever more central role in pedagogy to uphold and challenge democracy's commitments (Atay and Ashlock 2018).

Based on teaching experience spanning three decades, along with research gleaned from critical pedagogy, democratic theory, and communication studies, as well as conversations with more than 130 students and faculty at a Southeast US mid-size, research-intensive, minority-serving, community-engaged university, this chapter considers how to intensify communication's civic commitments as a needed and desired focus for Generation Z. Though Generation Z's interest in political engagement is keen, their knowledge and skills to participate are often lagging. More specifically, student knowledge of political practices and conventions is low, leading students to disparage political processes, institutions, and actors. To involve those in Generation Z who abstain from critical democratic practices requires teaching experiences that can advance the civic competencies expressed in communication, including ethics, justice, dialogue, diversity, and collaboration.

In structuring a curriculum to foster responsible, justice-oriented citizenship, communication studies instructors can provide a strong' foundation for students to enter public service in paid and volunteer capacities, as well as community organizing and activism. Instruction on current political issues and cultivating leadership practices creates opportunities for engagement and scholarship, by showcasing how communication is both practical and helpful in addressing local and global political issues. Planning multiple routes to collaboration and digital competencies provides students with critical 21st-century knowledge and skills necessary for meaningful democratic engagement.

This chapter initially details the challenges that communication instructors face when teaching Generation Z, whose members have endured economic instability and a sustained pandemic that fuel their distrust of traditional political processes and institutions. It then turns to how channeling and deepening communication instruction toward democratic ends helps learners increase their agency to forge collaborations and use and analyze digital platforms that in turn cultivate requisite critical thinking skills to express dissent, engage in dialogue and debate, and influence the direction of public discourse in the community. The conclusion offers suggestions and reflections on how the route to curricular change of this kind is messy, running parallel in many ways to the challenges of creating social change in the communities of which Generation Z is a part.

GENERATION Z AND TWENTY-FIRST CENTURY CHALLENGES

No exact scientific demarcation defines generations; however, researchers increasingly agree that the cohort born around the mid-90s presents unique characteristics that set them apart from Millennials (Dimock 2019; Seemiller and Grace 2016; Twenge 2017). They grew up in a more diverse American society where individuals from minority groups have reached leading positions, including the country's presidency (Seemiller and Grace 2016). Even though individuals have singular life experiences, some contextual factors cut across Gen Z as a whole and influence their communication modes, forms of civic engagement, and needs as college students.

The emergence of this new generation coincides with the proliferation of mobile technologies and a trend toward Internet ubiquity (Turner 2015). Born amid the digital revolution, these young people display affinity toward mediated forms of communication. A Kaiser Family Foundation survey of 2000 individuals, ages of 8 and 18, reveals that this generation engages with their electronic devices on average, eight hours a day, more time than any other activity during their waking hours (Rideout et al. 2010). Notably, there are discrepancies regarding access and skills among this generation. A Pew Research Center survey indicates that nearly one-in-five students cannot always finish their homework because they lack access to a high-speed Internet connection at home (Anderson and Perrin 2018). Black and Hispanic households with low incomes are particularly affected by this problem; nevertheless, cell phone connection is nearly ubiquitous (Pew Research Center 2013). Based on these facts, it is not surprising that Gen Zers prefer multitasking and engaging with others through their gadgets (Seemiller and Grace 2016). They tend to use text messages over phone calls, social media updates over emails, and on-demand services over traditional media.

Generation Z individuals use their high connectivity to be civically engaged and to become informed about topics that matter to them. Communication scholars point out that youth desire political expression that focuses on identity and affords them a political voice (Lane et al. 2018). Their weak ties to traditional groups and institutions (France 2007) prompt young people to use self-expression as a strategy for inventing their political selves (Wells 2015). Consequently, this generation often supports causes through lifestyle changes that can range from boycotting companies to altering diets and dress codes. Most of them have a negative view of traditional politics and its current polarization (Seemiller and Grace 2016). Many avoid voting and lack an understanding of the governance structure of organizations, such as governments and universities.

These trends create specific needs and challenges in higher education settings. Gen Zers have an overload of information at their fingertips, consuming news through social media platforms such as Facebook, Instagram, and Twitter (Kalogeropoulos 2019). However, research shows that young people do not always know how to filter the quality of online content (McGrew et al. 2017). Also, they avidly use on-demand services, such as Netflix and Amazon, which creates an expectation for constant connection and availability (Rue 2018; Seemiller and Grace 2016). Some speculate that excessive screen time contributes to the decline of mental health quality indicators observed in recent years. However, thus far, no study has established a direct causal link between these two variables, which suggests that the problem may have multiple sources (Livingstone 2017; Twenge 2017). Taken together, these contextual factors challenge educators on various fronts. Inside the classroom, instructors compete with electronic devices for students' attention. When developing the curriculum, instructors are starting to realize that students bring high expectations for services, response, and engagement. When engaging with students, instructors are faced with the task of bridging academic rigor and youths' mental health.

Although no singular cause explains the increase in mental distress problems, policies of austerity and abrupt human losses that Gen Zers witnessed nearly their whole lives probably aggravate the issue. A global economic recession, several epidemics (SARS, HIV/AIDS, swine flu, avian flu, Ebola, and the Zika virus), a pandemic, and terrorist attacks shaped the two first decades of the twenty-first century (Dimock 2019; Seemiller and Grace 2016). In particular, the COVID-19 crisis induced a rapid, makeshift migration to remote education.

This shift laid bare the inequities infusing the digital realm, especially in the United States. Effective delivery and student performance relied heavily on access to reliable broadband Internet, adequate hardware and software, and regular access to a physical and emotional environment conducive to learning—all factors that map to the socioeconomic status which in turn mirrors systemic demographic disparities such as racial inequities (Schwartzman 2020). While the recession, many epidemics, and the pandemic highlighted economic inequities, these crises also fueled a sense of outrage, helplessness, or despair about how to respond. COVID-19 paralyzed activism as entire communities sheltered in place, sequestered in isolation or at least distanced themselves from others who might transmit or be exposed to a highly contagious disease.

Together, sociotechnical shifts and the clouds of crises over the early twenty-first century test the capacity of students (and teachers) to prepare for, adapt to, and learn from uncertainty and change. The pedagogical landscape thus requires change under these conditions. How can students approach uncertainties as opportunities? Since learning arises from pushing past the comfort zone of familiar answers (Brown et al. 2014), what can empower students to confront and embrace challenges that resist simple solutions? What kind of educational practices can replace timidity amid crisis with the temerity to confront it? Finally, how can students build resilience to persist (Duckworth 2016) in building democratic institutions and practices despite setbacks?

CRITICAL COMMUNICATION PEDAGOGY

Education as a liberatory practice has as its starting point that students ought to acquire and develop the knowledge, skills, social relations, and values that lead to critical consciousness and action to challenge injustices where they exist in the political and economic landscape (Freire 1970, 1997). This call is all the more urgent for Generation Z as it faces unprecedented economic, ecological, and political challenges.

In the early twentieth century, John Dewey recognized the need to integrate traditional schooling with community experiences. He urged educators to introduce young people to community members so they could work together to understand better our collective history and contemporary concerns (2015, 1938). Putting Dewey's ideas into practice in the twenty-first century could mean that students discover that gender inequality is not a new problem, but one ensured by systems of control that disadvantage women, or that rules of capitalism require an abundance of low-wage workers in order to support the lifestyles of the wealthy. And, just as certain values are perpetuated in society—maximize efficiency to maximize profits, and reward competition among employees to name just a few—those same values must be confronted in the classroom in order to encourage constructive dialogue and dissent rather than silence, conformity, and obedience (hooks 2017).

Critical communication pedagogy's task, then, requires teaching students to use dialogue, critique, narratives, and dissent as vital resources for pursuing freedom and social justice. Or, as Henry Giroux (2012) says, pedagogy needs to be designed to:

> make sure that the future points the way to a more socially just world, a world in which critique and possibility--in conjunction with the values of reason, freedom, and equality—function to alter the grounds upon which life is lived. (119)

Teaching students to think independently, by pursuing multiple sources of knowledge, is the gateway to engaged learning and a critical citizenry.

STUDENT VOICES ILLUMINATE CIVIC PROMISE

We organized and hosted seven events in the fall of 2018, collecting the views and comments of 130 undergraduate students, approximately 25% of the department's communication studies majors. In 30-75 minute sessions, and working from a pre-planned discussion guide, five faculty members of various ranks facilitated conversations and activities with students, recording their responses to: a) word associations for community, civic engagement, activism, justice, politics, and democracy; b) what skills, experience, and knowledge students considered necessary for post-graduation civic activities; and c) what obstacles exist for them in working toward a more just world.

Through an iterative process, we collected the data using printed handouts in which students wrote word associations. We also took notes that summarized the pre-planned discussions and thematically grouped them to understand students' perspectives on civic commitments. To demonstrate the transparency of the research process, we framed large posters of the word clouds created by student word associations that call public attention to what matters to our students.

Students unanimously viewed community, civic engagement, and activism positively. Family and local ties were framed as positive aspects of community interactions. Participants said that they valued diversity in their communities, realized that an investment of personal time to fulfill responsibilities and duties as citizens was not a burden, and applauded the work of activists who advance their beliefs and ethical standing in efforts for needed social change.

Students regarded justice, politics, and democracy as institutions that fall short of their potential. They argued, convincingly, that justice is meted out differently in our society, depending on social class and wealth. They saw politics as dirty, corrupt, boring, dishonest, and a dated process of rancor and argument that rarely leads to positive outcomes. While they understood that democracy may be an ideal way of putting people first in governance, they noted flaws remain in the United States in actualizing equality and liberty.

To be better prepared for civic life, students said they wanted to know more about local and global political issues, as well as the political infrastructure for how to secure change. Doing so, they said, would improve their ability to discuss politics, and adjust communication and action to the demands of the moment. They called for instruction on interpersonal skills, organizational knowledge, and digital literacies in order to gain greater confidence in how to more effectively work with nonprofits, advocate for change, and apply their classroom knowledge to community concerns.

The students expressed a high degree of reflexivity in identifying their shortcomings in contributing to a more just world. They noted, for instance, that they lacked connections and even basic knowledge of where to start the process of introducing efforts to make the community better. They indicated a need for more practice and skills to be able to speak to others who have views unlike their own, rather than shying away from difficult conversations. They also noted the need to decenter themselves in favor of extending compassion toward other people's thoughts and actions.

Finally, the students demonstrated a keen awareness of how systems, institutions, and government structures are beholden to lobbying efforts, greed, and even corruption. The students lamented how partisan politics has led to the devaluing of minorities, the lack of willingness to overcome unequal applications of justice, and dogmatic ideologies.

COMMUNITY LITERACY

For Gen Zers, civic learning is confounded by a lack of interest and confidence in traditional politics, situating them as "disconnected, dissatisfied, and distrustful of government and political process—perhaps more than any other modern generation" (Twenge 2017, 278). Still, this generation voices a strong desire for social change, just not in the ways practiced by previous generations (Seemiller and Grace 2016). Toward that end, communication educators serve students best by introducing community and new literacies that speak to both ways of being in the world and skills necessary for students to develop as critical agents capable of advancing democracy.

DISCOURSES OF ORGANIZING

To teach students to develop a strong sense of agency, one that can provide the foundation for speaking out and encountering rejection, faculty need to nurture cooperative sensibilities. Classrooms, as instruments of higher education, are "a crucial anchoring institution of citizenship" to provide knowledge, but also to shape identities as students plan for future lives, involving career decisions and how they want to live in society (Boyte 2015, 3).

For generations, students have been raised to believe that *one person can make a difference*. While the impact of one person's commitment can indeed ignite important work by others, rarely does one person, alone, accomplish anything great. This heroic image of the *power of one* is situated squarely in the myth of American exceptionalism that suggests our country is unique in being able to advance the best interests of the world, a position that when ascribed to a single country or singular person has dangerous consequences (Levitz 2019). Among those are that the myth may lead to neglecting, or worse, dismissing the role of important partners, and also adopting a course of action that is blind to impacts in other, related areas.

Though stories are prevalent and enduring about what one person can do alone, what communication studies contributes to that narrative is a critical reminder that communication and action are dialogic at heart, involving more than the singular one to advance social change. What follows is an examination of discourses of organizing for developing deep civic commitments. They build on the dialogic impulse and lead students toward two distinct yet necessary paths for democratic engagement, one in favor of cooperative action and the other in raising critical expression through resistance and dissent.

FORGING COOPERATIVE EXCELLENCE

The joys of collaboration promise participants the opportunity to learn from and with others who may possess differing views, talents, and knowledge. This path argues that many standpoints are better than one in order to be as inclusive as possible toward achieving some goal, whether that be redressing the impact of racism in a community or advancing gender pay equity, as just two critical, public needs. Thus, while not guaranteed, the net result is (hopefully) a better outcome, one approaching what leading civic engagement scholar Harry Boyte calls "cooperative excellence" (2015). He explains:

> Cooperative excellence is the principle that a mix of people from highly varied backgrounds can achieve remarkable intellectual, social, political, and spiritual growth and can undertake generative public work if they have the right encouragement, resources, challenges, and calls to public purpose. (14)

Features that define discourses of collaboration include affirmation, support for the person and the cooperative enterprise, clear communication, flexibility to fill in when someone steps out, and a meaningful purpose.

In her study of a collaborative class project in a communication course, Lori Britt (2014) concluded that three related practices help shape meaningful experiences. First, the instructor needs to move away from the front of the classroom to model a democratic work relationship with students. Second, time needs to be offered both inside and outside of the classroom for relationship building activities among students and between students and professors. Third, faculty need to intentionally step away from the instructional lead so that students can explore, make mistakes, regroup, and create on their own, together. Hess and McAvoy (2015) note that among the many benefits of collaboration is when participants demonstrate thoughtful suggestions and guidance aimed at full inclusion by other collaborators, redirecting erroneous judgments, and in other ways mitigating mistakes throughout the activity or process. For these reasons, collaboration today is rightly considered a best practice both in government processes and in the classroom. At the same time, it is important to offer a cautionary note to how easily collaborative practices can be commandeered rhetorically toward objectionable ends.

"We just need to collaborate" is routinely considered an invitation, but sometimes it is, in fact, an intentional move to steal control of a situation by preemptively chilling dissent. When used in this way, collaboration is manhandled in indiscriminate, even misleading ways. That is, when collaboration is named and used, absent the meaningful practices to enact it, it becomes simply a contrived, linguistic measure expressly designed to stymie meaningful engagement. This approach is all too common around difficult matters and proceeds by one or more people suggesting we should all go along, and get along. Those who refuse are summarily dismissed as apathetic or if they resist, they are labeled troublemakers. This mode of pseudo collaboration is common in governance, causing frustration, discouragement and anger (Nabatchi and Leighninger 2015). Under these circumstances, collaboration is just a shadow of its potential that refuses to adequately address a host of interaction variables including differentials in power, particularities of narratives, value-based distinctions, and unequal access to information.

For collaboration to deliver on its hopeful process and products students need time and spaces where partners struggle together, an ethical endeavor that signals a profound desire to communicate, even when it may be difficult and even when participants hold opposing positions (Jovanovic 2014). Discomfort can pave the way for necessary questions that in turn press for better articulation of values and reasons for collaborating.

Communication is risky business, as is collaboration, for it engenders our vulnerability to the expectations, views, and judgments of others. Philosopher Emmanuel Levinas writes, "Communication with the other can be transcendent only as a dangerous life, a fine risk to be run" (1998, 120). The rewards, however, can be significant. Being exposed to new ideas and giving up control over the outcome in deference to curiosity and possibility can lead to unexpected and gratifying experiences (Edgoose and Edgoose 2017). Students can learn about collaboration in the community, by attending charrettes, working and voting with participatory budgeting processes, and joining public deliberation opportunities. Doing so yields increased learning and increased participation in public life.

JOINING OTHERS IN RESISTANCE AND DISSENT

By funneling collaborative efforts toward other ends, namely social justice, students learn deeper communication lessons, namely how collective voices assert power through resistance and expressions of dissent. They can learn important communicative lessons from historically under-represented members of our communities who have amassed decades of practice in pushing against the status quo that has left them absent the same resources as their wealthier or whiter or more educated brethren. The benefits of authentic engagement in our democracy accrue for students when they are exposed to and practice modes of resistance reflective of an understanding of history and the political grounding for broad-based social movements.

Importantly, as students learn of the enduring racism—on campus and in the United States—by reading reports of and hearing stories of disillusionment, discrimination, isolation, and alienation, they are better prepared to understand that more than just talk is required to influence social change. For instance, when instruction provides details of the background and context for the rise of the Black Lives Matter movement that has included protests and sometimes violence, students gain a deeper appreciation for the lingering frustrations and inequities that have disproportionately impacted Blacks through racial profiling and lack of equal access to housing, medical attention, and education. Recognizing that persistent inequalities in the world remain, it is critical for teachers to inspire students to consider ways to correct those injustices. Higher education's mission—in tandem with democracy's goals—must pursue equality, justice, and freedom. Toward that end, students need to learn of the "structural conditions that promote or limit access to the promise of democracy" (Pitts and Jovanovic 2016, 15). And, if a show of collective resistance to existing policies or procedures is necessary to call attention to wrongs that those in seats of power would prefer to ignore, then students ought to know what options exist for demonstrating dissent.

That student activism is on the rise again is a hopeful sign for democracy (Jason 2018). A generation ago, political action focused primarily on advocating for equitable representation of minority groups, while current action is more inclined to concentrate on affecting systemic social change (Pousson and Myers 2019). Protest action, sit-ins, and civil disobedience that have long been used to call attention to causes are increasingly augmented by student action through participation on key campus committees. All of these forms of resistance operate to raise questions and disrupt past performance in favor of new ways of operation (Kezar and Maxey 2014). Further, Kezar and Maxey (2014) note that when faculty and staff work as allies with students to express resistance and dissent, foundational learning emerges around key activist strategies useful as well in public settings, including:

> (a) developing plans for change, (b) determining strategies, (c) learning approaches to consciousness raising, (d) learning the language of those in power and how "the system" works, (e) understanding mediation and negotiation, (f) using data to influence decision makers, and (g) navigating and overcoming obstacles in the change process. (33)

These skills can be integrated into course curricula in the study of communication activism, the rhetoric of social movements, and organizational communication. Indeed, student activism itself leads to important learning and civic competencies including commitment to social involvement (action), awareness of current, political issues (knowledge), and heightened self-confidence and leadership (skills) necessary to advocate for change (Biddix 2014). That is, when resistance and dissent are taught as democratic values, instructors can provide important pathways to lifelong civic engagement.

NEW LITERACIES

Given the pervasiveness of networked technologies in our society, it is likely that students will forge collaborations and enact their democratic values across embodied and virtual spaces. Research highlights the fundamental role of media, information, and digital literacies for increasing participation in public life because Internet access alone does not solve knowledge gaps (Hobbs 2010; Martens and Hobbs 2015; Shaw and Hargittai 2018). For this reason, new literacies are needed as a fundamental aspect of curriculum to increase students' agency.

Students need knowledge and skills that afford a threefold approach to participation in public life: becoming informed, debating ideas, and taking action (Gordon et al. 2013). Also, students should understand how political, economic, and sociotechnical factors intersect in networked public spheres. Teaching new literacies within a critical framework can leverage their ability to influence public discourse. The following sections focus on three emerging communication challenges to articulate an approach for deepening civic engagement in the communication curriculum.

BECOMING INFORMED AMID CHAOS AND CONFUSION

Disinformation is not new; however, in the United States, the problem reached staggering levels after the 2016 presidential election that demanded a response from educators to help students navigate this new context. A study measuring the level of exposure to fake news among 1,208 participants estimated that the average American adult read and remembered at least one false story (Allcott and Gentzkow 2017). Despite growing awareness of the problem, the landscape of disinformation has not improved much since 2016. For instance, COVID–19 brought one of the biggest challenges fact-checkers have ever faced (Suárez 2020), which poses severe risks to public health.

False information spreads mainly through the Internet, which affects students because they are more likely to learn about the world through new media than traditional sources (Gasser et al. 2012). Young people's time in front of screens, however, does not necessarily improve their evaluative skills. In one study, almost 8,000 students from middle and high school, as well as college, completed 56 tasks designed to test their ability to assess the quality of online information (McGrew et al. 2017). The results revealed a lack of preparedness in all educational levels.

Teaching students how to identify trustworthy information is a fundamental step to foster civic engagement. Pairing these skills with a contextual perspective of why and how fake news spreads can leverage students' ability to influence public discourses. Circulating false information is a political strategy for making quality information unusable (Tufekci 2017). Chaos and confusion become the alternative to traditional forms of censorship in a media environment that makes it almost impossible to suppress messages. The business model of social media platforms also reinforces the problem because it favors user engagement over quality information (Lazer et al. 2018). Finally, fast-paced technological advancements automatize the fabrication of stories (Chesney and Citron 2018). Therefore, understanding the imperatives that contribute to online disinformation allows students to identify intervention points and become vocal advocates for political and social changes.

ENGAGING WITH DEBATES IN POLARIZED CONTEXTS

A high-choice media environment can enable echo chambers (Sunstein 2017) and filter bubbles (Pariser 2012) that polarize political conversations. Greater interest in politics and diversity in media consumption can reduce the likelihood of being in an echo-chamber (Dubois and Blank 2018), so instructors need to encourage learners to seek information that expands their worldviews. Students also need skills to engage with debates in polarized contexts. Knowing "how context, audience, and identity intersect is one of the central challenges people face in learning how to navigate social media" (boyd 2014, 30). The Internet blurs divisions between producers and audiences, making it harder to understand who is interacting with online information. Besides, it allows people from distinct social circles (family, friends, and co-workers) to be part of the same virtual spaces, which increases the chances of different social norms/identities clashing (boyd 2014). Communication classrooms should be spaces where students learn to navigate these tensions so they can thrive when finding common ground, and grow when negotiating differences through dialogue.

Pushing learners to critically analyze networked public spheres also enables them to understand the risks associated with their online activities. Renee Hobbs (2010) stresses that "literacy competencies are not only needed to strengthen people's capacity for engaging with information but also for addressing potential risks associated with mass media and digital media" (29). Most websites and apps profit from personal data collection; however, privacy agreements are far from clear or straightforward (Chee et al. 2012). In addition to corporate monitoring, online environments offer the potential for permanent government and peer surveillance (de Souza e Silva and Frith 2012). Also, political retaliation can take the form of doxing or bullying that can cause mental, social, and economic harm (Tufekci 2017). These concerns are particularly pressing for civic engagement courses because of the inherently controversial nature of the topic and the current polarized state of political discussions.

USING DIGITAL MEDIA TO FOSTER ACTIVISM

Civic engagement is taking place across embodied and virtual realities. Many social movements have capitalized on digital technologies for communication and coordination since the popularization of smartphones. The Internet emphasizes visual messages, so students need to learn multimedia skills to communicate not only through written language but also via images and sounds if they want to fully engage in the civic life of their communities (Hobbs 2010). Attention is the fuel for social movements (Tufekci 2017), so these skills can also leverage the power of communities and foster collective action.

It is imperative to teach multimedia production alongside a critical view of the role that technologies have in promoting social change. Students might come to the classroom with a *techno-deterministic perspective* (Slack and Wise 2005), and they might think that technological developments will determine the course of events in society. They might also bring the opposite belief that *culture determines* the fate of humanity regardless of other factors (Slack and Wise 2005). In this case, they may overlook aspects of how the Internet redefines the landscape for civic engagement. Encouraging students to analyze technological uses and affordances within specific contexts (Barney 2004) can avoid deterministic traps.

ADAPTING AND CONNECTING THE CURRICULUM TO FOCUS ON JUSTICE

In 2020, the rapid spread of the COVID-19 virus into a worldwide pandemic demonstrated that challenges come not only from evolving technologies but also from unknown forces in our social world. The economic, health, political, social, and technological features of everyone's lives are so intertwined that disruption to one inevitably impacts the others. Thus, students need to be prepared to adapt and connect communication to advance justice no matter the circumstances they confront. Practical engagement with digital tools and a critical societal outlook remain central foundations for strong civic engagement around which curriculum can pivot. In particular, valuable, critical possibilities for expanding student civic engagement grow by combining community and new literacies to advance student agency that is ethical, active, and in solidarity with others.

For Generation Z students, mastering the logic of digital communication's potential is critical, as one of many possibilities in a civic engagement toolbox, along with building relationships and alliances, to instigate and sustain social change. Voting and offering service to others are critical engagement actions, yet alone are insufficient to uphold democracy. That is, students need introduction to the basics of in-person actions and digital engagement as well as exposure to other, admittedly more time-consuming civic and public actions. For instance, students need guidance in how to introduce a bill, how to develop strategies to enact policy changes, how to navigate the structure of governance for organizations, and how to work with or resist the decisions of elected officials.

Forming unlikely alliances across ideological and identity-based boundaries has become a clarion call against the polarized political context which Generation Z has seen operate without much success. The success stories deserve airing, where seemingly disparate views converge to address critical areas of concern like improving automobile safety, fighting corporate welfare, protecting children from commercialism, bolstering civic education in schools, and protecting public lands (Nader 2014). What is possible—cooperation and unlikely alliances—is neither easy nor guaranteed, but still possible, and an avenue for civic engagement ripe for Generation Z.

In face-to-face interactions, students can be encouraged to join with others who may be older, younger, of a different race, and of a different social class to better understand a variety of perspectives that demonstrate the power of multicultural, multigenerational alliances. Grassroots organizers suggest, and their allies agree, that when we support the leadership of those who have historically been dismissed or silenced by institutions of power, such as the homeless, minority groups, and people with disabilities, greater opportunity exists to push forward agendas for meaningful social change (Tompkins 2009). In digital arenas, instead of mimicking social media algorithms that reinforce existing patterns of information exposure, students can actively investigate and interact with people and groups they do not already endorse.

CONCLUSION

The cascade of crises that Generation Z has endured could easily induce timidity. In times of insecurity and danger, people naturally become more risk-averse and reluctant to initiate change. The portrait of Generation Z presents more subtle contours than fear-induced political paralysis or apathy. They express enthusiasm toward social justice measures that would advance causes related to values such as equality and diversity. But they encounter difficulty in putting these commitments into action, as they may not have developed sufficient community literacy to navigate the avenues for change.

Given the discipline's historic connections with developing civic virtues, communication studies educators can broaden students' capacities to generate change. Communicating across differences in backgrounds and identities will open possibilities for learning new means of expression from people who have had to develop innovative ways to navigate systems designed to silence them. Expanding the communicative toolbox for activism will involve leveraging the technological interests and facility with technological tools that characterize Generation Z as digital natives. Instead of lamenting the alleged erosion of interpersonal skills attendant to digital technologies (Turkle 2011), educators can channel technological affinity into deeper collaborations directed toward energizing activism. The speed and reach of digital communication offer possibilities for large-scale mobilization far beyond traditional mass media (Castells 2015).

Admittedly, Generation Z students exhibit some trepidation about academic rigor and have recorded much higher rates of mental health challenges than previous generations (Twenge 2017). Thus, embracing the precarity of robust, substantive collaborative practices that reveal the challenging work involved in collective action may require unaccustomed effort. Future investigations should prioritize developing and assessing activities that treat the characteristics of Generation Z students as resources to build upon rather than as deficits to criticize and "fix." Subsequent studies can devote particular attention to building student confidence by helping them find avenues for expressing their views in public forums and transforming their passionate beliefs into practical actions. An important component of this future work will be acknowledging crisis-induced vulnerability as a stimulus for building strength (Brown 2012), especially through collaborative action. Perhaps developing greater skills at navigating democratic processes and using digital technologies in the service of advocacy will build more willingness to forge ahead despite resistance that can help students become more resilient when faced with the prospect of momentary failure.

REFERENCES

Allcott, Hunt, and Matthew Gentzkow. 2017. "Social Media and Fake News in the 2016 Election." *The Journal of Economic Perspectives* 31 (2): 211–236. DOI: 10.1257/jep.31.2.211.

Anderson, Monica, and Andrew Perrin. 2018. "Nearly One-in-Five Teens Can't Always Finish their Homework Because of the Digital Divide." *Pew Research Center*. Last Modified October 26, 2018. https://www.pewresearch.org/fact-tank/2018/10/26/nearly-one-in-five-teens-cant-always-finish-their-homework-because-of-the-digital-divide/.

Atay, Ahmet, and Mary Z. Ashlock. 2018. *Millennial Culture and Communication Pedagogies: Narratives from the Classroom and Higher Education*. Lanham, MD: Lexington Books.

Baldwin, James. 1963. "A Talk to Teachers." *The Saturday Review*, December 21, 1963, pp. 42–44. https://www.unz.com/print/SaturdayRev-1963dec21-00042.

Barney, Darin. 2004. *The Network Society*. Cambridge: Polity Press.

Biddix, J. Patrick. 2014. "Development Through Dissent: Campus Activism as Civic Learning." *New Directions for Higher Education* 167: 73–85.

boyd, danah. 2014. *It's Complicated: The Social Lives of Networked Teens*. New Haven: Yale University Press.

Boyte, Harry C. 2015. *Democracy's Education: Public Work, Citizenship, and the Future of Colleges and Universities*. Nashville, TN: Vanderbilt University.

Britt, Lori. 2014. "The Collaborative Benefits of Service-Learning." *Partnerships: A Journal of Service-Learning and Civic Engagement* 5 (1): 51–71.

Brown, Brené. 2012. *Daring Greatly: How the Courage to Be Vulnerable Transforms the Way We Live, Love, Parent, and Lead*. New York: Avery.

Brown, Peter C., Henry L. Roediger, and Mark A. McDaniel. 2014. *Make It Stick: The Science of Successful Learning*. Cambridge: Belknap.

Castells, Manuel. 2015. *Networks of Outrage and Hope: Social Movements in the Internet Age*. Cambridge: Polity.

Chee, Florence M., Nicholas T. Taylor, and Suzanne de Castell. 2012. "Re-Mediating Research Ethics: End-User License Agreements in Online Games." *Bulletin of Science, Technology and Society* 32 (6): 497–506. Accessed May 25, 2020. DOI: 10.1177/0270467612469074.

Chesney, Bobby, and Danielle Citron. 2019. "Deep Fakes: A Looming Challenge for Privacy, Democracy, and National Security." *California Law Review* 107 (6): 1753–1819. Accessed May 25, 2020. DOI: 10.15779/Z38RV0D15J.

de Souza e Silva, Adriana, and Jordan Frith. 2012. *Mobile Interfaces in Public Spaces: Locational Privacy, Control, and Urban Sociability*. New York: Routledge.

Dewey, John. 2015. *Experience and Education*. New York: Free Press. (Originally published 1938).

Dimock, Michael. 2019. "Defining Generations: Where Millennials End and Generation Z Begins." *Pew Research Center*. Last Modified January 17, 2019. http://www.pewresearch.org/fact-tank/2019/01/17/where-millennials-end-and-generation-z-begins/.

Dubois, Elizabeth, and Grant Blank. 2018. "The Echo Chamber is Overstated: The Moderating Effect of Political Interest and Diverse Media." *Information, Communication and Society* 21 (5): 729–745. Accessed May 25, 2020. DOI: 10.1080/1369118X.2018.1428656.

Duckworth, Angela. 2016. *Grit: The Power of Passion and Perseverance.* New York: Scribner.

Edgoose, Jennifer Y. C., and Julian M. Edgoose. 2017. "Finding Hope in the Face-to-Face." *Annals of Family Medicine* 15 (3): 272–274. DOI: 10.1370/afm.2076.

France, Alan. 2007. *Understanding Youth in Late Modernity.* Maidenhead: Open University Press.

Freire, Paulo. 1997. *Pedagogy of the Oppressed.* New York: Continuum. (Originally published 1970).

Frey, Lawrence R., and Kevin M. Carragee. 2007. *Communication Activism: Communication for Social Change* (Vol. 1). Cresskill, NJ: Hampton Press.

Gasser, Urs, Sandra C. Cortesi, Momin Malik, and Ashley Lee. 2012. *Youth and Digital Media: From Credibility to Information Quality.* Cambridge: The Berkman Center for Internet and Society.

Giroux, Henry A. 2012. *Education and the Crisis of Public Values.* New York: Peter Lang.

Gordon, Eric, Jesse Baldwin-Philippi, and Martina Balestra. 2013. *Why We Engage: How Theories of Human Behavior Contribute to Our Understanding of Civic Engagement in a Digital Era.* Cambridge: The Berkman Center for Internet and Society.

Hess, Diana E., and Paula McAvoy. 2015. *The Political Classroom: Evidence and Ethics in Democratic Education.* New York: Routledge.

Hobbs, Renee. 2010. *Digital and Media Literacy: A Plan of Action.* Washington, D.C.: Aspen Institute.

hooks, bell. 2017. "Confronting Class in the Classroom." In *The Critical Pedagogy Reader* (3rd Ed.), edited by Antonia Darder, Rodolfo D. Torres, and Marta P. Baltodano, 181–187. New York: Routledge.

Jason, Zachary. 2018. "Student Activism 2.0: A Look Back at the History of Student Activism and Whether Today's Protesters are Making a Difference." *Ed. Magazine.* https://www.gse.harvard.edu/news/ed/18/08/student-activism-20.

Jovanovic, Spoma. 2014. "Struggling Together: Collaboration as Ethical Practice." *Partnerships: A Journal of Service-Learning and Civic Engagement* 5 (1): 1–3.

Kalogeropoulos, Antonis. 2019. "How Younger Generations Consume News Differently." *Reuters Institute and University of Oxford.* Last Modified September, 2019. http://www.digitalnewsreport.org/survey/2019/how-younger-generations-consume-news-differently/.

Kezar, Adrianna, and Dan Maxey. 2014. "Collective Action on Campus Toward Student Development and Democratic Engagement." *New Directions for Higher Education* 167: 31–41.

Lane, Daniel S., Vishnupriya Das, and Dan Hiaeshutter-Rice. 2019. "Civic Laboratories: Youth Political Expression in Anonymous, Ephemeral, Geo-Bounded

Social Media." *Information, Communication and Society* 22 (14): 2171–2186. Accessed May 25, 2020. DOI: 10.1080/1369118X.2018.1477973.

Lazer, David M. J., Matthew A. Baum, Yochai Benkler, Adam J. Berinsky, Kelly M. Greenhill, Filippo Menczer, Miriam J. Metzger, Brendan Nyhan, Gordon Pennycook, David Rothschild, Michael Schudson, Steven A. Sloman, Cass R. Sunstein, Emily A. Thorson, Duncan J. Watts, and Jonathan L. Zittrain. 2018. "The Science of Fake News: Addressing Fake News Requires a Multidisciplinary Effort." *Science* 359 (6380): 1094–1096. Accessed May 25, 2020. DOI: 10.1126/science.aao2998.

Levinas, Emmanuel. 1998. *Otherwise Than Being or Beyond Essence*. Translated by Alphonso Lingis. Pittsburgh: Duquesne University Press.

Levitz, Eric. 2019. "American Exceptionalism is a Dangerous Myth." *New York Magazine*. Last Modified January 2, 2019. https://nymag.com/intelligencer/2019/01/american-exceptionalism-is-a-dangerous-myth.html.

Livingstone, Sonia. 2018. Review of *iGen: Why Today's Super-Connected Kids are Growing Up Less Rebellious, More Tolerant, Less Happy, and Completely Unprepared for Adulthood* by Jean Twenge. *Journal of Children and Media* 12 (1): 118–123. Accessed May 25, 2020. DOI: 10.1080/17482798.2017.1417091.

Martens, Hans, and Renee Hobbs. 2015. "How Media Literacy Supports Civic Engagement in a Digital Age." *Atlantic Journal of Communication* 23 (2): 120–137. Accessed May 25, 2020. DOI: 10.1080/15456870.2014.961636.

McGrew, Sarah, Teresa Ortega, Joel Breakstone, and Sam Wineburg. 2017. "The Challenge that's Bigger than Fake News: Civic Reasoning in a Social Media Environment." *American Educator* 41 (3): 4–9. Accessed May 25, 2020. https://files.eric.ed.gov/fulltext/EJ1156387.pdf.

Morris, Charles E., and Stephen H. Browne. 2013. *Readings on the Rhetoric of Social Protest* (3rd Ed.). State College, PA: Strata.

Nader, Ralph. 2014. *Unstoppable*. New York: Nation Books.

Pariser, Eli. 2012. *The Filter Bubble: How the New Personalized Web is Changing What We Read and How We Think*. New York: Penguin Books.

Pew Research Center. 2013. "A Closer Look at Generations and Cell Phone Ownership." *Pew Research Center*. Last Modified February 3, 2011. https://www.pewresearch.org/internet/2011/02/03/a-closer-look-at-generations-and-cell-phone-ownership/.

Pitts, Lewis, and Spoma Jovanovic, S. 2016. "What Will our Council Do in a Post-Truth Era?" *Greensboro News & Record*. Last Modified December 11, 2016. https://greensboro.com/opinion/columns/lewis-pitts-and-spoma-jovanovic-what-will-our-council-do-in-a-post-truth-era/article_75ec8f8e-59bf-503b-91b4-2f2d23474a11.html.

Pousson, J. Mark, and Karen A. Myers. 2019. "College Students with Disabilities and Their Activism." In *Student Activism in the Academy: Its Struggles and Promise*, edited by Joseph L. DeVitis and Pietro A. Sasso, 205–219. Gorham, ME: Myers Education Press.

Rideout, Victoria J., Ulla G. Foehr, and Donald F. Roberts. 2010. *Generation M2: Media in the Lives of 8–18-Year Olds*. Menlo Park: Kaiser Family Foundation.

Rue, Penny. 2018. "Make Way, Millennials, Here Comes Gen Z." *About Campus* 23 (3): 5–12. Accessed May 25, 2020. DOI: 10.1177/1086482218804251.

Schwartzman, Roy. 2020. "Performing Pandemic Pedagogy." *Communication Education* 69 (4): 502–517. DOI: 10.1080/03634523.2020.1804602.

Seemiller, Corey, and Meghan Grace. 2016. *Generation Z Goes to College* (1st Ed.). San Francisco, CA: Jossey Bass.

Shaw, Aaron, and Eszter Hargittai. 2018. "The Pipeline of Online Participation Inequalities: The Case of Wikipedia Editing." *Journal of Communication* 68 (1): 143–168. Accessed May 25, 2020. DOI: 10.1093/joc/jqx003.

Slack, Jennifer Daryl, and J. Macgregor Wise. 2005. *Culture+Technology: A Primer*. New York: Peter Lang Publishing.

Suárez, Eduardo. 2020. "How Fact-Checkers Are Fighting Coronavirus Misinformation Worldwide." *Reuters Institute*. Last Modified March 31, 2020. https://reutersinstitute.politics.ox.ac.uk/risj-review/how-fact-checkers-are-fighting-coronavirus-misinformation-worldwide.

Sunstein, Cass R. 2018. *#Republic: Divided Democracy in the Age of Social Media*. Princeton: Princeton University Press.

Tedford, Thomas L., and Dale A. Herbeck. 2017. *Freedom of Speech in the U.S.* (8th Ed.). State College, PA: Strata.

Tompkins, Phillip K. 2009. *Who is My Neighbor? Communicating and Organizing to End Homelessness*. Boulder, CO: Paradigm Publishers.

Tufekci, Zeynep. 2017. *Twitter and Tear Gas: The Power and Fragility of Networked Protest*. Yale: Yale University Press.

Turkle, Sherry. 2011. *Alone Together: Why We Expect More from Technology and Less from Each Other*. New York: Basic Books.

Turner, Anthony. 2015. "Generation Z: Technology and Social Interest." *The Journal of Individual Psychology* 71 (2): 103–113. Accessed May 25, 2020. DOI: 10.1353/jip.2015.0021.

Twenge, Jean M. 2017. *iGen: Why Today's Super-Connected Kids are Growing Up Less Rebellious, More Tolerant, Less Happy-and Completely Unprepared for Adulthood*. New York, NY: Atria.

Wells, Chris. 2015. *The Civic Organization and the Digital Citizen: Communicating Engagement in a Networked Age*. Oxford: Oxford University Press.

Bibliography

Abramovich, Samuel, Christian Schunn, and Ross Mitsuo Higashi. 2013. "Are Badges Useful in Education?: It Depends Upon the Type of Badge and Expertise of Learner." *Educational Technology Research and Development* 61 (2): 217–232. DOI: 10.1007/s11423-013-9289-2.

Adams, Nan B. 2004. "Digital Intelligence Fostered by Technology." *Journal of Technology Studies* 30 (2): 93–97. DOI: 10.21061/jots.v30i2.a.5.

Ahmed, Wondimu, Alexander Minnaert, Greetje van der Werf, and Hans Kuyper. 2010. "Perceived Social Support and Early Adolescents' Achievement: The Mediational Roles of Motivational Beliefs and Emotions." *Journal of Youth and Adolescence* 39 (1): 36–46. DOI: 10.1007/s10964-008-9367-7.

Allcott, Hunt, and Matthew Gentzkow. 2017. "Social Media and Fake News in the 2016 Election." *The Journal of Economic Perspectives* 31 (2): 211–236. DOI: 10.1257/jep.31.2.211.

Altman, Steven A. 2020. "Will Covid-19 Have a Lasting Impact on Globalization?" *Harvard Business Review*, May 20, 2020. https://hbr.org/2020/05/will-covid-19-have-a-lasting-impact-on-globalization.

American Psychological Association. 2020. "Building Your Resilience." Accessed July 21, 2020. http://www.apa.org/topics/resilience.

Ames, Carole, and Jenner J. Archer. 1988. "Achievement Goals in the Classroom: Students' Learning Strategies and Motivational Processes." *Journal of Educational Psychology* 80 (3): 260–267. DOI: 10.1037/0022-0663.80.3.260.

Anderson, Craig, Akiko Shibuya, Nobuko Ihori, Edward L. Swing, Brad J. Bushman, Akira Sakamoto, Hannah R. Rothstein, and Muniba Saleem. 2010. "Violent Video Game Effects on Aggression, Empathy, and Prosocial Behavior in Eastern and Western Countries: A Meta-Analytic Review." *Psychological Bulletin* 136 (2): 151–173. DOI: 10.1037/a0018251.

Anderson, Lorin W., and David R. Krathwohl (Eds). 2001. *A Taxonomy for Learning, Teaching, and Assessing: A Revision of Bloom's Taxonomy of Educational Objectives*. New York: Longman.

Anderson, Monica, and Andrew Perrin. 2018. "Nearly One-in-Five Teens Can't Always Finish Their Homework Because of the Digital Divide." *Pew Research Center.* Last Modified October 26, 2018. https://www.pewresearch.org/fact-tank/2018/10/26/nearly-one-in-five-teens-cant-always-finish-their-homework-because-of-the-digital-divide/.

Anderson, Monica, and Jingjing Jiang. 2018. "Teens, Social Media & Technology 2018." *Pew Research Center.* Last Modified May 31, 2018. https://www.pewresearch.org/internet/2018/05/31/teens-social-media-technology-2018/.

Andrews, Jane, and Helen Higson. 2008. "Graduate Employability, 'Soft Skills' Versus 'Hard' Business Knowledge: A European Study." *Higher Education in Europe* 33 (4): 411–422. DOI: 10.1080/03797720802552267.

Appleby, Drew. "The Soft Skills College Students Need to Succeed Now and in the Future: Transferable Skills for Success in College and the Workplace." *American Psychological Association,* September 2017. https://www.apa.org/ed/precollege/psn/2017/09/soft-skills.

Arnett, Ronald. 2008. "Pointing the Way to Communication Ethics Theory: The Life-Giving Gift of Acknowledgment." *Review of Communication* 8 (1): 21–28.

Arseven, Ilami. 2018. "The Use of Qualitative Case Studies as an Experiential Teaching Method in the Training of Pre-Service Teachers." *International Journal of Higher Education* 7 (1): 111–125.

Asikainen, Henna, Jaanika Blomster, and Viivi Virtanen. 2018. "From Functioning Communality to Hostile Behaviour: Students' and Teachers' Experiences of the Teacher-Student Relationship in the Academic Community." *Journal of Further and Higher Education* 42: 633–648. DOI: 10.1080/0309877X.2017.1302566.

Assor, Avi, and Haya Kaplan. 2001. "Mapping the Domain of Autonomy Support: Five Important Ways to Enhance or Undermine Students' Experience of Autonomy in Learning." In *Trends and Prospects in Motivation Research,* edited by Anastasia Efklides, Richard Sorrentino, and Julius Kuhl, 99–118. Dordrecht, The Netherlands: Kluwer.

Assor, Avi, Haya Kaplan, and Guy Roth. 2002. "Choice is Good, But Relevance is Excellent: Autonomy-Enhancing and Suppressing Teacher Behaviours Predicting Students' Engagement in Schoolwork." *British Journal of Educational Psychology* 72 (2): 261–278. DOI: 10.1348/000709902158883.

Atay, Ahmet, and Mary Z. Ashlock. 2018. *Millennial Culture and Communication Pedagogies: Narratives from the Classroom and Higher Education.* Lanham, MD: Lexington Books.

Baldwin, James. 1963. "A Talk to Teachers." *The Saturday Review,* December 21, 1963, pp. 42–44. https://www.unz.com/print/SaturdayRev-1963dec21-00042.

Barak, Miri. 2018. "Are Digital Natives Open to Change? Examining Flexible Thinking and Resistance to Change." *Computer & Education* 121: 115–123. DOI: 10.1016/j.compedu.2018.01.016.

Barak, Miri, Alberta Lipson, and Steven Lerman. 2006. "Wireless Laptops as Means for Promoting Active Learning in Large Lecture Halls." *Journal of Research on Technology in Education* 38 (3): 245–263. DOI: 10.1080/15391523.2006.10782459.

Barney, Darin. 2004. *The Network Society.* Cambridge: Polity Press.

Bibliography

Bauer-Wolf, Jeremy. 2019. "Survey: Employers Want 'Soft Skills' from Graduates." *Inside Higher Ed.* https://www.insidehighered.com/quicktakes/2019/01/17/survey-employers-want-soft-skills-graduates.

Baumeister, Roy F., and Mark R. Leary. 1995. "The Need to Belong: Desire for Interpersonal Attachments as a Fundamental Human Motivation." *Psychological Bulletin* 117 (3): 497–529. DOI: 10.1037/0033-2909.117.3.497.

Beall, Melissa, Jennifer Gill-Rosier, Jeanine Tate, and Amy Matten. 2008. "State of the Context: Listening in Education." *International Journal of Listening* 22 (2): 123–132. DOI: 10.1080/10904010802174826.

Belmont, Michael J., Ellen A. Skinner, James G. Wellborn, and James P. Connell. 1992. *Two Measures of Teacher Provision of Involvement, Structure, and Autonomy Support (Technical Report.)* Rochester, NY: University of Rochester.

Berry, Gregory R. 2016. "Can Computer-Mediated Asynchronous Communication Improve Team Processes and Decision Making? Learning from the Management Literature." *The Journal of Business Communication (1973)*, September. DOI: 10.1177/0021943606292352.

Bethune, Sophie. "Gen Z More Likely to Report Mental Health Concerns." Last Updated January 2019. https://www.apa.org/monitor/2019/01/gen-z.

Biddix, J. Patrick. 2014. "Development Through Dissent: Campus Activism as Civic Learning." *New Directions for Higher Education* 167: 73–85.

Bodie, G. D., D. L. Worthington, and C. C. Gearhart. 2013. "The Listening Styles Profile-Revised (LSP-R): A Scale Revision and Evidence for Validity." *Communication Quarterly* 61 (1): 72–90. DOI: 10.1080/01463373.2012.720343.

Bodie, Graham. 2011. "The Revised Listening Concepts Inventory (LCI-R): Assessing Individual and Situational Differences in the Conceptualization of Listening." *Imagination, Cognition and Personality* 30 (3): 301–339.

Boehrer, John. 1994. "On Teaching a Case." *International Studies Notes* 19 (2): 14–20.

Boggiano, Ann K., Cheryl Flink, Ann Shields, Aubyn Seelbach, and Marty Barrett. 1993. "Use of Techniques Promoting Students' Self-Determination: Effects on Students' Analytic Problem-Solving Skills." *Motivation and Emotion* 17: 319–336. DOI: 10.1007/bf00992323.

Bond, Christopher D. 2012. "An Overview of Best Practices to Teach Listening Skills." *International Journal of Listening* 26 (2): 61–63. DOI: 10.1080/10904018.2012.677660.

Bonney, Kevin. 2015. "Case Study Teaching Method Improves Performance and Perceptions of Learning Gains." *Journal of Microbiology & Biology Education* 16 (1): 21–28.

Boyd, Danah. 2014. *It's Complicated: The Social Lives of Networked Teens*. New Haven: Yale University Press.

Boyte, Harry C. 2015. *Democracy's Education: Public work, Citizenship, and the Future of Colleges and Universities*. Nashville, TN: Vanderbilt University.

Britt, Lori. 2014. "The Collaborative Benefits of Service-Learning." *Partnerships: A Journal of Service-Learning and Civic Engagement* 5 (1): 51–71.

Brockbank, Anne, and Ian McGill. 1998. *Facilitating Reflective Learning in Higher Education*. Philadelphia, PA: Society for Research into Higher Education & Open University Press.

Brown, Brené. 2012. *Daring Greatly: How the Courage to Be Vulnerable Transforms the Way We Live, Love, Parent, and Lead.* New York: Avery.

Brown, Peter C., Henry L. Roediger, and Mark A. McDaniel. 2014. *Make It Stick: The Science of Successful Learning.* Cambridge: Belknap.

Buhs, Eric S. 2005. "Peer Rejection, Negative Peer Treatment, and School Adjustment: Self-Concept and Classroom Engagement as Mediating Processes." *Journal of School Psychology* 43 (5): 407–424. DOI: 10.1016/j.jsp.2005.09.001.

Burgoon, Judee K. 1993. "Interpersonal Expectations, Expectancy Violations, and Emotional Communication." *Journal of Language and Social Psychology* 12 (1–2): 30–48. DOI: 10.1177/0261927X93121003.

Burgoon, Judee K., and Stephen B. Jones. 1976. "Toward a Theory of Personal Space Expectations and Their Violations." *Human Communication Research* 2 (2): 131–146. DOI: 10.1111/j.1468-2958.1976.tb00706.x.

Buskirk-Cohen, Allison, and Aria Plants. 2019. "Caring About Success: Students' Perceptions of Professors' Caring Matters More Than Grit." *International Journal of Teaching and Learning in Higher Education* 31 (1): 108–114. https://files.eric.ed.gov/fulltext/EJ1206948.pdf.

Cameron, Elizabeth, and Marisa A. Pagnattaro. 2017. "Beyond Millennials: Engaging Generation Z in Business Law Classes." *Journal of Legal Studies Education* 34 (2): 317–324. DOI: 10.1111/jlse.12064.

Carder, Linda, Patricia Willingham, and David Bibb. 2001. "Case-Based, Problem-Based Learning: Information Literacy for the Real World." *Research Strategies* 18 (3): 181–190.

Castells, Manuel. 2015. *Networks of Outrage and Hope: Social Movements in the Internet Age.* Cambridge: Polity.

CDC. 2021. "Operational Considerations for Schools." https://www.cdc.gov/coronavirus/2019-ncov/global-covid-19/schools.html.

Cennamo, Lucy, and Dianne Gardner. 2008. "Generational Differences in Work Values, Outcomes and Person-Organisation Values Fit." Edited by Keith Macky, Dianne Gardner, and Stewart Forsyth. *Journal of Managerial Psychology* 23 (8): 891–906. DOI: 10.1108/02683940810904385.

Centers for Disease Control and Prevention. 2020. "Mental Health, Substance Use, and Suicidal Ideation During the COVID-19 Pandemic – United States, June 24–30, 2020." August 13, 2020. https://www.cdc.gov/mmwr/volumes/69/wr/mm6932a1.htm.

Chang, Bo. 2019. "Reflection in Learning." *Online Learning* 23 (1): 95–110.

Chee, Florence M., Nicholas T. Taylor, and Suzanne de Castell. 2012. "Re-Mediating Research Ethics: End-User License Agreements in Online Games." *Bulletin of Science, Technology and Society* 32 (6): 497–506. Accessed May 25, 2020. DOI: 10.1177/0270467612469074.

Chesney, Bobby, and Danielle Citron. 2019. "Deep Fakes: A Looming Challenge for Privacy, Democracy, and National Security." *California Law Review* 107 (6): 1753–1819. Accessed May 25, 2020. DOI: 10.15779/Z38RV0D15J.

Chicca, Jennifer, and Teresa Shellenbarger. 2018. "Connecting with Generation Z: Approaches in Nursing Education." *Teaching and Learning in Nursing* 13 (3): 180–184. DOI: 10.1016/j.teln.2018.03.008.

Clarkson, Natalie. 2018. "How is Mental Health Affecting Generation Z's Ability to Achieve?" *Virgin Group*, January 18.

Coates, Hamish. 2007. "A Model of Online and General Campus-Based Student Engagement." *Assessment & Evaluation in Higher Education* 32 (2): 121–141. DOI: 10.1080/02602930600801878.

Collaboration for Academic, Social, and Emotional Learning (CASEL). "CASEL's Widely Used Framework Identifies Five Core Competencies." Accessed June 25, 2020. https://casel.org/what-is-sel/.

Connell, James P., and James G. Wellborn. 1990. "Competence, Autonomy and Relatedness: A Motivational Analysis of Self-System Processes." In *Minnesota Symposium on Child Psychology* 23, edited by Megan R. Gunnar and L. Alan Sroufe, 43–77. Hillsdale, NJ: Lawrence Erlbaum Associates, Inc.

Cooley, Sam, Victoria Burns, and Jennifer Cumming. 2015. "The Role of Outdoor Adventure Education in Facilitating Groupwork in Higher Education." *Higher Education* 69: 567–582. DOI: 10.1007/s10734-014-9791-4.

Coyle, K. J., and S. Bodor. 2020. "North American Association for Environmental Education and National Wildlife Federation: Guide to Advocating for Outdoor Classrooms in Coronavirus-Era School Reopening." https://www.nwf.org/-/media/Documents/PDFs/NWF-Reports/2020/COVID-19-Outdoor-Classroom-Policy-Guide.

Creswell, John W., and Cheryl N. Poth. 2016. *Qualitative Inquiry and Research Design: Choosing Among Five Approaches*. Thousand Oaks, CA: Sage Publications.

Creswell, John W., and Vicki Plano-Clark. 2006. *Designing and Conducting Mixed Methods Research*. Thousand Oaks, CA: Sage Publications. https://www.sagepub.com/sites/default/files/upm-binaries/10982_Chapter_4.pdf.

Cronon, William. 1998. "'Only Connect...' The Goals of a Liberal Education." *The American Scholar* 67 (4): 73–80.

Crowther, Emma, and Sarah Balliee. 2016. "A Method of Developing and Introducing Case-Based Learning to a Preclinical Veterinary Curriculum." *Anatomical Sciences Education* 9 (1): 80–89.

Daniels, Harvey, and Marilyn Bizar. 1998. *Methods That Matter: Six Structures for Best Practice Classrooms*. Portland, ME: Stenhouse.

Dannels, Deanna P. 2015. *8 Essential Questions Teachers Ask: A Guidebook for Communicating with Students*. New York: Oxford.

Davis, Barbara. 2009. *Tools for Teaching* (2nd Ed.). San Francisco: Jossey-Bass.

deCharms, R. Christopher. 1984. "Motivation Enhancement in Educational Settings." In *Research on Motivation in Education: Student Motivation* 1, edited by Russell Ames and Carole Ames, 275–310. Orlando, FL: Academic Press.

Deci, Edward L., Allan J. Schwartz, Louise Sheinman, and Richard M. Ryan. 1981. "An Instrument to Assess Adult's Orientations Toward Control Versus Autonomy in Children: Reflections on Intrinsic Motivation and Perceived Competence." *Journal of Educational Psychology* 73 (5): 642–650. DOI: 10.1037/0022-0663.73.5.642.

Deci, Edward L., and Richard M. Ryan. 1985. *Intrinsic Motivation and Self-Determination in Human Behavior*. New York: Plenum.

Deci, Edward L., and Richard M. Ryan. 2000. "The 'What' and 'Why' of Goal Pursuits: Human Needs and the Self-Determination of Behavior." *Psychological Inquiry* 11 (4): 227–268. DOI: 10.1207/S15327965PLI1104_01.

Deep Focus. 2015. "Deep Focus Cassandra Report: Gen Z Uncovers Massive Attitude Shifts Toward Money, Work and Communication Preferences." Accessed June 30, 2020. http://www.marketwired.com/press-release/deep-focus-cassandra-reprot-gen-z-uncovers-massisve-attitude-shifts-toward-money-work-2004889.htm.

Desai, Supriya, and Vishwanath Lele. 2017. "Correlating Internet, Social Networks and Workplace: A Case of Generation Z Students." *Journal of Commerce & Management Thought* 8 (4): 802–815.

de Souza e Silva, Adriana, and Jordan Frith. 2012. *Mobile Interfaces in Public Spaces: Locational Privacy, Control, and Urban Sociability.* New York: Routledge.

Dewey, John. 2015. *Experience and Education.* New York: Free Press. (Originally published 1938).

Dimock, Michael. 2019. "Defining Generations: Where Millennials End and Generation Z Begins." http://www.pewresearch.org/fact-tank/2019/01/17/where-millennials-end-and-generation-z-begins/.

Dismukes, R. Key, David Gaba, and Steven Howard. 2006. "So Many Roads: Facilitated Debriefing in Healthcare." *Simulation in Healthcare* 1 (1): 23–25.

Dixson, Marcia D. 2010. "Creating Effective Student Engagement in Online Classes: What Do Students Find Engaging?" *Journal of Scholarship of Teaching and Learning* 10 (1): 1–13.

Dixson, Marcia, Mackenzie Greenwell, Christie Rogers-Stacy, Tyson Weister, and Sara Lauer. 2016. "Nonverbal Immediacy Behaviors and Online Student Engagement: Bringing Past Instructional Research into the Present Virtual Classroom." *Communication Education* 66: 37–53. DOI: 10.1080/03634523.2016.1209222.

Dolby, Nadine. 2012. "There's No Learning When Nobody's Listening." *The Chronicle of Higher Education.* http://eres.regent.edu:2048/login?url=https://search-proquest-com.ezproxy.regent.edu/docview/1026558027?accountid=13479.

Donaghy, Roger. 2014. "Innovation Imperative: Meet Generation Z." Last Modified November 18, 2014. https://news.northeastern.edu/2014/11/18/innovation-imperative-meet-generation-z/.

Dori, Yehudit, Revital Tal, and Masha Tsaushu. 2003. "Teaching Biotechnology Through Case Studies: Can We Improve Higher Order Thinking Skills of Nonscience Majors?" *Science Education* 87 (6): 767–793.

Downs, Cal W., Paul Harper, and Gary Hunt. 1976. "Internships in Speech Communication." *Communication Education* 25 (4): 276–282. DOI: 10.1080/03634527609384641.

Dubois, Elizabeth, and Grant Blank. 2018. "The Echo Chamber is Overstated: The Moderating Effect of Political Interest and Diverse Media." *Information, Communication and Society* 21 (5): 729–745. Accessed May 25, 2020. DOI: 10.1080/1369118X.2018.1428656.

Duckworth, Angela. 2016. *Grit: The Power of Passion and Perseverance.* New York: Scribner.

Duran, Robert L., Lynne Kelly, and James A. Keaten. 2005. "College Faculty Use and Perceptions of Electronic Mail to Communicate with Students." *Communication Quarterly* 53 (2): 159–176. DOI: 10.1080/01463370500090118.

Durlak, Joseph, Roger P. Weissberg, Allison Dymnicki, Rebecca Taylor, and Kriston K. Schellinger. 2011. "The Impact of Enhancing Students' Social and Emotional Learning: A Meta-Analysis of School-Based Universal Interventions." *Child Development* 82 (1): 405–432. DOI: 10.1111/cdev.2011.82.issue-1.

Edgoose, Jennifer Y. C., and Julian M. Edgoose. 2017. "Finding Hope in the Face-to-Face." *Annals of Family Medicine* 15 (3): 272–274. DOI: 10.1370/afm.2076.

Elam, Elizabeth, and Harlan Spotts. 2004. "Achieving Marketing Curriculum Integration: A Live Case Study Approach." *Journal of Marketing Education* 26 (1): 50–65.

Elmore, Tim. 2014. "Homelanders: The Next Generation." Last Updated February 27, 2014. https://www.psychologytoday.com/us/blog/artificial-maturity/201402/homelanders-the-next-generation.

Elmore, Tim. 2017. *Marching Off the Map: Inspire Students to Navigate a Brand New World*. Atlanta: Poet Gardener Publishing.

Entertainment Software Association. 2019. "Essential Facts about the Computer and Video Game Industry." Accessed June 1, 2020. https://www.theesa.com/wp-content/uploads/2019/05/ESA_Essential_facts_2019_final.pdf.

Ferguson, Christopher J., and Adolfo Garza. 2011. "Call of (Civic) Duty: Action Games and Civic Behavior in a Large Sample of Youth." *Computers in Human Behavior* 27 (2): 770–775. DOI: 10.1016/j.chb.2010.10.026.

Ferguson, Christopher J., and Cheryl K. Olson. 2013. "Friends, Fun, Frustration and Fantasy: Child Motivations for Video Game Play." *Motivation and Emotion* 37 (1): 154–164. DOI: 10.1007/s11031-012-9284-7.

Finn, Jeremy D., and Donald A. Rock. 1997. "Academic Success Among Students at Risk for School Failure." *Journal of Applied Psychology* 82 (2): 221–234. DOI: 10.1037/0021-9010.82.2.221.

Firat, Mehmet. 2013. "Multitasking or Continuous Partial Attention: A Critical Bottleneck for Digital Natives." *Turkish Online Journal of Distance Education* 14 (1): Article 23. DOI: 10.17718/tojde.52102.

France, Alan. 2007. *Understanding Youth in Late Modernity*. Maidenhead: Open University Press.

Fratantuono, Michael. 1994. "Evaluating the Case Method." *International Studies Notes* 19 (2): 34–44.

Fredricks, Jennifer. 2014. *Eight Myths of Student Disengagement: Creating Classrooms of Deep Learning*. Thousand Oaks: Corwin Press.

Freire, Paulo. 1997. *Pedagogy of the Oppressed*. New York: Continuum. (Originally published 1970).

Frey, Lawrence R., and Kevin M. Carragee. 2007. *Communication Activism: Communication for Social Change* (Vol. 1). Cresskill, NJ: Hampton Press.

Fried, Carrie B. 2008. "In-Class Laptop Use and Its Effects on Student Learning." *Computers & Education* 50 (3): 906–914. DOI: 10.1016/j.compedu.2006.09.006.

Fry, Richard, and Kim Parker. 2018. "Early Benchmarks Show 'Post-Millennials' on Track to be Most Diverse, Best-Educated Generation Yet." *Pew Research Center*.

Last Modified November 15, 2018. Washington, D.C. https://www.pewsocialtrends.org/2018/11/15/early-benchmarks-show-post-millennials-on-track-to-be-most-diverse-best-educated-generation-yet/.

Frymier, Ann Bainbridge, and Marian L. Houser. 2000. "The Teacher-Student Relationship as an Interpersonal Relationship." *Communication Education* 49 (3): 207. DOI: 10.1080/03634520009379209.

Gallois, Cindy, Tania Ogay, and Howard Giles. 2005. "Theorizing About Intercultural Communication." In *Theorizing about Intercultural Communication*, edited by W. B. Gudykunst, 121–148. Thousand Oaks: Sage.

Gamble, Teri, and Michael Gamble. 2013. *Communication Works* (11th Ed.). New York: McGraw-Hill.

Gardner, Jolynn, Cynthia Ronzio, and Anastasia Snelling. 2018. "Transformational Learning in Undergraduate Public Health Education: Course Design for Generation Z." *Pedagogy in Health Promotion* 4 (2): 95–100. DOI: 10.1177/2373379917721722.

Gasser, Urs, Sandra C. Cortesi, Momin Malik, and Ashley Lee. 2012. *Youth and Digital Media: From Credibility to Information Quality*. Cambridge: The Berkman Center for Internet and Society.

Gay, Geneva. 2000. *Culturally Responsive Teaching*. New York: Teachers College Press.

Gayton, Jorge, and Beryl C. McEwen. 2007. "Effective Online Instructional and Assessment Strategies." *American Journal of Distance Education* 21 (3): 117–132. DOI: 10.1080/08923640701341653.

"Generation Z Goes to College: How They Compare to Previous Generations." 2018. *Lendkey*. Accessed July 20, 2020. https://www.lendkey.com/blog/paying-for-school/generation-z-goes-to-college-how-they-compare-to-previous-generations/.

Genota, Lauraine. 2018. "Why Generation Z Learners Prefer YouTube Lessons Over Printed Books; Video Learning Outranks Printed Books in Survey." *Education Week*. Last Modified September 11, 2018. https://www.edweek.org/ew/articles/2018/09/12/why-generation-z-learners-prefer-youtube-lessons.html.

George, Daniel R., Tomi D. Dreibelbis, and Betsy Aumiller. 2013. "How We Used Two Social Media Tools to Enhance Aspects of Active Learning During Lectures." *Medical Teacher* 35 (12): 985–988. DOI: 10.3109/0142159X.2013.818631.

Giddens, A. 1984. *The Constitution of Society: Outline of the Theory of Structuration*. Berkley, CA: University of California Press.

Giles, Howard. 1973. "Accent Mobility: A Model and Some Data." *Anthropological Linguistics* 15: 87–105.

Giroux, Henry A. 2012. *Education and the Crisis of Public Values*. New York: Peter Lang.

Giunta, Catherine. 2017. "An Emerging Awareness of Generation Z Students for Higher Education Professors." *Archives of Business Research* 5 (4): 90–104. DOI: 10.14738/abr.54.2962.

Goodboy, Alan K., and San Bolkan. 2009. "College Teacher Misbehaviors: Direct and Indirect Effects on Student Communication Behavior and Traditional Learning Outcomes." *Western Journal of Communication* 73 (2): 204–219. DOI: 10.1080/10570310902856089.

Gordon, Eric, Jesse Baldwin-Philippi, and Martina Balestra. 2013. *Why We Engage: How Theories of Human Behavior Contribute to Our Understanding of Civic Engagement in a Digital Era.* Cambridge: The Berkman Center for Internet and Society.

Granic, Isabela, Adam Lobel, and Rutger CME Engels. 2014. "The Benefits of Playing Video Games." *American Psychologist* 69 (1): 66–78. DOI: 10.1037/a0034857.

Grant, Janie, and Tim Grace. 2019. "Use of Diverse Case Studies in an Undergraduate Research Methods and Statistics Course." *Psychology Learning & Teaching* 18 (2): 197–211.

Grant, Richard. 1997. "A Claim for the Case Method in the Teaching of Geography." *Journal of Geography in Higher Education* 21 (2): 171–185.

Greenaway, Roger. 2007. "Dynamic Debriefing." In *The Handbook of Experiential Learning*, edited by Mel Silberman, 59–80. San Francisco, CA: John Wiley & Sons.

Griffiths, Mark D. 2002. "The Educational Benefits of Videogames." *Education and Health* 20 (3): 47–51.

Grolnick, Wendy S., and Richard M. Ryan. 1987. "Autonomy in Children's Learning: An Experimental and Individual Difference Investigation." *Journal of Personality and Social Psychology* 52 (5): 890–898. DOI: 10.1037/0022-3514.52.5.890.

Guthrie, Kathy, and Holly McCracken. 2010. "Making a Difference Online: Facilitating Service-Learning Through Distance Education." *The Internet and Higher Education* 13: 153–157. DOI: 10.1016/j.iheduc.2010.02.006.

Hampton, Debra, Darlene Welsh, and Amanda Wiggins. 2019. "Learning Preferences and Engagement Level of Generation Z Nursing Students." *Nurse Educator* 45 (3): 160–164.

Hardre, Patricia L., and Johnmarshall Reeve. 2003. "A Motivational Model of Rural Students' Intentions to Persist in, Versus Drop out of, High School." *Journal of Educational Psychology* 95 (2): 347–356. DOI: 10.1037/0022-0663.95.2.347.

Harper, Jeffrey, Steven Lamb, and James Buffington. 2008. "Effective Use of Case Studies in the MIS Capstone Course Through Semi-Formal Collaborative Teaching." *Journal of Information Systems Education* 19 (4): 411–418.

Hartman, Rita, Mary Townsend, and Marlo Jackson. 2019. "Educators' Perceptions of Technology Integration into the Classroom: A Descriptive Case Study." *Journal of Research in Innovative Teaching & Learning* 12: 236–249. DOI: 10.1108/JRIT-03-2019-0044.

Hassini, Elkafi. 2006. "Student–Instructor Communication: The Role of Email." *Computers & Education* 47 (1): 29–40. DOI: 10.1016/j.compedu.2004.08.014.

Healy, Kristen. 2019. "Using an Escape-Room-Themed Curriculum to Engage and Educate Generation Z Students About Entomology." *American Entomologist* 65 (1): 24–28.

Hemmi, A., S. Bayne, and R. Land. 2009. "The Appropriation and Repurposing of Social Technologies in Higher Education." *Journal of Computer Assisted Learning* 25 (1): 19–30. DOI: 10.1111/j.1365-2729.2008.00306.x.

Herreid, Clyde, and Nancy Schiller. 2013. "Case Studies and the Flipped Classroom." *Journal of College Science Teaching* 42 (5): 62–66.

Hess, Diana E., and Paula McAvoy. 2015. *The Political Classroom: Evidence and Ethics in Democratic Education.* New York: Routledge.

Hilcenko, Slavoljub. 2017. "How Generation Z Learns Better." *European Journal of Social Sciences Education and Research* 11 (2): 379–389.

Hobbs, Renee. 2010. *Digital and Media Literacy: A Plan of Action.* Washington, D.C.: Aspen Institute.

Hoffer, Erin. 2020. "Case-Based Teaching: Using Stories for Engagement and Inclusion." *International Journal on Social and Educational Sciences* 2 (2): 75–80.

Holsti, Ole. 1994. "Case Teaching: Transforming Foreign Policy Courses with Cases." *International Studies Notes* 19 (2): 7–13.

hooks, bell. 1994. *Teaching to Transgress: Education as the Practice of Freedom.* New York: Routledge-Falmer.

hooks, bell. 2017. "Confronting Class in the Classroom." In *The Critical Pedagogy Reader* (3rd Ed.), edited by Antonia Darder, Rodolfo D. Torres, and Marta P. Baltodano, 181–187. New York: Routledge.

Hope, Joan. 2016. "Get Your Campus Ready for Generation Z." *Student Affairs Today* 19 (7): 1–7. DOI: 10.1002/say.30253.

Horton, Charles. 1902. *Human Nature and Social Order.* New York: Scribner.

Hyde, Michael J. 2005. "Acknowledgment, Conscience, Rhetoric, and Teaching: The Case of Tuesdays with Morrie." *Rhetoric Society Quarterly* 35 (2): 23–46. https://www.jstor.org/stable/40232462.

Hyde, Michael J. 2006. *The Life-Giving Gift of Acknowledgment: A Philosophical and Rhetorical Inquiry.* West Lafayette, IN: Purdue University Press.

Ilguy, Mehmet, Dilhan Ilguy, Erdogan Fisekcioglu, and Inci Oktay. 2014. "Comparison of Case-Based and Lecture-Based Learning in Dental Education Using the SOLO Taxonomy." *Journal of Dental Education* 78 (11): 1521–1527.

Iorgulescu, Maria-Cristina. 2016. "Generation Z and Its Perception of Work." *Cross-Cultural Management Journal* 18 (1): 47–54.

Jackson, Linda A., Edward A. Witt, Alexander Ivan Games, Hiram E. Fitzgerald, Alexander Von Eye, and Yong Zhao. 2012. "Information Technology Use and Creativity: Findings from the Children and Technology Project." *Computers in Human Behavior* 28 (2): 370–376.

Jaleniauskienė, Evelina, and Palmira Jucevičienė. 2015. "Reconsidering University Educational Environment for the Learners of Generation Z." *Social Sciences* 88 (2): 38–53. DOI: 10.5755/j01.ss.88.2.12737.

Jang, Hyungshim, Johnmarshall Reeve, and Edward L. Deci. 2010. "Engaging Students in Learning Activities: It is Not Autonomy Support or Structure but Autonomy Support and Structure." *Journal of Educational Psychology* 102 (3): 588–600. DOI: 10.1037/a0019682.

Jason, Zachary. 2018. "Student Activism 2.0: A Look Back at the History of Student Activism and Whether Today's Protesters Are Making a Difference." *Ed. Magazine.* https://www.gse.harvard.edu/news/ed/18/08/student-activism-20.

Jovanovic, Spoma. 2014. "Struggling Together: Collaboration as Ethical Practice." *Partnerships: A Journal of Service-Learning and Civic Engagement* 5 (1): 1–3.

Junco, Reynol. 2013. "Comparing Actual and Self-Reported Measures of Facebook Use." *Computers in Human Behavior* 29 (3): 626–631. DOI: 10.1016/j.chb.2012.11.007.

Kaiser Family Foundation. 2010. "Generation M2: Media in the Lives of 8- to 18-Year-Olds." https://www.kff.org/other/event/generation-m2-media-in-the-lives-of/.

Kalogeropoulos, Antonis. 2019. "How Younger Generations Consume News Differently." *Reuters Institute and University of Oxford*. Last Modified September 2019. http://www.digitalnewsreport.org/survey/2019/how-younger-generations-consume-news-differently/.

Kantorova, Katerina, Hana Jonasova, Jan Panus, and Roman Lipka. 2017. "A Study of Generation Z from the Communication Perspective of Universities." *Scientific Papers of the University of Pardubice* 24 (1): 83–94.

Karou, Ki. n.d. "5 Video Game Principles that Motivate Endless Play and Learning." *Mind Research Institute*. Accessed June 2, 2020. https://blog.mindresearch.org/blog/video-game-principles-play-learning.

Kezar, Adrianna, and Dan Maxey. 2014. "Collective Action on Campus Toward Student Development and Democratic Engagement." *New Directions for Higher Education* 167: 31–41.

King, Stephanie. B. 2014. "Graduate Student Perceptions of the Use of Online Course Tools to Support Engagement." *International Journal for the Scholarship of Teaching and Learning* 8 (1). DOI: 10.20429/ijsotl.2014.080105.

Knoop, R. 1984. *Case Studies in Education*. Ontario: Praise Publishing.

Kozinsky, Sieva. 2017. "How Generation Z Is Shaping the Change in Education." *Forbes*. Accessed July 20, 2020. https://www.forbes.com/sites/sievakozinsky/2017/07/24/how-generation-z-is-shaping-the-change-in-education/#ffdb15d65208.

Kreber, Caroline. 2001. "Learning Experientially Through Case Studies? A Conceptual Analysis." *Teaching in Higher Education* 6 (2): 217–228.

Kuh, George D. 2008. *High-Impact Educational Practices: What They Are, Who Has Access to Them, and Why They Matter*. Washington, D.C.: American Association of Colleges and Universities.

Ladson-Billings, Gloria. 1994. *The Dreamkeepers: Successful Teachers of African American Children* (1st Ed.). San Francisco: Jossey-Bass Publishing Company.

Lane, Daniel S., Vishnupriya Das, and Dan Hiaeshutter-Rice. 2019. "Civic Laboratories: Youth Political Expression in Anonymous, Ephemeral, Geo-Bounded Social Media." *Information, Communication and Society* 22 (14): 2171–2186. Accessed May 25, 2020. DOI: 10.1080/1369118X.2018.1477973.

Lazer, David M. J., Matthew A. Baum, Yochai Benkler, Adam J. Berinsky, Kelly M. Greenhill, Filippo Menczer, Miriam J. Metzger, Brendan Nyhan, Gordon Pennycook, David Rothschild, Michael Schudson, Steven A. Sloman, Cass R. Sunstein, Emily A. Thorson, Duncan J. Watts, and Jonathan L. Zittrain. 2018. "The Science of Fake News: Addressing Fake News Requires a Multidisciplinary Effort." *Science* 359 (6380): 1094–1096. Accessed May 25, 2020. DOI: 10.1126/science.aao2998.

Lee, Joyce. 2020. "Mental Health Effects of School Closures During Covid-19". *The Lancet Child and Adolescent Health* 4. Accessed July 20, 2020. https://www.thelancet.com/action/showPdf?pii=S2352-4642%2820%2930109-7.

Lehmann, Thomas, Inka Haehnlein, and Dirk Ifenthaler. 2014. "Cognitive, Metacognitive and Motivational Perspectives on Preflection in Self-Regulated Online Learning." *Computers in Human Behavior* 32: 313–323. DOI: 10.1016/j.chb.2013.07.051.

Lei, Jing. 2010. "Quantity Versus Quality: A New Approach to Examine the Relationship Between Technology Use and Student Outcomes." *British Journal of Educational Technology* 41 (3): 455–472.

Levinas, Emmanuel. 1972. *Humanism of the Other*. Translated by Nidra Poller. Chicago: University of Illinois Press.

Levinas, Emmanuel. 1998. *Otherwise Than Being or Beyond Essence*. Translated by Alphonso Lingis. Pittsburgh: Duquesne University Press.

Levitz, Eric. 2019. "American Exceptionalism is a Dangerous Myth." *New York Magazine*. Last Modified January 2, 2019. https://nymag.com/intelligencer/2019/01/american-exceptionalism-is-a-dangerous-myth.html.

Lewin, Kurt. 1951. "Problems of Research in Social Psychology." In *Field Theory in Social Science: Selected Theoretical Papers*, edited by Dorwin Cartwright, 155–169. New York: Harper & Row.

Lipari, Lisbeth. 2004. "Listening for the Other: Ethical Implications of the Buber-Levinas Encounter." *Communication Theory* 14 (2): 122–141. DOI: 10.1111/j.1468-2885.2004.tb00308.

Livingston, Gretchen, and Amanda Barroso. 2019. "For U.S. Teens Today, Summer Means More Schooling and Less Leisure Time Than in the Past." *Pew Research Center*. Last Modified August 13, 2019. https://www.pewresearch.org/fact-tank/2019/08/13/for-u-s-teens-today-summer-means-more-schooling-and-less-leisure-time-than-in-the-past/.

Livingstone, Sonia. 2018. "Review of *iGen: Why Today's Super-Connected Kids are Growing Up Less Rebellious, More Tolerant, Less Happy, and Completely Unprepared for Adulthood* by Jean Twenge." *Journal of Children and Media* 12 (1): 118–123. Accessed May 25, 2020. DOI: 10.1080/17482798.2017.1417091.

Loveland, Elaina. 2017. "Instant Generation." *The Journal of College Admission* 234: 34–38.

Malroutu, Y. 2017. "Enhancing Student Learning Experience in Blended Classroom Teaching." *Journal of Advances in Humanities and Social Sciences* 3 (6): 324–331.

Mangiapane, Ernesto, and Gabrielle Ilse Viscuso. 2020. "Pandemic Covid-19: Psychodynamic Analysis of a Global Trauma. Clinical Considerations Pre/Post Lock Down." *Journal of Medical Research and Health Sciences* 3 (6): 976–990. DOI: 10.15520/jmrhs.v3i6.194.

Mani, B. Venkat. 2020. "Inclusive Teaching Is Needed to Help Combat the Xenophobia, Racism and Discrimination Brought on by COVID-19|Inside Higher Ed." *Inside Higher Ed*. Last Modified May 14, 2020. https://www.insidehighered.com/views/2020/05/14/inclusive-teaching-needed-help-combat-xenophobia-racism-and-discrimination-brought.

Marron, Maria B. 2015. "New Generations Require Changes Beyond the Digital." *Journalism & Mass Communication Educator* 70 (2): 123–124. DOI: 10.1177/1077695815588912.

Martens, Hans, and Renee Hobbs. 2015. "How Media Literacy Supports Civic Engagement in a Digital Age." *Atlantic Journal of Communication* 23 (2): 120–137. Accessed May 25, 2020.

Martin, Florence, and Doris U. Bolliger. 2018. "Engagement Matters: Student Perceptions on the Importance of Engagement Strategies in the Online Learning Environment." *Online Learning* 22 (1): 205–222. DOI: 10.24059/olj.v22i1.1092.

McCroskey, James C., and Linda L. McCroskey. 2016. "Instructional Communication: The Historical Perspective." In *Handbook of Instructional Communication: Rhetorical and Relational Perspectives*, edited by Timothy P. Mottet, Virginia P. Richmond, and James C. McCroskey, 33–47. London: Routledge, Taylor and Francis Group.

McGonigal, Jane. 2011. *Reality is Broken: Why Games Make Us Better and How They Can Change the World*. New York: Penguin Press.

McGrew, Sarah, Teresa Ortega, Joel Breakstone, and Sam Wineburg. 2017. "The Challenge That's Bigger Than Fake News: Civic Reasoning in a Social Media Environment." *American Educator* 41 (3): 4–9. Accessed May 25, 2020. https://files.eric.ed.gov/fulltext/EJ1156387.pdf.

McMurtrie, Beth. 2019. "Many Professors Want to Change Their Teaching But Don't. One University Found Out Why." *The Chronicle of Higher Education*. Last Modified March 21, 2019. https://www.chronicle.com/article/Many-Professors-Want-to-Change/245945?cid=at&utm_source=at&utm_medium=en&cid=at.

Meerts-Brandsma, Lisa, Jim Sibthorp, and Shannon Rochelle. 2019. "Using Transformative Learning Theory to Understand Outdoor Adventure Education." *Journal of Adventure Education and Outdoor Learning* 1–14. DOI: 10.1080/14729679.2019.1686040.

Milczarski, Vivian, and Amanda Maynard. 2015. "Improving Information Literacy Skills for Psychology Majors: The Development of a Case Study Technique." *College & Undergraduate Libraries* 22 (1): 35–44.

Miller, Amy, and Brooklyn B. Mills. 2019. "'If They Don't Care, I Don't Care': Millennial and Generation Z Students and the Impact of Faculty Caring." *The Journal of the Scholarship of Teaching and Learning* 19 (4): 78–89. https://files.eric.ed.gov/fulltext/EJ1234123.pdf.

Miller, Amy Chasteen, and Brooklyn Mills. 2019. "'If They Don't Care, I Don't Care': Millennial and Generation Z Students and the Impact of Faculty Caring." *Journal of the Scholarship of Teaching and Learning* 19 (4): 78–89. DOI: 10.14434/josotl.v19i4.24167.

Mingst, Karen. 1994. "Cases and the Interactive Classroom." *International Studies Notes* 19 (2): 1–6.

Mintz, Steven. 2019. "Are Colleges Ready for Generation Z?" *Higher Ed Gamma* [Blog]. Last Modified March 18, 2019. https://www.insidehighered.com/blogs/higher-ed-gamma/are-colleges-ready-generation-z.

Mirivel, Julien C. 2014. *The Art of Positive Communication: Theory and Practice*. New York: Peter Lang.

Mocek, Evelyn Anne. 2017. "The Effects of Syllabus Design on Information Retention by At-Risk First Semester Students." *Syllabus* 6 (2). Accessed June 25, 2020. http://www.syllabusjournal.org/syllabus/article/view/222/Mocek.

Mohr, Kathleen, and Eric Mohr. 2017. "Understanding Generation Z Students to Promote a Contemporary Learning Environment." *Journal on Empowering Teaching Excellence* 1 (1): 84–94. DOI: 10.15142/T3M05T.

Molla, Rani. 2017. "Millennials Have a Netflix Account. Gen Z is Playing Video Games." Accessed June 2, 2020. https://www.vox.com/2017/7/17/15961370/millennials-netflix-account-gen-z-video-games-mobile-phone-nielsen.

Molnar, Alex, G. Miron, N. Elgeberi, M. K. Barbour, L. Huerta, S. R. Shafer, and J. K. Rice. 2019. "Virtual Schools in the U.S. 2019." *National Education Policy Center*. https://nepc.colorado.edu/publication/virtual-schools-annual-2019.

Moore, Kevin, Carol Jones, and Robert Frazier. 2017. "Engineering Education for Generation Z." *American Journal of Engineering Education* 8 (2): 111–126.

Morreale, Sherwyn, Janice Thorpe, and Joshua N. Westwick. 2021. "Online Teaching: Challenge or Opportunity for Communication Education Scholars?" *Communication Education* 70 (1): 117–119. DOI: 10.1080/03634523.2020.1811360.

Morris, Charles E., and Stephen H. Browne. 2013. *Readings on the Rhetoric of Social Protest* (3rd Ed.). State College, PA: Strata.

Mottet, Timothy P., Virginia P. Richmond, and James C. McCroskey. 2016. *Handbook of Instructional Communication: Rhetorical and Relational Perspectives*. London: Routledge, Taylor and Francis Group. http://search.ebscohost.com/login.aspx?direct=true&AuthType=sso&db=cat00991a&AN=sth.ocn925332681&site=eds-live.

Moyer-Gusé, Emily. 2008. "Toward a Theory of Entertainment Persuasion: Explaining the Persuasive Effects of Entertainment-Education Messages." *Communication Theory* 18 (3): 407–425. DOI: 10.1111/j.1468-2885.2008.00328.x.

Mustoe, L. R., and A. C. Croft. 1999. "Motivating Engineering Students by Using Modern Case Studies." *International Journal of Engineering Education* 15 (6): 469–476.

Nader, Ralph. 2014. *Unstoppable*. New York: Nation Books.

National Association of Colleges and Employers. n.d. "Job Outlook 2016: The Attributes Employers Want to See on New College Graduates' Resumes." Accessed June 30, 2020. https://www.naceweb.org/career-development/trends-and-predictions/job-outlook-2016-attributes-employers-want-to-see-on-new-college-graduates-resumes/.

National Association of Colleges and Employers (NACE) Center for Career Development and Talent Acquisition. 2018. "Are College Graduates 'Career Ready'?" Last Modified February 19, 2018. https://www.naceweb.org/career-readiness/competencies/are-college-graduates-career-ready/.

National Center for Education Statistics, U.S. Department of Education. 2019. "Number and Percentage Distribution of Students Enrolled at Title IV Institutions, by Control of Institution, Student Level, Level of Institution, Distance Education Status of Student, and Distance Education Status of Institution: United States, Fall 2018." In *Integrated Postsecondary Education Data System*, edited by U.S. Department of Education, National Center for Education Statistics. https://nces.ed.gov/ipeds/Search/ViewTable?tableId=26394&returnUrl=%2Fipeds%2FSearch.

"National COVID-19 Outdoor Learning Initiative." 2020. https://www.greenschoolyards.org/covid-learn-outside.

Nemko, Marty. 2015. "Generation Z." *Psychology Today*. Last Modified October 25, 2015. https://www.psychologytoday.com/us/blog/how-do-life/201510/generation-z.

O'Sullivan, Patrick, Steven Hunt, and Lance Lippert. "Mediated Immediacy: A Language of Affiliation in a Technological Age." *Journal of Language and Social Psychology* 23: 464–490. DOI: 10.1177%2F0261927X04269588.

Pace, Wayne R., and Robert F. Ross. 1983. "The Basic Course in Organizational Communication." *Communication Education* 32 (4): 402–412. DOI: 10.1080/03634528309378561.

Palfrey, John, and Urs Gasser. 2016. *Born Digital: How Children Grow Up in a Digital Age* (Revised, Expanded Ed.). New York: Basic Books.

Palley, Will. 2012. "Gen Z: Digital in Their DNA." Last Modified April 23, 2012. http://www.jwtintelligence.com/wpcontent/uploads/2012/04/F_INTERNAL_Gen_Z_0418122.pdf.

Pariser, Eli. 2012. *The Filter Bubble: How the New Personalized Web is Changing What We Read and How We Think*. New York: Penguin Books.

Parker, Kim, and Ruth Igielnik. 2020. "On the Cusp of Adulthood and Facing an Uncertain Future: What We Know About Gen Z So Far." *Pew Research Center*. Last Modified May 14, 2020. https://www.pewsocialtrends.org/essay/on-the-cusp-of-adulthood-and-facing-an-uncertain-future-what-we-know-about-gen-z-so-far/.

Parks, Elizabeth. 2020. "Listening Through the Ages: Measuring Generational Listening Differences with the LCI-R." *International Journal of Listening* 34 (3). DOI: 10.1080/10904018.2020.1748503.

Passarelli, Angela, Eric Hall, and Mallory Anderson. 2010. "A Strengths-Based Approach to Outdoor and Adventure Education: Possibilities for Personal Growth." *Journal of Experiential Education* 33 (2): 120–135.

Payne, Phillip. 2002. "On the Construction, Deconstruction and Reconstruction of Experience in 'Critical' Outdoor Education." *Australian Journal of Outdoor Education* 6 (2): 4–21.

Pearson. 2018. "Beyond Millennials: The Next Generation Learners." https://www.pearson.com/content/dam/one-dot-com/one-dot-com/global/Files/news/news-annoucements/2018/The-Next-Generation-of-Learners_final.pdf.

Pew Research Center. 2008. "Teens, Video Games, and Civics: Teens' Gaming Experiences Are Diverse and Include Significant Social Interaction and Civic Engagement." Accessed May 28, 2020. https://www.pewresearch.org/internet/2008/09/16/teens-video-games-and-civics/.

Pew Research Center. 2013. "A Closer Look at Generations and Cell Phone Ownership." *Pew Research Center*. Last Modified February 3, 2011. https://www.pewresearch.org/internet/2011/02/03/a-closer-look-at-generations-and-cell-phone-ownership/.

Pew Research Center. 2019a. "Generations and Age." https://www.pewresearch.org/topics/generations-and-age/.

Pew Research Center. 2019b. "Defining Generations: Where Millennials End and Generation Z Begins." https://www.pewresearch.org/fact-tank/2019/01/17/where-millennials-end-and-generation-z-begins/.

Pew Research Center. 2020. "Worries About Coronavirus Surge, as Most Americans Expect a Recession – or Worse." Last Modified March 26, 2020. https://www.people-press.org/2020/03/26/worries-about-coronavirus-surge-as-most-americans-expect-a-recession-or-worse/.

Pfefferbaum, Betty, and Carol S. North. 2020. "Mental Health and the Covid-19 Pandemic." *The New England Journal of Medicine*. DOI: 10.1056/NEJMp2008017. https://www.nejm.org/doi/full/10.1056/NEJMp2008017#article_introduction.

Pitts, Lewis, and Spoma Jovanovic, S. 2016. "What Will Our Council Do in a Post-Truth Era?" *Greensboro's News & Record*. Last Modified December 11, 2016. https://greensboro.com/opinion/columns/lewis-pitts-and-spoma-jovanovic-what-will-our-council-do-in-a-post-truth-era/article_75ec8f8e-59bf-503b-91b4-2f2d23474a11.html.

Plochocki, Jeffrey. 2019. "Several Ways Generation Z May Shape the Medical School Landscape." *Journal of Medical Education and Curricular Development*. DOI: 10.1177/2382120519884325.

Popil, Inna. 2011. "Promotion of Critical Thinking by Using Case Studies as Teaching Method." *Nurse Education Today* 31 (2): 204–207.

Postman, Neil. 2011. *Technopoly: The Surrender of Culture to Technology*. New York: Vintage.

Poulos, Chris. 2004. "Disruption, Silence, and Creation: The Search for Dialogic Civility in the Age of Anxiety." *Qualitative Inquiry* 10 (4): 534–547.

Pousson, J. Mark, and Karen Myers. 2018. "Ignatian Pedagogy as a Frame for Universal Design in College: Meeting Learning Needs of Generation Z." *Education Sciences* 8 (4): 1–10. DOI: 10.3390/educsci8040193.

Pousson, J. Mark, and Karen A. Myers. 2019. "College Students with Disabilities and Their Activism." In *Student Activism in the Academy: Its Struggles and Promise*, edited by Joseph L. DeVitis and Pietro A. Sasso, 205–219. Gorham, ME: Myers Education Press.

Prensky, Marc R. 2012. *From Digital Natives to Digital Wisdom: Hopeful Essays for 21st Century Learning*. Thousand Oaks: Corwin Press.

Raju, P. K., and Chetan Sankar. 1999. "Teaching Real-World Issues Through Case Studies." *Journal of Engineering Education* 88 (4): 501–508.

Ramirez, Artemio, and Zuoming Wang. 2008. "When Online Meets Offline: An Expectancy Violations Theory Perspective on Modality Switching." *Journal of Communication* 58 (1): 20–39. DOI: 10.1111/j.1460-2466.2007.00372.x.

Rawal, Sangtia, and U. S. Pandey. 2013. "E-Learning: Learning from Smart Generation Z." *International Journal of Scientific and Research Publications* 3 (5): 564–568.

Reeve, Johnmarshall, and Hyungshim Jang. 2006. "What Teachers Say and Do to Support Students' Autonomy During a Learning Activity." *Journal of Educational Psychology* 98 (1): 209–218. DOI: 10.1037/0022-0663.98.1.209.

Reeve, Johnmarshall, Hyungshim Jang, Dan Carrell, Soohyun Jeon, and Jon Barch. 2004. "Enhancing Students' Engagement by Increasing Teachers' Autonomy Support." *Motivation and Emotion* 28 (2): 147–169. DOI: 10.1023/B:MOEM.00 00032312.95499.6f.

Richards, Larry, Michael Gorman, William Scherer, and Robert Landel. 1995. "Promoting Active Learning with Cases and Instructional Modules." *Journal of Engineering Education* 84 (4): 375–381.

Rickes, Persis C. 2016. "Generations in Flux: How Gen Z Will Continue to Transform Higher Education Space." *Planning for Higher Education* 44 (4): 21–45. http://eres.regent.edu:2048/login?url=https://search-proquest-com.ezproxy.regent.edu/docview/1838982286?accountid=13479.

Ricketts, Miriam, and James Willis. 2001. *Experience AI: A Practitioner's Guide to Integrating Appreciative Inquiry with Experiential Learning*. Chagrin Falls, OH: Taos Institute.

Ridberg, Maia. 2006. "Professors Want Their Classes 'Unwired'." *The Christian Science Monitor*, May 4, 2006. http://eres.regent.edu:2048/login?url=https://search-proquest-com.ezproxy.regent.edu/docview/405555725?accountid=13479.

Rideout, Victoria J., Ulla G. Foehr, and Donald F. 2010. *Generation M2: Media in the Lives of 8–18-Year Olds*. Menlo Park: Kaiser Family Foundation.

Robles, Marcel. 2012. "Executive Perceptions of the Top 10 Soft Skills Needed in Today's Workplace." *Business Communication Quarterly* 75 (4): 453–465. DOI: 10.1177/1080569912460400.

Rohnke, Karl. 1984. *Silver Bullets: A Guide to Initiative Problems, Adventure Games, Stunts and Trust Activities*. Hamilton, MA: Project Adventure, Inc.

Rohnke, Karl. 1989. *Cowstails and Cobras II: A Guide to Games, Initiatives, Ropes Courses & Adventure Curriculum*. Hamilton, MA: Project Adventure, Inc.

Rohnke, Karl, and Steve Butler. 1995. *Quicksilver: Adventure Games, Initiative Problems, Trust Activities, and a Guide to Effective Leadership*. Thousand Oaks, CA: SAGE Publications.

Roll, Kate. 2020. "Lecturer and Student Relationships Matter Even More Online Than on Campus." *The Guardian*. Last Modified June 8, 2020. https://www.theguardian.com/education/2020/jun/08/lecturer-and-student-relationships-matter-even-more-online-than-on-campus?fbclid=IwAR3UEXOlJd1aJ6JwUTM2L95DaSF1BtZsfMY5tjDbtQWbJCtk57jigKVwwGo.

Rospigliosi, Pericles. "The Role of Social Media as a Learning Environment in the Fully Functioning University: Preparing for Generation Z." *Interactive Learning Environments* 27 (4): 429–431.

Rue, Penny. 2018. "Make Way, Millennials, Here Comes Gen Z." *About Campus* 23 (3): 5–12. Accessed May 25, 2020. DOI: 10.1177/1086482218804251.

Ryan, Richard M., and Edward L. Deci. 2000. "Self-Determination Theory and the Facilitation of Intrinsic Motivation, Social Development, and Well-Being." *American Psychologist* 55 (1): 68–78. DOI: 10.7717/peerj-cs.230/fig-3.

Ryan, Richard M., and Edward L. Deci. 2002. "Overview of Self-Determination Theory: An Organismic Dialectical Perspective." In *Handbook of Self-determination*

Research, edited by Edward L. Deci and Richard M. Ryan, 3–33. Rochester, NY: University of Rochester.

Safapour, Elnaz, Sharareh Kermanshachi, and Piyush Taneja. 2019. "A Review of Nontraditional Teaching Methods: Flipped Classroom, Gamification, Case Study, Self-Learning, and Social Media." *Education Sciences* 9 (4): 273–292.

Safranova, Margarita, Caleb Miller, and Colin Kuehl. 2019. "When Are We Ever Going to Have to Use This? Discussing Programmatic Learning Outcomes in the Classroom." *Journal of Political Science Education* 4 (4): 421–432.

Samuels-Peretza, Debbie, Lana Dvorkin Camielb, Karen Teeleyc, and Gouri Banerjeed. 2017. "Digitally Inspired Thinking: Can Social Media Lead to Deep Learning in Higher Education?" *College Teaching* 65 (1): 32–39. DOI: 10.1080/87567555.2016.1225663.

Sanford, Kathy, Lisa J. Starr, Liz Merkel, and Sarah Bonsor Kurki. 2015. "Serious Games: Video Games for Good?" *E-Learning and Digital Media* 12 (1): 90–106. DOI: 10.1177/2042753014558380.

Schonell, Stuart, and Rob Macklin. 2019. "Work Integrated Learning Initiatives: Live Case Studies as a Mainstream WIL Assessment." *Studies in Higher Education* 44 (7): 1197–1208.

Schwartzman, Roy. 2020. "Performing Pandemic Pedagogy." *Communication Education* 69 (4): 502–517. DOI: 10.1080/03634523.2020.1804602.

Schwieger, Dana, and Christine Ladwig. 2018. "Reaching and Retaining the Next Generation: Adapting to the Expectations of Gen Z in the Classroom." *Information Systems Education Journal* 16 (3): 45–54.

Seemiller, Corey, and Jason Clayton. 2019. "Developing the Strengths of Generation Z College Students." *Journal of College and Character* 20: 268–275. DOI: 10.1080/2194587X.2019.1631187.

Seemiller, Corey, and Meghan Grace. 2016a. *Generation Z Goes to College*. Hoboken, NJ: John Wiley & Sons.

Seemiller, Corey, and Meghan Grace. 2016b. *Generation Z Goes to College* (1st Ed.). San Francisco, CA: Jossey Bass.

Seemiller, Corey, and Meghan Grace. 2017. "Generation Z: Educating and Engaging the Next Generation of Students." *About Campus: Enriching the Student Learning Experience* 22 (3): 21–26. DOI: 10.1002/abc.21293.

Seemiller, Corey, Meghan Grace, Paula Dal Bo Campagnolo, Isa Mara Da Rosa Alves, and Gustavo Severo De Borba. 2021. "What Makes Learning Enjoyable? Perspectives of Today's College Students in the U.S. and Brazil." *Journal of Pedagogical Research* 5 (1): 1–17.

Sellnow, Deanna, and Renee Kaufmann. 2018. "Instructional Communication and the Online Learning Environment: Then, Now, Next." In *The Handbook of Instructional Communication: Rhetorical and Relational Perspectives* (2nd Ed.), edited by M. L. Houser and A. M. Hosek, 195–206. Taylor and Francis.

Shatto, Bobbi, and Kelly Erwin. 2016. "Moving on From Millennials: Preparing for Generation Z." *The Journal of Continuing Education in Nursing* 47 (6): 253–254. DOI: 10.3928/00220124-20160518-05.

Shatto, Bobbi, and Kelly Erwin. 2017. "Teaching Millennials and Generation Z: Bridging the Generational Divide." *Creative Nursing* 23 (1): 24–28.

Shaw, Aaron, and Eszter Hargittai. 2018. "The Pipeline of Online Participation Inequalities: The Case of Wikipedia Editing." *Journal of Communication* 68 (1): 143–168. Accessed May 25, 2020. DOI: 10.1093/joc/jqx003.

Shearer, Rick, Tugce Aldemir, Jann Hitchcock, Jessie Resig, Jessica Driver, and Megan Kohler. 2020. "What Students Want: A Vision of a Future Online Learning Experience Grounded in Distance Education Theory." *American Journal of Distance Education* 34 (1): 36–52. DOI: 10.1080/08923647.2019.1706019.

Sherblom, John. 2010. "The Computer-Mediated Communication (CMC) Classroom: A Challenge of Medium, Presence, Interaction, Identity, and Relationship." *Communication Education* 59: 497–523. DOI: 10.1080/03634523.2010.486440.

Sherstad, Pamela S. 2019. "Exploring the Higher Education Listening Experiences of Generation Z." PhD Dissertation, Regent University.

Singh, Anjali. 2014. "Challenges and Issues of Generation Z." *Journal of Business and Management* 16 (7): 59–63.

Singhal, Arvind, and Everett M. Rogers. 2002. "A Theoretical Agenda for Entertainment—Education." *Communication Theory* 12 (2): 117–135. DOI: 10.1111/j.1468-2885.2002.tb00262.x.

Skinner, Ellen, Carrie Furrer, Gwen Marchand, and Thomas Kindermann. 2008. "Engagement and Disaffection in the Classroom: Part of a Larger Motivational Dynamic?" *Journal of Educational Psychology* 100 (4): 765–781. DOI: 10.1037/a0012840.

Skinner, Ellen A., and Michael J. Belmont. 1993. "Motivation in the Classroom: Reciprocal Effects of Teacher Behavior and Student Engagement Across the School Year." *Journal of Educational Psychology* 85 (4): 571–581. DOI: 10.1037/0022-0663.85.4.571.

Slack, Jennifer Daryl, and J. Macgregor Wise. 2005. *Culture+Technology: A Primer.* New York: Peter Lang Publishing.

Slater, Michael D., and Donna Rouner. 2002. "Entertainment—Education and Elaboration Likelihood: Understanding the Processing of Narrative Persuasion." *Communication Theory* 12 (2): 173–191.

Slefo, George. 2019. "Fortnite Emerges as a Social Media Platform for Gen Z." Accessed May 27, 2020. https://adage.com/article/digital/fortnite-emerges-social-media-platform-gen-z/2176301.

Spackman, Andy, and Leticia Camacho. 2009. "Rendering Information Literacy Relevant: A Case-Based Pedagogy." *The Journal of Academic Librarianship* 35 (6): 548–554.

Spears, Julia, Stephanie Zobac, Allison Spillane, and Shannon Thomas. 2015. "Marketing Learning Communities to Generation Z: The Importance of Face-to-Face Interaction in a Digitally Driven World." *Learning Communities Research and Practice* 3 (1): 1–10.

Squire, Kurt. 2006. "From Content to Context: Videogames as Designed Experience." *Educational Researcher* 35 (8): 19–29.

Staton-Spicer, Ann Q., and Cheryl R. Marty-White. 1981. "A Framework for Instructional Communication Theory: The Relationship Between Teacher

Communication Concerns and Classroom Behavior." *Communication Education* 30 (4): 354–366.

Stefanou, Candice R., Kathleen C. Perencevich, Matthew DiCintio, and Julianne C. Turner. 2004. "Supporting Autonomy in the Classroom: Ways Teachers Encourage Student Decision Making and Ownership." *Educational Psychologist* 39 (2): 97–110. DOI: 10.1207/s15326985ep3902_2.

Steinkuehler, Constance. 2012. "The Mismeasure of Boys: Reading and Online Videogames." WCER Working Paper No. 2011-3. Madison: Wisconsin Center for Education Research, University of Wisconsin. Accessed May 28, 2020. https://wcer.wisc.edu/docs/working-papers/Working_Paper_No_2011_03.pdf.

Steinkuehler, Constance, and Sean Duncan. 2008. "Scientific Habits of Mind in Virtual Worlds." *Journal of Science Education and Technology* 17 (6): 530–543. DOI: 10.1007/s10956-008-9120-8.

Stillman, Jessica. 2016. "Gen Z is Anxious, Distrustful, and Often Downright Miserable, New Poll Reveals." Inc., March 23, 2016. https://www.inc.com/jessica-stillman/gen-z-is-anxious-distrustful-and-often-downright-miserable-new-poll-reveals.html.

Stocker, Shevaun L., and Kristel M. Gallagher. 2019. "Alleviating Anxiety and Altering Appraisals: Social-Emotional Learning in the College Classroom." *College Teaching* 67 (1): 23–35. DOI: 10.1080/87567555.2018.1515722.

Strait, Jean, and Tim Sauer. 2004. "Constructing Experiential Learning for Online Courses: The Birth of E-Service." *Educause Quarterly* 1: 62–65.

Strawser, Michael. 2018. *Transformative Student Experiences in Higher Education: Meeting the Needs of the Twenty-First-Century Student 2 and Modern Workplace.* Hoboken: Lexington Books.

Strelan, Peter, Amanda Osborn, and Edward Palmer. 2020. "The Flipped Classroom: A Meta-analysis of Effects on Student Performance Across Disciplines and Education Levels." *Educational Research Review* 30: 100314. DOI: 10.1016/j.edurev.2020.100314.

Suárez, Eduardo. 2020. "How Fact-Checkers Are Fighting Coronavirus Misinformation Worldwide." *Reuters Institute*. Last Modified March 31, 2020. https://reutersinstitute.politics.ox.ac.uk/risj-review/how-fact-checkers-are-fighting-coronavirus-misinformation-worldwide.

Sunstein, Cass R. 2018. *#Republic: Divided Democracy in the Age of Social Media.* Princeton: Princeton University Press.

Sypher, Beverly. 1997. *Case Studies in Organizational Communication 2: Perspectives on Contemporary Work Life.* New York: The Guilford Press.

Tatum, Nicholas T., and T. Kody Frey. 2021. "(In)flexibility During Uncertainty? Conceptualizing Instructor Strictness During a Global Pandemic." *Communication Education* 70 (2): 214–216. DOI: 10.1080/03634523.2020.1857419.

Tedford, Thomas L., and Dale A. Herbeck. 2017. *Freedom of Speech in the U.S.* (8th Ed.). State College, PA: Strata.

Terry, Gareth, Nikki Hayfield, Victoria Clarke, and Virginia Braun. 2017. "Thematic Analysis." In *the SAGE Handbook of Qualitative Research in Psychology*, edited by Carla Willig and Wendy Stainton Rogers, 17–36. London: SAGE Publications Ltd. DOI: 10.4135/9781526405555.n2.

The NPD Group. 2017. "Three Ways to Win Over the Thrifty Gen Z Consumer." Accessed May 27, 2020. https://www.npd.com/wps/portal/npd/us/news/thought-leadership/2019/3-ways-to-win-over-the-thrifty-gen-z-consumer/.

Thompson, Penny. 2017. "Communication Technology Use and Study Skills." *Active Learning in Higher Education* 18 (3): 257–270. DOI: 10.1177/1469787417715204.

Thurston, Travis. 2018. "Design Case: Implementing Gamification with ARCS to Engage Digital Natives." *Journal on Empowering Teaching Excellence* 2 (1): 23–52. DOI: 10.26077/vsk-5613.

Tindall, Evie, and Deanna Nisbet. 2008. "Listening: A Vital Skill for Learning." *International Journal of Learning* 15 (6): 121–127. DOI: 10.18848/1447-9494/CGP/v15i06/45802.

Tinto, Vladimir. 1987. "The Principles of Effective Retention." Paper Presented at Fall Conference of the Maryland College Personnel Association (LARGO, MD, November 20, 1987): 1–15. https://eric.ed.gov/?id=ED301267.

Tompkins, Phillip K. 2009. *Who is My Neighbor? Communicating and Organizing to End Homelessness*. Boulder, CO: Paradigm Publishers.

Townend, M. 2001. "Integrating Case Studies in Engineering Mathematics: A Response to SARTOR 3." *Teaching in Higher Education* 6 (2): 203–215.

Trenholm, Sarah. 2018. *Thinking Through Communication: An Introduction to the Study of Human Communication* (8th Ed.). New York: Routledge.

Tufekci, Zeynep. 2017. *Twitter and Tear Gas: The Power and Fragility of Networked Protest*. Yale: Yale University Press.

Turkle, S. 2011. *Alone Together: Why We Expect More from Technology and Less from Each Other*. New York: Basic Books.

Turkle, Sherry. 2012. "Connected, But Alone?" Filmed February 2012 in Long Beach, California. TED video, 19:32. https://www.ted.com/talks/sherry_turkle_connected_but_alone?language=en.

Turner, Anthony. 2015. "Generation Z: Technology and Social Interest." *The Journal of Individual Psychology* 71 (2): 103–113. Accessed May 25, 2020. DOI: 10.1353/jip.2015.0021.

Turner, Julianne C., Debra K. Meyer, Kathleen E. Cox, Candice Logan, Matthew DiCintio, and Cynthia T. Thomas. 1998. "Involvement in Mathematics: Teachers' Strategies and Students' Perceptions." *Journal of Educational Psychology* 90 (4): 730–745. DOI: 10.1037/0022-0663.90.4.730.

Twenge, Jean M. 2009. "Generational Changes and Their Impact in the Classroom: Teaching Generation Me." *Medical Education* 43 (5): 398–405. DOI: 10.1111/j.1365-2923.2009.03310.x.

Twenge, Jean M. 2017. *iGen: Why Today's Super-Connected Kids Are Growing Up Less Rebellious, More Tolerant, Less Happy-and Completely Unprepared for Adulthood*. New York, NY: Atria.

Uttal, David H., Nathaniel G. Meadow, Elizabeth Tipton, Linda L. Hand, Alison R. Alden, Christopher Warren, and Nora S. Newcombe. 2013. "The Malleability of Spatial Skills: A Meta-Analysis of Training Studies." *Psychological Bulletin* 139 (2): 352–402. DOI: 10.1037/a0028446.

Vallade, Jessalyn, and Renee Kaufmann. 2018. "Investigating Instructor Misbehaviors in the Online Classroom." *Communication Education* 67: 363–381. DOI: 10.1080/03634523.2018.1467027.

Varallo, Sharon M. 2008. "Motherwork in Academe: Intensive Caring for the Millennial Student." *Women's Studies in Communication* 31 (2): 151–157. DOI: 10.1080/07491409.2008.10162527.

Vorderer, Peter, and Ute Ritterfeld. 2009. "Digital Games." In *The SAGE Handbook of Media Processes and Effects*, edited by Robin L. Nabi and Mary Beth Oliver, 455–468. Los Angeles: Sage.

Wang, Hua, and Arvind Singhal. 2009. "Entertainment-Education Through Digital Games." In *Serious Games: Mechanisms and Effects*, edited by Ute Ritterfeld, Michael Cody, and Peter Vorderer, 271–292. New York: Routledge.

Waxman, K. T. 2010. "The Development of Evidence-Based Clinical Simulation Scenarios: Guidelines for Nurse Educators." *Journal of Nursing Education* 49 (1): 29–35. DOI: 10.3928/01484834-20090916-07.

Weick, Karl, and Kathleen Sutcliffe. 2007. *Managing the Unexpected: Resilient Performance in an Age of Uncertainty* (2nd Ed.). San Francisco, CA: Jossey-Bass.

Weick, Karl E. 1995. *Sensemaking in Organizations* (Vol. 3). Thousand Oaks, CA: Sage.

Weick, Karl E., and Karlene H. Roberts. 1993. "Collective Mind in Organizations: Heedful Interrelating on Flight Decks." *Administrative Science Quarterly*: 357–381.

Weick, Karl E., and Susan J. Ashford. 2001. "Learning in Organizations." *The New Handbook of Organizational Communication: Advances in Theory, Research, and Methods* 704: 731.

Wells, Chris. 2015. *The Civic Organization and the Digital Citizen: Communicating Engagement in a Networked Age*. Oxford: Oxford University Press.

Westwick, Joshua N., and Sherwyn P. Morreale. 2021. "Advancing an Agenda for Instructional Preparedness: Lessons Learned from the Transition to Remote Learning." *Communication Education* 70 (2): 217–222. DOI: 10.1080/03634523.2020.1857416.

Whistle. 2019. "Two-Thirds of Gen Z Males Say Gaming is a Core Component of Who They Are." Accessed May 26, 2020. https://www.aaaa.org/gen-z-males-say-gaming-core-component-who-they-are/.

Williams, Andy, and Nalda Wainwright. 2016. "A New Pedagogical Model for Adventure in the Curriculum: Part Two – Outlining the Model." *Physical Education and Sport Pedagogy* 21 (6): 589–602. DOI: 10.1080/17408989.2015.1048212.

Wolvin, Andrew D. 2012. "Listening in the General Education Curriculum." *International Journal of Listening* 26 (2): 122–128. DOI: 10.1080/10904018.2012.678201.

Wombacher, Kevin, Christina Harris, Marjorie Buckner, Brandi Frisby, and Anthony Limperos. 2017. "The Effects of Computer-Mediated Communication Anxiety on Student Perceptions of Instructor Behaviors, Perceived Learning, and Quiz Performance." *Communication Education* 66: 299–312. DOI: 10.1080/03634523.2015.1221511.

Wrage, Stephen. 1994. "Best Case Analysis: What Makes a Good Case and Where to Find the One You Need." *International Studies Notes* 19 (2): 21–27.

Wrench, Jason. 2012. *Casing Organizational Communication.* Dubuque: Kendall Hunt.

Yang, C., and Y. S. Chang. 2012. "Assessing the Effects of Interactive Blogging on Student Attitudes Towards Peer Interaction, Learning Motivation, and Academic Achievements." *Journal of Computer Assisted Learning* 28 (2): 126–135. DOI: 10.1111/j.1365-2729.2011.00423.x.

Yoo, Moon-Sook, and Hyung-Ran Park. 2015. "Effects of Case-Based Learning on Communication Skills, Problem-Solving Ability, and Learning Motivation in Nursing Students." *Nursing and Health Sciences* 17 (2): 166–172.

Zhang, Jie, and Ann Giralico Pearlman. 2018. "Expanding Access to International Education Through Technology Enhanced Collaborative Online International Learning (COIL) Courses." *The International Journal of Technology in Teaching and Learning* 14 (1): 1–11. https://sicet.org/main/wp-content/uploads/2019/03/1_Zhang_Jie.pdf.

Zhou, Chun, Aurora Occa, Soyoon Kim, and Susan Morgan. 2020. A Meta-Analysis of Narrative Game-Based Interventions for Promoting Healthy Behaviors. *Journal of Health Communication* 25 (1): 54–65. DOI: 10.1080/10810730.2019.1701586.

Zumbrunn, Sharon, Courtney McKim, Eric Buhs, and Leslie R. Hawley. 2014. "Support, Belonging, Motivation, and Engagement in the College Classroom: A Mixed Method Study." *Instructional Science* 42 (5): 661–684.

Index

Note: *Italic* page number refer to figures and tables.

acknowledgment, 25–27, 29–31, 36; benefits of, 28, 32; from college instructors, 40, 41; in communication and ethics, 35; importance of, 33; modeling, 36; prior to and during spring 2020, 38; received during spring 2020, 39; received prior to spring 2020, 40; role in facilitating resiliency and consequently retention, 34
action-based learning, 119–20
active learning, 93; classroom, 89; strategies, 96; techniques, 15
activism: communicative toolbox for, 143; digital media to foster, 141; student, 138–39
adaptive pedagogy, groundwork for, 76
American exceptionalism, 135
American Psychological Association, 34
Anderson, Monica, 13
antagonistic relationship, 12
AntConc, 50
Arnett, Ronald, 36
Arseven, Ilami, 94, 95, 97
Association of American Colleges and Universities (AAC&U), 16
attention span, 88
authentic engagement, benefits of, 137–38

autonomy, 10, 73–74
autonomy supportive (*versus* controlling), 9, 11, 12; antagonistic relationship, 12; complementary relationship, 13; curvilinear relationship, 12–13
autonomy-supportive instruction online, 77–78

Baby Boomers, 4
Baldwin, James, 129
Balliee, Sarah, 92
best practices: for Generation Z, 125; video games, 111–12
Blackboard Announcements, 17
Black Lives Matter movement, 138
board game, 107–8
Boehrer, John, 98
Bolliger, Doris U., 26
Britt, Lori, 136
Burgoon, Judee K., 47, 54

Camacho, Leticia, 91, 96
Carder, Linda, 91, 97, 98
case-based, problem-based learning (CBPBL), 91
case-based instruction (CBI), 91
case-based learning (CBL), 91

case study method, 91–96
Centers for Disease Control and Prevention, 60
chaos, 139–40
Chicca, Jennifer, 90
The Christian Science Monitor (Ridberg), 62
civic engagement, 140, 141
civic learning, 135
Clarkson, Natalie, 61
Clayton, Jason, 74
Coley, Charles Horton, 85
Collaboration for Academic, Social, and Emotional Learning (CASEL), 19
collaborative learning, 15–17
Collaborative Online International Learning (COIL) course, 16
communal behavior, 105
communication, 1, 137; listening, 45–46
Communication Accommodation Theory (CAT), 47, 54
communication behaviors, 2, 3, 65
communication classrooms, 140
communication education, 1–2, 5, 6
communication instruction, 129
communication instructors, 1, 2, 80–81, 130
communication scholars, 131
communication scholarship, 46; listening and, 59
communication technology, 64
communicators, 54, 55
community literacy, 135
competence, 10
complementary relationship, 13
computer-mediated technologies, 87
confusion, 139–40
constructivist pedagogies, 28–29
continuous partial attention, 88–89
cooperative excellence, 136–37
core mechanic design model, 108, *108*
coronavirus, 45
COVID-19 pandemic, 6, 14, 17, 26, 30, 31, 34, 86, 95, 103, 112, 116, 118, 126, 132, 139, 141; behavioral changes during, 59; mental health conditions, 60; and online learning, 81
Creswell, John W., 30
crisis-induced vulnerability, 143
crisis pedagogy, 27
crisis space, 26; mid-March 2020, 26–27
critical communication pedagogy, 133
critical thinking skills, 96; engagement and development of, 93
Croft, A. C., 92
Cronon, William, 64
Crowther, Emma, 92
culturally responsive teaching, 17–19, *18*
curvilinear relationship, 12–13

Dannels, Deanna P., 37
Davis, Barbara, 97
debriefing, 122; to enhance soft skills, 122, *123–24*
deep learning, 93
Desai, Supriya, 88, 91
Dewey, John, 133
digital age, 59
digital communication, logic of, 142
digital communication interactions, 47
digital game design tools, 109–11, *110*
digital games, 106
digital gamification, 115
digitalized media environment, 60
digital learning games, 103
digital media, to foster activism, 141
digital natives, 60, 71, 72, 103, 115, 126, 143; online courses for, 79; technology for, 13–14; (re)thinking assumptions about, 116–17
digital pedagogy, 115–16
digital platforms, 47; digital natives in, 72
digital spaces, 45; digital natives in, 72
digital technologies, 45, 47, 54, 55, 143
discourses, of organizing, 135–36
discussion board, 77–78
disinformation, 139
dissent, 137–39
diversity, 134, 140, 143

diversity and global learning, 15–17
Dixson, Marcia, 76
doing stage, team-building, 119–20
Dolby, Nadine, 62
Dori, Yehudit, 93

education: hurdles in black hole, 115; as liberatory practice, 133; self-determination theory, 10–13, *12*
educational games, 111
educational landscape, 87–91
educational process, 87
educational systems, 6
educators, 85
effective learning environments, pedagogy to co-create engaging and, 64–66, *66*
effective online instruction: applications to, 75–80; autonomy-supportive instruction online, 77–78; practicing student-centric pedagogy online, 75–77; promoting practicality and utility online, 78–80
effective online teaching, knowledge of, 72
effective pedagogical approach, higher education, 94–95
Elam, Elizabeth, 95, 98
Electronic Entertainment Design and Research Company (EEDAR), 104–5
Elmore, Tim, 60, 61
engagement, 96; in academic learning, 9; in classroom, 19–20; in games, 106; in learning activities, 14
Entertainment-Education research, 106
Entertainment Software Association, 104
Erwin, Kelly, 13, 60, 72, 90, 96
escape room, 89
Expectancy Violation Theory (EVT), 47, 54
experiential learning, 90
experiential learning theory, 94, 125
extraordinary space, 34–37

face-to-face context, 26, 47
face-to-face educational environments, 60
face-to-face interactions, 142
face-to-face meetings, with students, 45
face-to-face teamwork, for digital natives, 117
false information, 139, 140
Firat, Mehmet, 88–89
flipped classroom, 79
focus groups, 49–50; results, 50–54, *51*, *52*
fosters interactive learning, 89
Fratantuono, Michael, 98
Fried, Carrie B., 63
Fry, Richard, 72

Gamble, Michael, 61, 63
Gamble, Teri, 61, 63
game adjacent tools, 105
Game Design Challenge, 109
game design models, *107*, 107–9, *108*
Game Design Rubric, 110
game mechanics, 107
games. *See* video games
Gardner, Jolynn, 96
Generation X, 4
Generation Y, 4
Generation Z, 46, 143; characteristics and considerations, 3–4; as college students, 60–62, 115; educational landscape, 94; expectations of, 30; generational research, 4; instructional design strategies to support, 13–19; instructional practices for, 116; learning experiences, 61; (re)learning teamwork through OAE, 118; listening expectations, 48; listening processes, 59; listening tips from, 66, *66*; literature on, 4; need-supportive instructional strategies, *12*, 13; potential advantage of, 5; scholarship, 64; teachers' instructional styles, 10; and twenty-

first century challenges, 130–32; video games for, 103
Generation Z Goes to College (Seemiller and Grace), 3, 4
Generation Z (Gen Z) students, 71; with instant gratification, 90; learning preferences, 72–75; overarching characteristics, 87; preferences and attitudes of, 72
Gen Z classroom, games in, 104–5
Gen Z focus group, 49, *51*
Giles, Howard, 47, 54
Giroux, Henry, 133
Giunta, Catherine, 87, 88
globalization, health crisis impacts, 45
Google Hangout, 36
Grace, Meghan, 5, 60, 74, 86, 89, 90; *Generation Z Goes to College,* 3, 4
Grace, Tim, 93, 94
Grant, Janie, 93, 94
Grant, Richard, 98, 99
Great Recession, 17

Hampton, Debra, 98
handheld technology, 64, 67
hands-on learning approach, 89
hard skills, 88, 117
Herreid, Clyde, 93
Hess, Diana E., 136
higher education: with COVID-19, 60; dialectical tension, 86; effective pedagogical approach, 94–95; (re)introducing soft skills to, 117–19; lecture-laden landscape of, 90; mission, 138; needs and challenges in, 131; role of, 87; technology in, 115; technology influence on listening in, 62–63
higher-order thinking skills, 104
high-impact practices (HIPs), 16, 17
Hilcenko, Slavoljub, 89, 96
Hoaxes & Havoc game, 110, *110*
Hobbs, Renee, 140
Hoffer, Erin, 97
Homelanders, 4
Hope, Joan, 61
Hyde, Michael J., 29, 33, 36

identity categorization, 46; impact on classroom listening, 49–54
iGeneration, 4
Ilguy, Mehmet, 91
immediacy, 76
impact, 65
instructional communication, 2, 5, 6
instructional communication theory framework, 65
instructional design strategies, 13; culturally responsive teaching and social-emotional learning, 17–19, *18*; multidimensional learning, 14–15; service learning, collaborative learning, and diversity and global learning, 15–17; technology for digital natives, 13–14
instructional flexibility, 77
instructional space, 55; real-world implications for, 46
instructors, 64; encourage effective listening, 66; groundwork for adaptive pedagogy, 76; scaffolding assignments, 80; students and, 47, 55; students' individual needs, 73; utilize relational behaviors, 46
instrumental and course related benefits, 32
integrated case study (ICS), 91
integrating stage, team-building, 124–25
intergenerational listening: and technology, 46–48; tips for, 55–56
Internet, 132, 139–41
involvement, 11
Iorgulescu, Maria-Cristina, 88
island hopping survival, 120–22

Jaleniauskienė, Evelina, 61
Jiang, Jingjing, 13
Jucevičienė, Palmira, 61

justice-oriented citizenship, 130

K–12 education, 14
Kaiser Family Foundation survey, 131
Kantorova, Katerina, 92
Kezar, Adrianna, 138
Knoop, R., 97
Kreber, Carolin, 94, 96

Ladwig, Christine, 74
learn-by-doing pedagogical philosophy, 92
learning: collaborative, 15–17; diversity and global, 15–17; game design as, 107; instructional design strategies and approaches, *18*, 19; multidimensional, 14–15; self-direction in, 96; service, 15–17; social-emotional, 17–19, *18*
learning contracts, 78
Learning Management System (LMS), 17
learning preferences, 72; autonomy, 73–74; personalization, 72–73; practicality, 74–75
learning space, 5, 6
Lele, Vishwanath, 88, 91
Levinas, Emmanuel, 137
Lewin, Kurt, 87
listening, 45–47; and communication scholarship, 59; demographic traits perceived to influence, 50, *51*; expectations of Generation Z, 48; in higher education, technology influence on, 62–63; role in co-creating an effective academic community, 67–68; student-centric pedagogy by, 77
Listening Concepts Inventory (LCI-R), 48
listening space, 29–33
Listening Styles Profile (LSP-R), 48
live case study (LCS), 95

Macklin, Rob, 95

Malroutu, Y., 89, 94
Mangiapane, Ernesto, 27
Marsi, Y. Lakshmi, (2019), 118
Martin, Florence, 26
Marty-White, Cheryl R., 65, 66
Maxey, Dan, 138
Maynard, Amanda, 99
McAvoy, Paula, 136
McCroskey, James C., 1
McCroskey, Linda L., 1
Me Generation, 4
mental health, 59, 60
mental presence, 62
Milczarski, Vivian, 99
Millennials, 4, 104, 130
Miller, Amy, 29
Mills, Brooklyn B., 29
mindful listening, 63
modules/self-pacing, 78
Moore, Kevin, 93, 98
Morreale, Sherwyn, 27
motivation: in learning activities, 14; self-determination theory, 10–13, *12*
multidimensional learning, 14–15
multidisciplinary education, 86
Mustoe, L. R., 92
Myers, Karen, 73

National Association of Colleges and Employers (NACE) Center for Career Development and Talent Acquisition, 15–16
National Association of Colleges and Employers Job Outlook Survey, 117
National Communication Association CommNotes, 5
National COVID-19 Outdoor Learning Initiative (2020), 126
natural-forced space: early April 2020, 28–29; late March 2020, 27–28
Nemko, Marty, 61
Net Generation, 4
neurological perspective, 88
new literacies, 139

North, Carol S., 27

on-demand services, 131
online group decision support systems, 87
online learning, COVID-19 Pandemic and, 81
online pedagogy, 72
online platforms, 14
online spaces, 76
online survey: results, 50–54, *51*, *52*; study procedure, 48–49
open communication, 17
organizational communication, 86
O'Sullivan, Patrick, 76
outdoor adventure education (OAE), 116; Generation Z (re)learning teamwork through, 118; Transformative Learning Theory in, 118–19

Pandey, U. S., 94
Parker, Kim, 72
Pearson report (2018), 71
pedagogical practices, 34, 88
pedagogy: to co-create engaging and effective learning environments, 64–66, *66*; tool, 86, 94, 115
personalization, 72–73
personal/relational and holistic benefits, 32
Pew Research Center, 3–4
Pfefferbaum, Betty, 27
Playable Media, 110, *110*
Play Lab, 110
polarized contexts, debates in, 140–41
Popil, Inna, 89, 91, 97
Post-Gen Z focus group, 49, *51*
Postman, Neil, 117; *Technolopy: The Surrender of Culture to Technology*, 116
Post-millennials, 4
Poth, Cheryl N., 30
Pousson, J. Mark, 73
practicality, 74–75; and utility online, 78–80
pragmatic problem-solving model, 97

problem-based learning, 93
prosocial skills, 105
psychological needs, 10–11

racism, 138
Raju, P. K., 85, 89, 98
Rawal, Sangtia, 94
readiness competencies, 15–16
reflecting stage, team-building, 122, *123*–24, 124
reflection, 79–80
relatedness, 10, 11
research question (RQ), 46
resistance, 137–39
responsible citizenship, 129
Richards, Larry, 91, 95, 97
Rickes, Persis C., 87, 89, 92
Ridberg, Maia: *The Christian Science Monitor*, 62
Rohnke, Karl, 120
Roll, Kate, 35
Rospigliosi, Pericles, 89

Safranova, Margarita, 90
Sankar, Chetan, 85, 89, 98
scaffolding process, 74
Schiller, Nancy, 93
Schonell, Stuart, 95
Schwieger, Dana, 74
Seemiller, Corey, 3, 5, 60, 74, 86, 89, 90; *Generation Z Goes to College*, 3, 4
self, 65
self-determination theory (SDT), 9; motivation and education, 10–13, *12*
serious games, 106
service learning, 15–17, 79
shallow learning, 93
Shatto, Bobbi, 13, 60, 72, 90, 96
Shearer, Rick, 75
Shellenbarger, Teresa, 90
shooter video games, 105
Singh, Anjali, 87
single-phase mixed methods, 30
single-player games, 105
six-step analytic process, 50

smartphones, 13–14
social distancing, 45
social-emotional learning (SEL), 17–19, *18*, 19
social media, 14, 73, 131
social networks, 61
socio-contextual factors, 9
sociotechnical shifts, 132
Socratic approach, 91
soft skill, 5, 88; debriefing to enhance, 122, *123*–24; (re)introducing to higher learning, 117–19
Spackman, Andy, 91, 96
Spears, Julia, 90
Spotts, Harlan, 95, 98
Staton-Spicer, Ann Q., 65, 66
streaming services, 105
structure (*versus* chaos), 9, 11, 12; antagonistic relationship, 12; complementary relationship, 13; curvilinear relationship, 12–13
student: examples and reviews, 78; face-to-face interactions, 142; face-to-face meetings with, 45; and instructors, 47, 55; internal and external opportunities for, 75; listening processes, 59; listening tips from, 66, *66*; media devices, 64–65; need knowledge and skills, 139; voices illuminate civic promise, 133–35; working on case studies, 93
student activism, 138–39
student-centered teaching, 18
student-centric approach, 73
student-centric pedagogy online, 75–76; brief student assessments, 76; building immediacy, 76; instructional flexibility, 77
student-regulated learning (SRL), 77
study procedure, 48; focus groups, 49–50; online survey, 48–49
survey responses: to academic classification question, 38; to race/ethnicity classification question, 38
sustained openness, 33

Sypherz, Beverly Davenport, 92

tabletop game tools, 109
task, 65
Taylor, James, 85
teachers' instructional styles, 9, 10
teacher-student communication, 6
teacher-student interaction, 26
teacher-student relationship, 11–12, 28
teaching, culturally responsive, 17–19, *18*
teaching style, engagement-promoting aspect of, 12
team-based learning, 118
team-building, TLT design of OAE: best practices for Generation Z, 125; doing stage, 119–20; integrating stage, 124–25; island hopping survival, 120–22; reflecting stage, 122, *123*–24, 124
teamwork: face-to-face, 117; (re)learning through OAE, 118
techno-deterministic perspective, 141
technologically advanced learning tools, 14
technological pedagogy, 116
technology: collaborative projects using, 16; in communication interactions, 47; for digital natives, 13–14; in higher education, 115; in-class use of, 63; influence on listening in higher education, 62–63; in instructional contexts, 52; intergenerational listening and, 46–48; use of, 60
technology platforms, 14
Technology: The Surrender of Culture to Technology (Postman), 116
Terry, Gareth, 50
text-based materials, 14
text conceptualization, 2–3; Generation Z, 3–5; procedures, 5–7
Thompson, Penny, 63
Tompkins, Phillip K., 35
Townend, M., 91, 93

traditional lecture-based classrooms, 14
traditional teaching pedagogies, 28–29
transformative learning, 75
Transformative Learning Theory (TLT), 125; in outdoor adventure education, 118–19
transparency, 78
Trenholm, Sarah, 62
Turner, Anthony, 88
Twenge, Jean M., 65, 66

uncomfortable space, 33–34
university administration, recommendations for, 80–81
utility online, 78–80

video-based instruction, 73, 76

video games, 103; benefits of, 105; engagement in, 104; in Gen Z classroom, 104–5; long-term effects of, 105; popularity of, 104–5; tips and best practices, 111–12
virtual connectivity, 15
virtual schools, 71
Viscuso, Gabrielle Ilse, 27

Wong et al., Jacqueline (2018), 77
Wrage, Stephen, 97, 98
Wrench, Jason, 86

YouTube, 71, 73

Zhou, Chun, 108
Zoom, 115, 117
Zoom-based instruction, 93

About the Authors

Sadia E. Cheema (PhD, Texas Tech University) is an assistant professor of Public Relations at State University of New York (SUNY) Brockport. Her scholarly research lies at the intersection of gamification, activism, and corporate social responsibility. In particular, she is interested in examining the motivational processes underlying new media technologies that enhance youth's broader involvement in social and political causes.

Kristen T. Christman (PhD, University of North Carolina at Greensboro) is an instructor at The University of North Carolina, Greensboro. Dr. Christman's teaching, facilitation and research focus on positive communication, relationships, communication and community, and lifespan communication and aging. Christman is an affiliate faculty member for the Lloyd International Honors College and The School of Health and Human Science Gerontology Program. In addition to her higher education experience, Christman worked for a national nonprofit, Say Yes to Education.

Troy B. Cooper (PhD, University of Illinois, 2014) is an assistant professor and director of Undergraduate Studies in the School of Information Science at the University of Kentucky. His research focuses on instructional communication, the basic communication course, and critical analysis of technology.

Cristiane S. Damasceno (PhD, North Carolina State University) is an assistant professor in the Department of Communication Studies at the University of North Carolina at Greensboro. After receiving her bachelor's degree from Sao Paulo State University, she moved to the United States to pursue an MS and a PhD at North Carolina State University. Dr. Damasceno's research focuses on networked learning communities, online disinformation, and new literacies. She is also a researcher affiliated with the National Communication Association Center for Communication, Community Collaboration, and Change.

T. Kody Frey (PhD, University of Kentucky, 2019) is an assistant professor in the School of Information Science at the University of Kentucky. His research focuses on applied and instructional communication primarily within the context of classrooms and higher education. His agenda connects scholarship related to classroom communication technologies, the basic communication course, interpersonal communication, and communication research methods.

Juli James is an adjunct instructor at the Mayborn School of Journalism, University of North Texas, and owner of Playable Media, an educational games and online learning design company. Before moving to Texas, Juli worked at Arizona State University's Center for Games & Impact where she developed and lead a collaborative innovation initiative to bring together journalism and game design. Juli is also an army veteran.

Spoma Jovanovic (PhD, University of Denver) is professor in the Department of Communication Studies at the University of North Carolina, Greensboro (UNCG). Her research centers on collaborations with community members and activists to enhance ethical conversations and action in democratic participation and social justice. She is the author of *Democracy, Dialogue and Community Action: Truth and Reconciliation in Greensboro* and co-author of *Communication Ethics: Activities for Critical Thinking and Reflection*. Her work as a 2019-2020 Fellow with the University of California's National Center for Free Speech and Civic Engagement led to the development of the edited volume, *Expressions in Contested Public Spaces: Free Speech and Civic Engagement*. She is the director of the UNCG-National Communication Association Center for Communication, Community Collaboration, and Change.

Corey Jay Liberman (PhD, Rutgers University, 2008) is an associate professor of Public Relations and Strategic Communication in the Department of Communication and Media Arts at Marymount Manhattan College. His research spans the interpersonal communication, group communication, and organizational communication worlds, and he is currently interested in studying the social practices of dissent within organizations, specifically the antecedents, processes, and effects associated with effective employee dissent communication, as well as risk and crisis communication. He is currently working on a co-edited book entitled *Casing*

Nonverbal Communication and a co-authored book entitled *Organizational Communication: Strategies for Success (3rd Edition)*. He is coauthor of *Organizational Communication: Strategies for Success (2nd Edition)* and *Risk and Crisis Communication: Communicating in a Disruptive Age*, editor of *Casing Persuasive Communication*, and co-editor of *Casing Crisis and Risk Communication, Casing Communication Theory, and Casing Mediated Communication*: all published by Kendall Hunt.

Jessica D. McCall (PhD, University of North Carolina at Greensboro) is an instructor and basic course director at The University of North Carolina, Greensboro. Dr. McCall's teaching, facilitation, and research focus on building effective communities, relationships, and skill sets for leadership and growth both in and out of the classroom. McCall is an adjunct facilitator and moderator with the Center for Creative Leadership. She also serves as a facilitator with UNCG's Team Development program

Gwendelyn S. Nisbett received her PhD from the University of Oklahoma in Social Influence and Political Communication in 2011. She is an associate professor of strategic communication in the Mayborn School of Journalism at the University of North Texas. Dr. Nisbett's research examines the intersection of mediated social influence, political communication, and popular culture. Her research incorporates a multi-method approach to understanding the influence of fandom and celebrity in political and civic engagement.

Emeline Ojeda-Hecht is a PhD student at Colorado State University pursing a degree in Communication Studies with an emphasis in relational and organizational communication. She received a bachelor's and master's degree in Organizational Communication from Murray State University. Her research interests include the use of social media among coworkers in organizations and the influence of generational differences among workplace relationships.

Elizabeth S. Parks (PhD, University of Washington) is currently an assistant professor at Colorado State University and adjunct assistant professor with the Colorado School of Public Health. Her scholarship blends social scientific and humanistic methods to improve listening and dialogue across difference and includes her book-length publication *The Ethics of Listening: Creating Space for Sustainable Dialogue*.

Newly Paul is a media and politics researcher and assistant professor of journalism in the Mayborn School of Journalism at the University of North Texas. Her research areas include political communication, race and gender in politics, and media coverage of elections. She has taught principles of news, news reporting, copyediting, political reporting, and minorities in media. Dr. Paul received her PhD from the Louisiana State University in Media and Public Affairs in 2015.

Renee Robinson, PhD, is a professor and chair of the Department of Communication and the Arts at Seton Hall University. Robinson has two areas of expertise, Instructional Communication and Organizational Communication. She has published in the areas of assessment, communication instruction and pedagogy, computer-mediated and digital communication, and mobile learning. Robinson is a curriculum developer who has taught face-to-face, hybrid, and online courses. She possesses a master of online teaching certificate and has created over 35 communication courses spanning delivery systems. Robinson is also a former faculty trainer and developer and has worked in various leadership positions at several higher education institutions.

Roy Schwartzman (PhD, University of Iowa) is a professor in the Department of Communication Studies and affiliate faculty with the Department of Peace and Conflict Studies and the Joint School of Nanoscience and Nanoengineering at the University of North Carolina, Greensboro. He is past president of the Association for the Rhetoric of Science, Technology, and Medicine and has held fellowships from the Holocaust Educational Foundation as well as the USC Shoah Foundation Institute. He has published more than 140 scholarly articles and book chapters and has received grants from the Southern poverty Law Center, the Jewish Chautauqua Society, the North Carolina Council on the Holocaust, the University of North Carolina System, and many other organizations. He is principal investigator for *Cultivate Resilient Communities*, the grant that establishes UNCG as the inaugural National Communication Association Center for Communication, Community Collaboration, and Change.

Pamela Sherstad, PhD, is a professor of Communication and serves as the dean of the School of Arts and Sciences at Grace Christian University. Dr. Sherstad's teaching experience began in Tanzania, East Africa, where she realized a passion for communication and culture. In addition to global communication, listening research in higher education provides opportunities to engage Generation Z to co-create effective learning environments. In January 2021, Dr. Sherstad was the recipient of the Grace Christian University Faculty Leadership Award.

R. Tyler Spradley, PhD (Texas A&M University), is a professor of Communication at Stephen F. Austin State University and a faculty associate at Arizona State University in the Hugh Downs School of Human Communication. Distinguished honors include induction into the Texas A&M Chapter of the Honor Society of Phi Kappa Phi, two-time recipient of the Jim Towns Endowed Mentoring Professorship, and honorary faculty memberships in the Stephen F. Austin State University chapters of Lambda Pi Eta and Omicron Delta Kappa. He currently serves as Coordinator of the interdisciplinary Leadership Minor as well as the Leadership and the Risk and Crisis Communication Certificates. Dr. Spradley researches organizational communication, specifically high reliability organizations, risk and crisis communication, sociomateriality, and mentoring. Research can be found in publications such as: *The International Encyclopedia of Organizational Communication, Sage Research Methods Cases, Journal of Leadership, Accountability and Ethics, Journal of Human Services,* and the *International Research Journal of Public Health.*

Dr. Jie Zhang is a professor of Special Education at State University of New York (SUNY) Brockport, where she has been a faculty member since 2008. Zhang completed her PhD in Exceptional Learning at Tennessee Technological University and undergraduate study at Changzhou University, China. She received the SUNY Chancellor's Award for Excellence in Teaching in 2017.

www.ingramcontent.com/pod-product-compliance
Lightning Source LLC
Chambersburg PA
CBHW061715300426
44115CB00014B/2702